*Eating the Flowers of Paradise*

# *Eating the Flowers of Paradise*

## A JOURNEY THROUGH THE DRUG
## FIELDS OF ETHIOPIA AND YEMEN

## KEVIN RUSHBY

St. Martin's Griffin
New York

ISBN 0-312-22969-0

Library of Congress Cataloging-in-Publication Data

Rushby, Kevin.
  Eating the flowers of paradise : one man's journey
through Ethiopia and Yemen / Kevin Rushby.
    p.   cm.
  Includes bibliographical references and index.
  ISBN 0-312-21794-3 (cloth)   0-312-22969-0 (pbk)
  1. Qat—Ethiopia. 2. Qat—Yeme. 3. Rushby, Kevin—
Journeys—Ethiopia. 4. Rushby, Kevin—Journeys—
Yemen. 5. Yemen—Description and travel. 6. Ethiopia—
Description and travel. 7. Narcotic habit—Ethiopia.
8. Narcotic habit—Yemen. I. Title.
HV5822.Q3R87   1999
362.29'3'092—dc
[B]
                                          99-10666
                                          CIP

First published in Great Britain in 1998 by
Constable and Company limited

First published by St. Martin's Press in hardcover
in the United States of America in 1999

First St. Martin's Griffin edition: May 2000

10 9 8 7 6 5 4 3 2 1

For Judith, Caitlin, Conor and Niall

# Contents

*All the photographs were taken by the author*

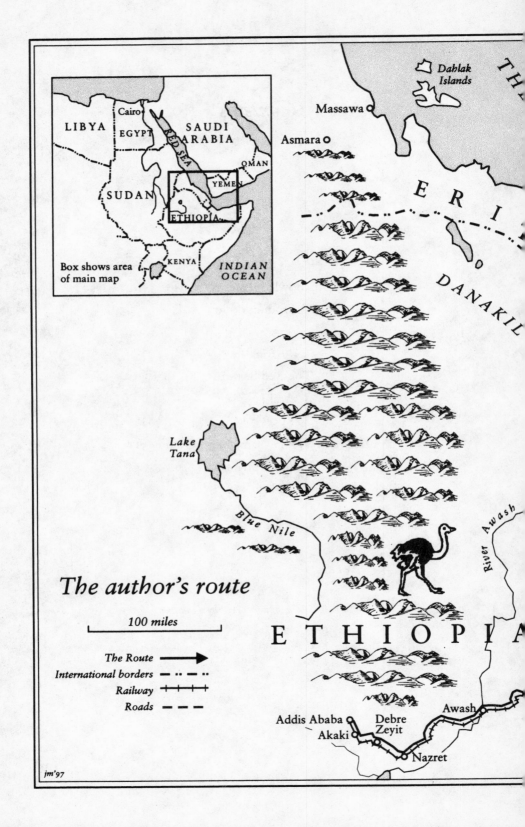

Dahlak
Islands

Massawa

Asmara

E R I

DANAKIL

Lake
Tana

Blue Nile

River Awash

*The author's route*

|———————| 100 miles

The Route ——————▶
International borders —·—··—··
Railway ++++++
Roads — — —

E T H I O P I A

Addis Ababa    Debre    Awash
Akaki          Zeyit

Nazret

jm'97

# *Acknowledgements*

Anyone who has walked and travelled through both Ethiopia and Yemen will have experienced the hospitality that the people give to strangers; I benefited a great deal from such kindness and without it this book would never have been possible.

In Yemen I am also indebted to Hassan al-Shumahi and Tim Mackintosh Smith for sharing their ideas, knowledge, and powers of translation, usually over a few bundles of Hamdani qat. Mike Gowman and Debbie Dorman helped me track down some interesting qat sessions in San'a, while Abera Teshome did so in Harar. During the writing of the book I heard with sadness that Sheikh Hajj Abdulsatar of Harar had died: his scholarship and knowledge will certainly be missed. Tim Mackintosh Smith also helped with checking the manuscript, as did Judith Rushby, Bruce Wannell, Alex MacCormick and Maggie Body. Any mistakes are, or course, mine. In London I was assisted by Dr Nigel Hepper with botanical information and Hajj Ali Ahmed Saleh with botanical samples; Rebecca Baldwin and my sister Joanne Rushby generously allowed me to spread these samples all over their living room on numerous occasions. The photographs were printed by myself with the benefit of Pat Whitaker's experience, knowledge and a clock liberated from wartime Berlin. Further support came from June and Geoffrey Hall and my mother, Averyl Rushby. I also wish to thank my agent Carolyn Whitaker and Carol O'Brien at Constable, who have been invaluable for their enthusiasm and good advice throughout.

In using Arabic in the text I have tried to use accepted English spellings, where available, and simple phonetic transliterations elsewhere.

I am grateful to Picador for permission to quote from *Complete Works of Rimbaud* translated by Paul Schmidt.

# *Introduction*

'Let us swear an oath, and keep it with an equal mind,
In the hollow Lotos-land to live and lie reclined
On the hills like Gods together, careless of mankind.'

Tennyson, 'The Lotos Eaters'

My first ever contact with the drug had been in 1982, a brief and unsatisfying experience significant only in the light of later events. I was in Juba,
the main settlement of southern Sudan and a place where I hoped to hitch
a ride to Uganda. Going out to the market, I came across a United Nations
lorry with a Somali driver who smiled dreamily at me from the cab and
revealed in the corner of his mouth, flashing like a broken traffic light, a
quid of brilliant green leaves.

'We call it *chat*,' he said, using the Somali name. 'And with it I can drive
right across Uganda without stopping.'

That seemed like a very good idea, as Uganda was at war with itself. 'But
we cannot take passengers – UN rules.' A few shiny green leaves were
passed down to me with that same dreamy smile. And so it was that my
introduction to the drug came as a gift from the United Nations, but on
this occasion they were no more than unwanted salad which I found bitter
and spat out as soon as politeness allowed. Like most first-timers I felt
nothing and assumed that it did nothing, that qat was a quack medicine for
the gullible. And if my head was full of romantic notions about travel and
adventure, it did not include taking leaves from lorry drivers.

Five years later, seated on cushions, qat leaves in my lap, watching the
shadows of Arabian night fill the dusty alleyways below the window of a
stone tower house, I had learnt differently and become as much a qat-lover
as the Somali driver. Yemen held me as Lotos-land held Ulysses's crew. I
passed the hours listening to the gentle lubalub of the hookah and whispered conversations about dead poets and fine deeds. In San'a, qat

governs. Each day at three, climbing the steps to a smoky room with a bundle under the arm; then closing the door to the outside world, choosing the leaves, gently crushing them with the teeth and waiting for the drug to take effect. No rush, just a silky transition, scarcely noticed, and then the room casts loose its moorings. 'Capturing moments of eternity', someone once called the subtle tinkering with time that qat effects.

After two years I no longer knew if life was good because of Yemen or because of qat. I left for Malaysia and went into mourning for the life I had lost, but the question remained unanswered. I remember taking a holiday on Tioman Island off Malaysia's east coast, as idyllic a tropical paradise as any travel agent ever came up with, and I spent my days trying to telephone someone in Yemen who thought he had a job for me.

There had been an expatriate in Yemen who always brought up his time in Pakistan, 'When we were in Islamabad . . . ', 'It's funny you should say that because when we were in . . . ', 'Did I ever tell you about the North-West Frontier . . . ' Those wonderful pearl strings of memory that no one else cared to see, lost behind a stony wall of other people's indifference, for two decades in his case. Some unkind soul even said to him: 'If it was so good, why did you leave?', and he added, quietly, 'Or why not go back?'

I watched him suffer without sympathy until, in a Kuala Lumpur staffroom, I found myself saying, again and again, like a reformed drinker whose conversation is bottles and booze: 'When I was in Yemen . . . ' But almost as often it was, 'There's this leaf they have in Yemen – it's called qat . . . ' And I knew all along, despite the passing years and even one false dawn when my return was abruptly cut short by Yemen's civil war, I knew that I would have to return and see if those pearl strings were anything more than piles of dusty discarded leaves and memories polished by time – the Lotos-land would have to be revisited, the paradise regained.

# Africa

# I

'perhaps all pleasure is relief'

William Burroughs, *Junky*

The first man I stopped was helpful.

'You want qat? What's that then – drugs?'

There were two Pakistani ladies passing us, dressed in chunky cardies and silky shalwar; I scanned their faces anxiously, but there was no reaction.

'Well, sort of drugs – yes, I suppose it might be . . . '

He nodded. 'You want drugs – blow? I'll get you some blow. How much you want?'

'No, I don't want any blow.'

'Good stuff, mate, don't worry.'

'Look, I don't want blow, I want qat. It's a leaf from Ethiopia and Yemen. You chew it.'

His face clouded over into sullen disinterest. 'Never heard of it. I do blow, that's all.'

He strolled away. The street was soon empty of people. On one side was a railway viaduct, a line that had once served London's docklands; on the other were some low-rise flats with beady-eyed little windows and security doors. It was possible of course that the qat-seller was in there, behind a dead-locked door with a spyhole and surveillance equipment, handing out little packets of happiness through an armoured grill. It was also possible that the local Yemeni greengrocer would have it, labelled salad, sitting between the red peppers and purple onions. Qat is nothing if not adaptable: should the President of the United States be caught holding state meetings the same way they do in Yemen and Somaliland, over a few bundles of qat leaves, he would get the same treatment as any crack addict. It's legal in Britain, banned in the USA, celebrated in Yemen, vilified in Saudi Arabia.

Unfortunately, I had no map for the qat-shop in the East End and the directions I'd been given were horribly vague: 'a kind-of shop place, a room, it's his house, loads of people coming and going – you'll find it', so I ended up loitering outside a café waiting for inspiration, accosting a second passer-by, a young West Indian who came from the café.

'Excuse me. Do you know where I can buy qat?'

'Drugs, right?'

'Well, sort of.'

'You want powder?'

'No, it's a leaf.'

'You want powder. Leaf's shit. Wait here.' He started to move away. 'Just wait, right? One minute.'

'No, I want qat – it's a leaf, green stuff – and legal.'

He was already ten yards away, but he stopped. It was as though the dread word 'legal' had let the air out of his trainers, a warrant card flashed in his face.

'Yeah, right, leaf.' He set off down a side street, slam-dunking a balled-up paper napkin over the fence.

I walked a few yards up the street and stopped, wondering what to try next. Then I noticed the door next to me was ajar, a red door of what I had taken to be an empty shop lot next to a bookie's. Peering inside I could make out one end of a chiller display cabinet of the sort that fishmongers use, only this one was stocked with bottles of mineral water and Coke cans. I put my hand on the door and eased it open a couple more inches. The rest of the display cabinet swung into view: a case of soft drinks and in the little white plastic trays where the filleted cod steaks should have been, piles of smooth green pods each about a foot long, carefully stacked in tidy pyramids of fifteen and looking like some alien seed stock on the brink of hatching out and invading the East End. I had never seen qat wrapped in banana leaves before but I knew I had found what I was looking for. With a push, I opened the door and stepped inside.

Qat, khat, chat, cat, jima, mira – the London Institute for the Study of Drug Dependence issues a factsheet stating that it is a green leafy plant cultivated throughout eastern Africa and the Arabian peninsula, and containing two pharmacologically active ingredients, cathinone and cathine, the effects of which are something like amphetamine sulphate. 'The khat plant is not controlled under UK domestic law,' the factsheet says. However, 'Cathinone and cathine . . . are controlled under the United Nations' Convention on Psychotropic Substances.' In the United States, Canada, Switzerland, Scandinavia and most of the Middle East, excluding Yemen, the leaf itself is banned. In a lecture given at a UN conference in 1983 it was stated that cathinone, the main active constituent, could 'create the same problem as cocaine if it was available'. Only twelve years later, in Manchester, a smiling young nightclubber held out his hand and showed me the tablets of cathinone that would make him dance all night and never lose that smile. In his pocket were some thin stems of Kenyan qat which he stripped and ate one-handed with the same skill as a Somali gunman clutching a Kalashnikov: the Ecstasy generation was branching out. No quiet room with a view, no water-pipe gently bubbling, no contemplation or poems or fine words, not even a closed door and a carpet to sit on. I wanted to press my hands to my ears and shout: 'Stop! This can't be right!'

As an eight-year-old at primary school I remember being handed a strip of paper and told to twist it once and stick the ends together. When I ran my finger along one side I can still recall my amazed discovery that there was no edge, no end, my finger just kept going on and on. Qat does that: challenges the borders and boundaries. It is legal and illegal, safe and unsafe, addictive and non-addictive, it makes you dance all night, it makes you sit and stare, it moves you to hallucinate or has no effect at all – it all depends on where you are and who you are talking to. In the USA, where it is demonised along with all the other substances, it also grows as an ornamental tree in various botanical parks and gardens. Occasionally, mysterious 'prunings' occur, much to the bafflement of gardeners and park-keepers. It is a substance that an initiate can quite calmly sit and chew while calling for it to be banned. Qat sits on the fence of our preconceived ideas and on either side of it too, challenging our conceptions of what a drug is, of what addiction is, of what an addicted society should be like. It questions where we draw the limits and makes those limits look as ridiculous as those straight-line colonial borders on maps of Africa.

[7]

As to its effects, the Institute's bulletin declares: 'In cultures where its use is indigenous, khat has traditionally been used socially, much like coffee in western culture.'

When I first read that bland, easy statement, I laughed: here was a leaf that in Yemen has a pivotal role in poetry, music, architecture, family relations, wedding and funerary rites, home furnishings, clothes, what people eat, when restaurants open and close, where roads go to and where not, who owns a car and who does not, office hours, television schedules, even whether couples have sex and how long it lasts. At a conservative estimate, it accounts for one third of the gross national product, politicians take decisons on it, businessmen strike deals over it, even Texan oil men will force themselves to accept bouquets of it, 'exchanging green gold for black gold', one of them told me; from the centre of the capital to the outermost desert reaches, tribesmen will accept judgements made by men with qat in their cheek. It had consumed my money, decided my friends, chosen my house, taught me some Arabic, and given me a love for the country more powerful than for my own, and all of that, this all-pervasive substance, was to be neatly summarised 'much like coffee in western cultures'.

In his backroom qat-shop in London's East End, Haj Ali had tried to evoke a little of his homeland. Along the right-hand wall were propped hard cushions to rest the qat-eater's back, the cloth a rich maroon velvet with lacy antimacassars draped along the tops. For seating there was a long thin cotton-stuffed mattress overlaid with oriental rugs. Elbows could slouch upon simple square bolsters, also in maroon velvet, and to supplement these were softer slip cushions with lace-edged cotton covers. If this was the Orient, the opium den of the dreamy east, then it was based on a sketch by Queen Victoria.

One man in a gold-embroidered skullcap was sitting on the mattress, two others were standing in front of the chiller examining the qat. As I came in they all looked up and frowned, not in an unfriendly fashion, just puzzled at the intrusion. They did not speak, so I greeted them, going over to shake hands with the seated man first as he was oldest and obviously the owner.

'As-salaam aleikum.'

The instant they heard Arabic, their faces relaxed. The old man smiled. 'Wa aleikum as-salaam. You speak Arabic? And you know qat?' He got up and went behind the chiller to select some bundles for me. 'How many do you want?'

'There are two of us. Don't you have Yemeni qat?'

'No, this is all from Harar in Ethiopia.'

He passed across a bundle and I inspected it. The smooth green wrapping was a banana leaf tied with a thin strip of dry raffia. At the top it tapered to a point, at the base it was open, revealing the cut ends of about twenty stalks. I made a show of looking at these although they appeared to be exactly the same as all the others in the display: red-barked with a dirty white pith.

'It's not fresh,' he apologised, 'Not like you buy in San'a – but then it takes two days to get here.'

The two other customers interrupted our conversation to take their leave. 'We've got three bundles.' One of them searched through his pockets for money while Haj Ali waved at him, protesting: 'No, no, no. Next time – no problem.'

But the customer found his cash and a brief battle ensued which the shopkeeper won, successfully repulsing the customer's attempt to pay. When they had gone I asked Haj Ali if he had ever visited Harar.

'Yes, many years ago. It is an Arab town in the hills of Ethiopia and they grow the best qat. Some people say that the tree came from there and was taken to Yemen.' He took the qat from me and put it with another bundle in a white plastic bag. 'We used to trade there and up to Djibouti, Eritrea and Sudan.'

'Was it an old route?'

'Yes, for taking slaves from Africa to Arabia. They would come down from Harar to the coast at Zeila, which is now very small. Then they would cross the Red Sea by dhow to Mokha – you know Mokha? Famous for coffee? – or Aden. These were the old routes: when I was a young man we used them.'

I knew that the same Aden-Zeila-Harar route was that taken by the explorer Richard Burton in 1854-55, when he became the first European to see Harar and live – non-Muslims having been barred from the holy city on pain of death.

'And qat came from Harar?'

'This qat? Yes.' He handed me the white bag.

'But originally – the first qat?'

He shook his head. 'They say Sheikh Shadhili took it from Harar to Mokha because the people wanted something to keep them awake. But who knows – that is more than five hundred years ago.'

He shuffled towards the cushions by the wall, indicating that I should sit down too. But at that moment a large party of customers, a group of Ethiopians, arrived and he was distracted. I tried to get one last question across as more men came inside and the room filled with voices and different languages.

'Is it still possible – I mean, the old route? Do the dhows still go from Zeila or Djibouti?'

He was loading another white carrier bag from the chiller, holding up another conversation with the large group. 'How many? Six? You British were in Aden then. We'd go across to Somaliland or down the coast to Zanzibar and Tanganyika then back to Aden.'

'By boat?'

'By boat – sambuk – or plane. They took Harari qat to Aden in those days by plane – that was how the Ethiopian Airlines started. The British were always fighting with the Imam in the north of Yemen, you see, so the qat camels were often held up.'

'But what about now – is it possible now?'

He shrugged. A fellow Yemeni had come in and the conversation had switched to Arabic: mine was rusty after two years of neglect, but his answer was clear enough.

'As-sambuk? Ma'arifsh. I don't know.'

More customers arrived, a group of Somali men and an Ethiopian, so I paid for the qat and said goodbye, passing through the doorway from the warmth of Yemen into the grimy grey autumn of London.

Haj Ali had not been wrong in suggesting Harar as a possible origin for the qat tree. Many sources give dates for the substance being sent to Yemen from Harar: brought by Ethiopians between 1301 and 1349, brought to the Yemeni city of Ta'izz in 1222, taken by a sufi named Sheikh Shadhili (there were a few by that name) in 1429 – but there was nothing definite, no precise documentary evidence. Although qat is mentioned by savants and sufis like al-Miswari of Ta'izz in the thirteenth century, they might have been referring to the tea made from the leaves of qat, rather than the plant – an explanation for the absence of the tree in the plant register drawn up

[10]

for the King of Yemen in about 1271 and also for the great traveller Ibn Battuta failing to spot it in 1330. Quite when this strange leaf started on its long journey from innocuous and unnoticed tree to cultural mainstay is a mystery but it seems likely that religious men first discovered its properties, using it to ward off sleep during long, night-time meditations, and carrying this useful spiritual helpmate with them on missionary journeys. The cultural beginnings of qat would have been born out of travel and movement just as Napoleon's expedition to Egypt brought hashish to Europe and nineteenth-century Bayer company salesmen had taken a marvellous new cough remedy called heroin across to the USA.

The distance covered by qat on that first movement was not so great but the route from Harar to the coast has always been fraught with difficulties. When Richard Burton went back down that road in January 1855 after just ten days in Harar, heartily relieved to have survived the Emir's uncertain hospitality, he was attacked and took a spear-thrust through his cheek. He was fortunate to survive with only the savage mark you can see in Leighton's painting of him in the National Portrait Gallery.

The other great literary figure of the nineteenth century associated with Harar fared worse. Arthur Rimbaud, poetic prodigy, retired at twenty with the valedictory *A Season in Hell* in which he wrote: 'My day is done; I am leaving Europe . . . I shall return with limbs of iron, dark skin, a furious eye: from my mask, I shall be judged as belonging to a mighty race.' But in reality he returned physically shattered and died in Marseilles soon after.

North of Harar, towards the French-speaking enclave of Djibouti, lies a region of Africa about which few good words have been said. Early travellers found the people had the disagreeable habit of slicing off testicles as trophies. The average temperatures, day and night, summer or winter, are the highest in the world. When I thought of qat being carried east across this volatile wilderness, I thought of the tins of Golden Syrup that fill the shelves of San'a's grocery shops and the picture of a dead lion above the Biblical quotation: 'Out of the strong shall come forth sweetness.'

I took my bundles off to Hackney, where I sat with Khaled, a Yemeni friend, in the garret window of my sister's flat overlooking the railway, slipping the little leaves and shoots past our lips while Khaled said, 'Isn't it wonderful to sit together again like this? I'm in San'a now, really, at

[11]

Muthana's place — the best place to take qat. This room reminds me of San'a somehow.'

This was not entirely by accident. I had pulled all the cushions onto the floor, hidden the sofa on the landing, swathed parts of a vegetable rack in stripy ethnic rugs to make armrests, and covered everything in yards of the bright scarlet and blue Indian cloth that San'a ladies use as shawls. But not only that, the room had two garret windows set down long dormers and these channelled the light into twin columns of dusty gold. By sitting on the floor we could no longer see the grim viaduct curling away from Hackney Central station, only the sky and this golden light pouring in. And if the gold had more to do with the reflections off the garish tandoori house opposite, then it only added to the eastern flavour. Khaled had brought his lute which he began to strum: his high plaintive voice gaining in confidence as he played, the sound of it hauntingly sad yet nailed to the driving beat of his right hand on the strings. Then I could see myself in a shared taxi on the road to San'a from the south, qat in lap, whacking the dust from a cassette tape before putting it in the machine and listening to that same bitter-sweet sound as the landscape of distant tawny mountains rolled by in slow motion.

My first experience of a Yemeni qat session was in a beautiful old Jewish house in the Al-Qaa quarter of San'a. There were alabaster windows threading the sunlight into amber ribbons, cushions covered in rich fabrics, the gentle curl of the hookah hose across the floor and conversations fascinating and varied. Through the open door was a sunny courtyard where trellised vines grew above a fountain and pool. This was the type of house that Jamal al-Din al-Shahari wrote about in 1747 in his book that glorified San'a as 'the City of Divine and Earthly Joy'. Like the poet, we chewed qat that was well chosen, washed and gleaming, the shoots were both supple and crisp. And I hated it.

For an hour or two it was pleasant to relax and talk, though there was obviously nothing to be gained from these bitter leaves. After five hours I never wanted to see it again. Like many other outsiders, I was waiting for the drug to happen and it didn't.

Then one night around Christmas-time a few months later, there was a knock at my door. It was past midnight and I went down in some irritation to find a strange figure in gentleman's walking brogues, twill trousers and what appeared to be a coat made from a bedouin tent. He was carrying a knobkerrie which he waggled at the street dogs. It was Tim, a colleague at the school where I was teaching and a long-time San'a resident.

'They really are beautiful animals, aren't they?' he said as the hounds formed a snarling semi-circle around us and the door. 'But probably rabid.'

We went inside and he explained the reason for his visit: 'I wondered if you would like to come round tomorrow? I'll be having qat, but you don't have to. There's this high room on top of my house – the seventh floor – it has a wonderful view over the Old City and you could photograph it.'

My first experience was still fresh in my mind and I muttered something uncharitable about 'expensive placebos' but agreed.

Tim's house was a magnificent tower, daubed with zig-zags of whitewash and entered via a stout castle door that had sunk two steps below street level as the centuries of dust piled up. I climbed the stairs to the roof, then up again on a narrow stone staircase to an extra little room that seemed to float over the surrounding houses, a place that could seat only four in comfort with tall arched windows of stained glass and a hand grenade that held a cigarette lighter. I took my photographs and Tim and two Yemeni friends talked about Yemen, about a lost city on top of an unclimbable crag that Tim had tried to reach, about one-legged poets and a place where wild tribes still traded in large silver coins stamped with the image of Empress Maria Theresa of Austria. I didn't buy any qat and I did not accept any from the others, but it was on that day that I became an addict because I began to understand that the pleasure of a qat session was not really about qat at all, but about the companionship of the sessions in cave-like rooms floating high above the ancient city.

Khaled understood this immediately when I told him about it. 'I have not had qat for eight months,' he told me. 'Who would I sit with? And where?'

He came from a remote area in northern Yemen, a place famed for its fiercely traditional tribal law. When he had first won his scholarship to study translation, I had worried that he would find London an appalling sewer of dissolution and moral decay without even basic civilising amenities such as a proper qat market. But when I suggested as much, he recoiled in amazement.

[13]

'You think that? No, believe me, London is a paradise. As for qat I can manage without it. Qat is an evil thing, it would be better if it was banned.'

So saying, he sighed and selected another sappy little sprig from the plastic bag. But I was less than enthusiastic about London myself: I had spent ten years abroad, before returning in 1994. Now I was pining for Yemen.

Khaled gave me short shrift on that score. 'I'd stay here forever if I could. Let me give you an example: in our area if someone kills another man from another tribe, then those people can come and kill me in revenge, even though I had nothing to do with the murder.' I had a vision of a tribesman armed with a matchlock rifle, face weathered by desert winds, sauntering up Hackney High Street in search of vengeance, a Yemeni Clint Eastwood.

Determined that I should not take such a rosy view of his country and such a dim one of my own, Khaled pressed his case.

'In our village I cannot even play music – it's forbidden for someone of my background. Can you imagine such a restriction on your life? Once I was living in San'a in a single room with my wife and children. I had my lute, and one day my father-in-law paid a surprise visit. We saw him from the window and panicked – where could we hide the lute? There was only one room and just two mattresses for furniture. If he saw the lute our shame would be terrible. I was running around with the thing in my hands, shaking with fear. Eventually we put it in the toilet on top of the cistern and prayed that he wouldn't visit the bathroom. Thank God, he didn't. Can you imagine that? Would you let anyone tell you not to play the guitar? Here in London you can live how you want and no one tells you it's wrong. That is paradise. Stay here, Kevin, this is a good place. Yemen is full of problems. Stay here. Paradise.'

Later, when Khaled was out in the bathroom, I picked up the phone and tried some travel agents for ticket prices. I wasn't really thinking straight. It was qat: sometimes it gives you strange ideas: once I drew up careful plans to rebuild my car as the diwan of an oriental despot, complete with gorgeous fabrics, central fountain and belly-dancing chauffeuse. Now I had this irrational urge to get out of paradise. I would do it. I would take that ancient trail, following in the footsteps of Haj Ali, Rimbaud and Burton, then cross by boat and travel through Yemen until I reached San'a, the Lotos-land, the paradise lost.

Next day, determined that I should not let this idea fade like all the others qat had given me, I went into the School of Oriental and African Studies library and began my preparations by consulting the experts: men like the Edwardian political agent, Wyman Bury, who travelled widely in Yemen before the First World War. His packing list was a masterpiece of asceticism and imperialism.

| | |
|---|---|
| Blankets: | One each for the men. Two for yourself. |
| Personal weapons: | Light carbine, a 0.30 Winchester or a Savage Automatic pistol, a 0.32 Browning + lead-nosed bullets. |
| | 500 rounds for the carbine. |
| | 200 rounds for the pistol. |
| Saddle: | Reverse hide, polo pattern. This is easy to clean and the Arabs think it is not pig-skin. |

There followed some peremptory words on personal habits.

I suppose you will have to carry handkerchiefs. Avoid white, and do not blow your nose in public, it startles folk. Above all avoid the topi of civilisation, goggles or sun umbrella. You will never be able to live them down.

On the frontispiece photograph he was pictured swathed in an indigo-stained cloak, bearing no more than a long spear and vast black beard, probably labelled 'Spy equipment – property of British Quartermaster Stores, Aden'. This was the old way to gain acceptance and pass through dangerous places: pretend to be someone else. Arabian exploration and travel always had the attraction of dressing-up games, of escaping into another identity. Wyman Bury became Abdullah Mansur of the Zaraniq tribe, Burton was a Turkish doctor or an Arab merchant, and Rimbaud became all kinds of people, including the trader Abdo Rinbo: all of them were liberated by stepping out of themselves, beyond the borders, and into another identity.

But there would be no indigo-stained wraps for my journey, I decided, and no disguise at all, except that by accepting qat I myself might be

[15]

accepted. The leaf would be all I needed to open doors. 'I have made qat my way up,' wrote Abdullah ibn Shariaf al-Din, the sixteenth-century Yemeni mystic. And I would do exactly the same, though the qat would add to my journey, not replace it; and where he had been searching for unity with God, my own goal was a paradise whose existence, perhaps, was no more than a memory.

The single air ticket I bought to the Ethiopian capital of Addis Ababa proved to be as expensive as a return to San'a, something the travel agent kindly pointed out to me when I explained my route to him.

'I sold a single ticket to Addis Ababa one time,' he told me. 'It was to this Rastafarian who thought Ethiopia was the Promised Land and he wouldn't be coming back. Six weeks later I saw him walking down Charing Cross Road. Why don't you just fly direct to Yemen? It'll save money.'

I told him about my memories of San'a. 'I need to approach things a little more slowly.'

He nodded. 'You may be right.'

The office was shabby and run-down: travel agents who admit that the slow route is better do not prosper.

'Did you speak to the Rasta?' I asked.

'Yes, I said to him "What about Ethiopia? Promised Land and all that?" He said – don't ask me to do a Jamaican accent, right – he said, the problem wasn't Ethiopia but he wasn't ready for it. He needed more preparation.'

He began to trace the outline of Africa on the map he had. 'Syrian Air are cheap – you get three days in Damascus airport. You can't rush these things, can you?'

# 2

In Addis Ababa I checked into a cheap chalet-style hotel with a guard on the gate and doors that locked. Along the path outside the room, like a miraculous fall of virginal snow under the eucalyptus trees, was a sprinkling of white condom wrappers. On the bedside cabinet was an information booklet advising guests that 'Making fire is not allowed in the room' and ending with the suggestion 'Please give maximum attention for spring mattress.'

After a dutiful hour on the mattress, I went through to the leafy courtyard where a group of Kenyans were chatting to two Saudi businessmen and getting drunk. It was still early morning, the air crisp and cool, and I was keen to start arrangements for my journey from Addis to Harar, so I walked out onto the main road and headed towards the centre of town.

Both sides of the route were thick with walkers making for the city. Most were people on their way to work, some of the women in white shawls, the men in shirt and trousers. Others had an out-of-town style: dusty feet and bundles over the shoulder, looking as if they had just tramped up from the coast – all 8,500 feet and 350 miles. As they passed a church a few of the older women stopped to bow and cross themselves. Barefoot shoeshine boys danced before me like mosquitoes and offered to put a polish on my canvas sneakers.

Closer in to the city some new buildings were going up, most of them hotels or offices for international companies, but recovery following the 1991 anti-communist victory was obviously proceeding slowly. Between the new concrete blocks were clusters of wooden shacks, roofed with crinkled, rain-stained tin and tied together with tangles of banana trees, purple convolvulus and prickly euphorbia. The summer rains had just finished so everywhere was brilliant with greenery, though the eucalyptus, as ever, managed to look tired and thirsty. In places the land had been ripped out by torrents, leaving deep red gulches strewn with boulders. From a cabin on the edge of such a ravine came a girl in a smart business suit with immaculately plaited hair, picking her way across some carefully laid stones to keep her shoes pristine.

When the traveller Herbert Vivien arrived in Addis Ababa in 1900, these ravines had yet to be bridged by anything more than a single wooden rail which no one used anyway. At that time the city was almost new, the Emperor Menelik II having founded it only thirteen years before, and Vivien was astonished that this could claim to be the capital of a great empire: 'I looked around incredulously, and saw nothing but a few summer-house huts and an occasional white tent, all scattered very far from each other over a rough hilly basin at the foot of steep hills.'

This was one of Africa's attempts at a new beginning, an Abyssinian Adelaide, but it grew in its own haphazard way and the attempt to make the great square and the railway station the focal points has failed – the centre of Addis, the African heart of the matter, is Mercato, a cacophanous, claustrophobic, and often dangerous market area where you can buy lion skins, crocodile teeth or nuggets of river gold, much as in Vivien's day. I had no intention of diving into that maelstrom immediately, planning to walk a little, change some money and investigate getting a Djiboutian visa.

I walked on past shops stacked to the rickety rafters with huge yellow-streaked papayas, green oranges and purple onions. A mini-bus had stopped and two ladies, one entering and one leaving, were exchanging greetings, deep bows and three kisses on each cheek with right hands clasped, then stepping gently back with eyes cast down and the muttered words dying like echoes. The driver waited. I was consulted by a man in a smart windcheater as to whether he should go on a weightlifting course to Morocco. Another offered to find me a girlfriend: 'Very clean. All girlfriends are university students but we must hurry or they will go to church.'

I jumped on the mini-bus to escape him and got out at Meskal Square, a vast tarmac gladiatorial ring where unwary pedestrians are hunted down by battered old Lada taxis. On one side are the grey monoliths of concrete modernity upon which, until 1991, were hung vast heroic revolutionary pictures. A *National Geographic* magazine photographer caught one in 1982 of a muscular young Ethiopian whacking a Yankie octopus labelled 'Imperialism' with a hammer. The communist government, known as the Dergue, had begun in 1974 with the overthrow of Emperor Haile Selassie but eventually had fallen to a federation of regional secessionists under the umbrella title of Ethiopian Peoples' Revolutionary Democratic Front, the EPRDF. Since this new government took over, the symbols of communist power have been slowly disappearing: the Soviet realist pictures are gone and the square has reverted from being Revolution Square to Meskal, the Holy Cross. In one former hall of communist utopianism, I changed Yankee dollars at a blackmarket rate and discussed the forthcoming football match between Ethiopia and Senegal. Some months later the entire Ethiopian team took the opportunity of a trip to Italy to defect, proving, perhaps, that not everything has changed. With money in my pocket, I then hailed a taxi.

Wubate, the taxi driver, was a young man with a pleasant honest face. He was a Christian from Gondar, he told me, and curious to know why I wanted to go to Djibouti. I explained my route through Ethiopia to the coast.

'Will you visit Harar? You should try the chat there – it's the best in the world.'

'Do you take qat?'

He grinned and gave me a sidelong glance. 'Sometimes – not often.' I told him I had sampled qat many times in Yemen and enjoyed it. This seemed to establish a bond between us – something that was to happen many times with other people over the following months.

'You want chat today?' he said enthusiastically, 'I can take you to a good chat-seller.'

'Yes, okay – after I've got my visa.'

But the Djiboutian Embassy wanted a letter from the British Embassy and we drove up an unmade track past butter-coloured villas that were disappearing under their own rebellious gardens, drowned by a rising tide of dark-leafed shrubbery and creeper-choked trees, eventually to emerge opposite a familiar royal crest on a pair of double gates.

One of the first buildings of Menelik's new capital was this outpost of another, more far-flung empire, still on the same spot where Herbert Vivien found it, though no longer an arduous mule ride from the centre. Inside the security wall I found ponies grazing contentedly under the trees and tidy lawns set with tables and parasols, waiting for tired expatriates to come and unwind.

The thatched-roof consular office is where the explorer Wilfred Thesiger was born in 1919, though it is now air-conditioned and as smartly anodyne as any modern business office. I read the noticeboard while waiting for my letter. Almost every African country had its own alarming bulletin: 'We advise against travel to Somalia', 'The political situation in Nigeria is uncertain', 'Security in South of Sudan and Nuba Mountains is unstable', 'Travel to Rwanda and Burundi is not advisable', 'Ethiopian border areas are to be avoided', and 'A bomb exploded at the Wabe Shebelle Hotel in Addis Ababa killing one person on 5 August. Be vigilant at all times.' But most worrying was the line 'Dire Dowa and Harar and the road between are unsafe at present', plus 'Avoid travelling at night in Djibouti and avoid main roads between Ethiopia and Djibouti where there is a strong risk of banditry.' Finally, there was a note advertising 'chips, beans and fried eggs' at the Friday night social evening in the British Club. It was all rather worrying.

My letter was soon ready and passed under the glass divide on production of about sixty dollars' worth of Ethiopian birr: around a dollar a word for a recommendation from a person I did not even see. I walked back to the gate.

'Who put the bomb in the Wabe Shebelle Hotel?' I asked Wubate when I was safely back in the taxi.

He shrugged. 'Nobody knows.'

'Are Dire Dowa and Harar safe now?'

He laughed. 'Nobody knows. The situation is vague.'

As he drove he began to question me closely on my links with the British Embassy. The salute I had been given on entering and leaving had left a big impression on him: not only that but I had a letter from the Ambassador personally recommending me as a suitable man to visit Djibouti. I was clearly an important and well-connected individual who probably knew someone who needed a personal driver, handyman or bodyguard. My humble rejections of such status only seemed to make him more certain of this – he began to talk about 'looking after' me during my stay in Ethiopia.

When I got back to the taxi with my Djiboutian visa safely stamped in my passport, there was a large green package on the passenger seat looking like a jade tusk.

'I bought chat,' said Wubate. 'The place is near here and it's cheaper if I buy without you – when they see you they will want more money. You must pay me sixteen birr.'

A quick glance at the bottom of the banana leaf wrapping revealed that Wubate knew how to buy qat: the stems there had a nailhead-type base, showing they were side shoots off a main trunk and so very good quality. I did not unwrap the covering which was tied up with thin raffia; qat dries out in the open air and I would certainly struggle to retie it.

Heading back towards the hotel, Wubate sang softly under his breath. He had a slightly asymmetric face, as though it had been wrenched to one side, leaving no visible scars but some underlying deformity of the bones. When he sang or smiled, his mouth became even more twisted, giving an expression of almost demonic cruelty. I asked what the song was.

'It's in Tigrinya language – a battle song.'

'Did you fight?'

He smiled. 'Yes.'

The Tigrinya battle song meant he had been with the Tigrean rebels in the north, mainstay of the EPRDF victory.

'What happened? Did you train as a soldier?'

'Yes – in Sudan. Do you know who that is?' He tapped the speedometer which was completely hidden behind a colourful sticker portraying a bearded holy man. 'It is St George. We had some training but they had tanks and fighter planes and rockets. We were few but they were many. Some of us didn't even have shoes. But we won.'

He began to sing again and said no more.


I had lunch in the hotel; then, after a nap, began to arrange the room so I could chew qat. This involved wrapping up a pillow with a blanket to make an armrest and I was just finishing this when there was a knock at the door. It was Wubate.

'You are taking chat alone? But why? Go to Room 10.' The door closed.

Room 10 was in a separate block through the courtyard and up some stairs. Next to the open door was a large mural of a haloed saint with a malevolent green serpent wrapped around his midriff preventing him from reaching a holy shrine on a distant mountain. I called out: 'As-salaam aleikum.'

A portly middle-aged man in spectacles, white vest and checked purple futa scrambled to his feet from the floor by the bed. 'Wa-aleikum as-salaam. Welcome! Welcome! Come in friend. I am Abdi and you are welcome.'

I left my shoes next to his outside the door and entered. He hurried to prepare a space for me, turning his suitcase into an armrest and laying a blanket out as a seat.

'Hassan will come later,' he said, though I hadn't a clue who Hassan might be. 'Are you Britishman? Very good. You must sit here.'

I protested: this gave me all the blankets and cushions. A waitress appeared at the door and was immediately despatched to fetch more pillows, plus soda water, Coca-Cola and cigarettes.

'You want coffee? No? So you take your qat like the Arabs not the Africans!'

Soon we had made three comfortable little nests on the floor between the bed, bathroom door and outside door. I went in the bathroom and slipped into a sarong I had brought along. This length of cloth is called a futa in Arabic and there is some art to sitting correctly in them. The right knee is drawn up while the left, also flexed, goes flat to the floor, the right elbow then rests naturally on the right knee, leaving the right hand, the clean hand in Arab custom, ready to rub the dust from the qat leaves. The left hand holds the stems and rests on the bolster. The only problem is that the futa can ride up at the front, flashing ones underwear to all present. To avoid embarrassment then, the rear hem is kept tight behind the knees as you sit, ensuring a polite tight veil of decency. The excess cloth at the front is then folded into your lap.

Only this is something of a skill and easily forgotten without regular practice. Abdi had seated himself opposite and was watching with interest. As I bent to sit, the waist slipped and before I could grab the cloth it was down around my ankles.

Abdi's left eyebrow twitched. 'I worked for the British Army in Aden for eight years,' he said coolly. I hurriedly retied the futa. 'But now I am in Saudi Arabia.'

I sat down. He had already opened his qat and was busily picking the choice leaves and building a wad in his right cheek. 'Hassan bought this chat. It looks okay. You take chat every day?'

'First time for some weeks.'

'In Saudi we take it once a week. It's illegal there, you know. But people still want it – probably more. They make plenty money with chat there. The police and soldiers are all selling it. For one afternoon you can spend eighty dollars.'

I opened the banana leaf wrapper and took out the qat bundle – about thirty two-foot long stems tied at the base with some grass. The leaves were very dark green while the stems had a maroon tint that shaded into grey-brown lower down. I undid the grass and threw it on the floor in front of me, then plucked out the last five inches of one stem.

The taste of qat varies but generally it is bitter. Western travellers from times past until the present are fond of describing its taste as being 'like privet' – as though that clarified the matter for most readers. The first reliable account from a European who definitely tried the leaf was by Carsten Niebuhr, leader of a Danish expedition to Yemen in 1761. He was not impressed with the 'disagreeable' and 'insipid' substance, adding, 'We did not relish this drug.'

William Makin, who wrote a melodramatic account of adventures in the Red Sea in the 1930s, gave it, not inaccurately, the flavour of dry lettuce and radishes, adding in distaste, 'I swilled the mess down with some coffee and lit a cigarette.' Presumably, he was initiated by an Ethiopian as the Yemenis neither swallow the qat, nor drink coffee with it. But at least he tried it: Norman Stone Pearn, an American of the same era, did not approve at all. Gamely setting off into Yemen, despite having heard that 'Maxwell Darling, the locust hunter from the Sudan, had been manhandled by beduins in the interior', he barred his guide from using the leaf, telling him that, 'I had no whisky and he should not have the advantage of me in Carte leaves, Carte blanche or Carte anything.'

Like a two-year-old who knows perfectly well that Brussel sprouts are disgusting without trying them, many European travellers were quick to condemn. Those that did experiment were no less critical: 'I have never met one [European] yet who liked it,' wrote Wyman Bury. 'The habit has become a serious social evil, undermining the mental and physical health of the native population; the foe alike of thrift and industry.' Bury dedicated his book *The Land of Uz* in a manner Maxwell Darling might have approved, to 'All who have supported a firm hinterland policy.'

But some qat can be pleasant to open-minded first-timers: the thickened tips of stems yield and snap in your fingers like young carrots or asparagus, then give the same tactile pleasure as crunching through an iceberg lettuce. Others can be pretty astringent, requiring a developed palate or large accompanying doses of sweet drinks, some have the fizz of a rocket salad or a lingering nuttiness, many varieties will make water taste sublime and tobacco, too. But the scent never varies: when I first detect that delicate, almost herb-like fragrance, then I am in San'a as surely as the smell of a newly cut lawn takes me to an English summer evening. And what is certain is that to the qat regular, nothing tastes better.

My companion was certainly a regular, tucking in with relish and frequent small grunts of pleasure.

'Are you from Saudi Arabia?' I asked, knowing from his African features that he was probably not.

'Somali,' he said. 'Born near Hargeisa, you know it because it was the capital of what was British Somaliland. I'm working in Jeddah.'

He had left Somalia as an eight-year-old and never returned except for short visits, spending his life working on the fringes of the Arabian peninsula: Aden, Abu Dhabi, Bharain, Kuwait, and now Jeddah. Although in exile for so long, he could still recite the names of his camels which relatives looked after for him in the countryside around Hargeisa. In 1992 his wife had been killed in the Somali War and his son disappeared while living in Mogadishu.

'A year later I was in Jeddah and a man came to my house. He said he had news of my son – that he was alive and in Najran near the Saudi-Yemeni border.'

Abdi had travelled down to see him and given him some money. The youth had escaped by dhow from Mogadishu and survived a gruelling journey across the Arabian Gulf to Yemen. With 180 people aboard and water running low, the armed crew had taken to selling drinks to those who

could pay. They landed at night on a deserted beach where most of the passengers, too weak to move fast, were soon picked up by the Yemeni Army
and taken to refugee camps. Abdi's son managed to evade them, walking
by night through the mountains until he reached San'a. There a distant relative was called on and helped him on his way north, eventually crossing
the border into Saudi Arabia.

'Is he still there?'

'Yes, he's got a good job now – plenty money.'

'What does he do?'

'He smuggles qat from Yemen. When he walked across, you see, he
found out some special paths that the smugglers use and got to know some
of them. They carry about sixty kilos in a sack on their backs and that
brings a very good price in Najran. The border is very dangerous though:
there are spies everywhere because there is a reward for information on qat
smugglers. Sometimes they get shot at but usually that's just the guards
trying to get them to drop the qat and run away – then they can take it and
sell it, you see.'

'But the penalty if he's caught – it must be tough?'

'Fifteen years and forty lashes.'

It is one of the remarkable features of qat that societies and cultures
have reacted so differently to its use, but nowhere is that difference so
clearly seen as across the Saudi-Yemen border. Abdi described qat sessions
in Saudi: behind closed curtains with trusted friends, each bringing his own
qat hidden down his trousers.

'What about other drugs?'

'Plenty problems. There's nothing to do for young people so they get
pills or qat or whisky – anything. Everything is smuggled into Saudi Arabia.
And qat is very mild really and it is a sociable thing – it gives people chance
to meet and talk. Is that not good? And the Koran does not forbid it. Now
they make qat-eaters criminals just like cocaine or heroin addicts. For the
young people, they think there is no difference – try qat, then try something else. It is all drugs.'

'Where do all these drugs come from?'

'Qat and guns from Yemen, whisky and pills from Djibouti. The Red
Sea is full of smugglers.'

I asked about Somalia, or at least Somaliland, the northern region.

'Yes, they smuggle a lot: they take things to Ethiopia by camel at night through the desert. Then qat goes down to Hargeisa by fast four-wheel-drive trucks. Everything is smuggling.'

He talked about the politics of the area: names coming thick and fast, factions and acronyms. For a man who had not been home since 1984, his grasp of events was impressive. It was from Abdi that I first heard the name Ittihad.

'They are fundamentalists and want Dire Dowa and Harar to be part of a Somali nation. You should not travel down from Harar to the Somali border. They will kill you. For me, no problem; for you, very dangerous.'

I thought of Richard Burton who had passed along that route, disguised as an Arab merchant for the same reasons of religious and racial intolerance.

'But I want to take that route – the old trade road.'

'It is all smuggling now, the only real trade route is the railway to Djibouti and that is no good either. I tell you these people will do bad things to you.'

Abdi's view of the region's politics was pessimistic and tinged with black humour.

'The leaders of America, Russia and Somalia all died and went to heaven and God called them all in separately to tell them what they did wrong in life. The Americans went in and after an hour they came out the room, crying and wailing. The Russians went in and after two hours came out, crying and wailing. Then the Somalis went in and a long time passed – many hours – then God came out crying and wailing.'

We were interrupted by Wubate arriving.

'Hassan!' cried Abdi, jumping up.

'Wubate,' I said.

He smiled at me a little sheepishly. 'My mother was Muslim so I have Christian and Muslim names.'

Abdi sat him down and gave him some qat. 'If you are a Muslim, you can come and live in Jeddah – plenty money there for you!'

Wubate just gave his twisted smile. 'It is not possible.'

Abdi began to persuade him, expounding on all the great advantages of Saudi Arabia – all of which involved getting 'plenty money'. They talked dreamily of riches, of made-good merchants from Yemen and Ethiopia with private jets and houses in London, New York and Addis Ababa.

'There is one man,' said Wubate, 'he drives in Addis in a gold Mercedes and every beggar he sees he gives a hundred birr.'

'True,' said Abdi emphatically.

Wubate was gazing out the open door. 'I want to go somewhere,' he said, 'America, Italy, Britain – but not Saudi.'

They talked in circles for a while: Wubate endlessly coming back to the rich merchant, untouchable and mysterious whose car door would open and money pour out. This was the early stages of qat, when conversation tumbles forward without a stop and the hours pass unnoticed.

The waitress appeared at the door. 'Telephone, Mister Abdi.'

Abdi went out.

'Why were you in Sudan?' I asked Wubate.

He smiled. 'Do you know the Geshebe?'

I nodded. The Geshebe, or Red Terror, had been unleashed by Lieutenant-Colonel Mengistu's communists two years after taking power in 1974, a horrific killing spree, supposedly directed against counter-revolutionaries but also securing Mengistu dictatorial powers. No one suspected of opposition survived unscathed: three million people left the country in the years that followed. Mengistu rode out nine coup attempts in 1978 alone, parading with the severed head of one general in the streets of Addis Ababa, murdering another by publicly squashing him under a tank. When the EPRDF soldiers finally fought their way into Menelik's palace in May 1991, they found a forty-foot-tall picture of Mengistu placed in front of the church altar.

Wubate's story was not untypical. As he was walking with a friend outside school, some soldiers opened fire and killed the friend. Wubate had fled to Sudan with some others, one of whom died in the desert from a snake bite. In the three years that followed he joined the EPRDF, while his companions had made it to a Red Cross camp and were now doctors in Italy and Canada. He sighed, 'Only myself and the boy who died from the snake did not escape.'

He took some more qat from the banana leaf wrapper. He was gently crushing the leaves then swallowing them, something I baulked at doing, having become accustomed to the Yemeni habit of storing in the cheek and rinsing out later.

'Do you read your Bible?' he asked.

[27]

I shook my head.

'You should. It's a good book. I read it every morning. There's one story I read over and over again – the one about Job.'

'I went to his tomb once.'

His eyes lit up. 'Really, where is it?'

'On a mountain-top in Yemen.'

This did not go down well. 'Yemen? I thought maybe Israel – I have a friend there. He's a Falasha from Gondar. He keeps writing to me, so one day I might try and get there. I'll say I'm a Jew – it's not difficult, we grew up together all Christians, Jews and Muslims mixed in together so we know each others' customs.'

I asked if he was married.

'Yes, but she went to Sudan in the war and I never heard from her again. Someone told me she made it to Italy and married an Italian man.'

Abdi appeared in the door. 'Who got married – you Hassan, you married?'

'Not now.'

'No need to marry here – too many girlfriends. I had one here last night but there was no power. The qat – what do you think, is it better with qat?'

'Of course,' said Wubate. 'For me it is very good.'

I was not convinced. 'I think a few leaves makes it better but who takes just a few leaves? A full afternoon of qat makes you dream too much – your mind drifts away and cannot concentrate on physical things.'

Wubate laughed. 'Nonsense. Don't you know how chat was discovered? A goatherd noticed that his herd liked to eat the leaves of a certain tree. Then he also noticed that at night they would not sleep but the males were very busy with the women goats. So one day he tried these leaves himself. Both he and his wife were very happy with the results and they took chat every day after that.'

Abdi shook his head ruefully. 'For me this is not true.'

It should not surprise anyone that this contradictory plant should be both good and bad for sex but other, less ambivalent, qualities have long made it popular with herbalists. One sixteenth-century text lauds the leaf for 'alleviating swelling and pustules, smarting of scrofula, wounds and ulcers, epilepsy, nightmares, nose bleeds, bad breath, eye itching, eye-lid tumours, watery eyes, throbbing eyes . . . and in moderation removes anxieties and melancholy'. Unfortunately, there are side-effects: 'it sets up borborygma and winds and is utterly harmful to those affected with haemorrhoids.'

We subsided into silence, thankfully undisturbed by borborygma or wind. Outside, the shadows were lengthening across the dusty golden square of the courtyard. The waitress brought a small glass of black coffee for Wubate. The currents of our thoughts had become deeper, moving too fast to relate to the others and so we sat in silence. Anyone glancing inside the room would have seen three men, comfortably slouched on cushions, eyes liquid and shining in the fading light, their hands moving occasionally to carry a leaf or a cigarette to the mouth but otherwise at rest. Like an audience lost in music that no others can hear and afterwards unable to explain what thoughts had danced through our minds, only that some kind of peace had been found.

After dark, Wubate quietly departed. The electricity did not come on with nightfall and in the gloom all I could see was Abdi's white vest and teeth, hovering in the dark. An hour later I left too.

I had not felt greatly affected by the qat, it being my first for some weeks, but still sleep did not come until late. Eventually I fell into a half-wakeful dream where I was in a beautiful stone house that was a bizarre amalgam of my mother's house in Nottingham and a Yemeni tower house, and a Chinese girl was feeding me grass stalks on which tiny heiroglyphs were inscribed.

# 3

If I recall that first week in Addis it is a memory of darkness, of nights in rooms with dim bulbs – bulbs with barely sufficient strength to cast a shadow. Abdi moaned about it constantly, missing the buzz of neon at night in Jeddah. Sometimes I walked along streets where you could not see your feet in the darkness, then drank beer in bars where customers with sick yellow faces stared unswervingly. Once a man slipped down beside me and whispered, 'This government is not good.' But when I asked why he just giggled. At a church behind the old presidential palace I was gripped by the bony, feverish hand of a madman and propelled forwards into the building towards a trap door, tripping over the prostrate, groaning figures of old women, hearing his crazed voice in my ear 'Three-in-one, one-in-three, Holy Trinity. Three-in-one . . . ' I went down a staircase into a crypt and came face to face with Menelik's white marble sarcophagus and the remains of Haile Selassie, only recently transferred from the presidential palace.

'Menelik II,' whispered the madman, 'modernised Ethiopia very good. First the bicycle, then the motor car, finally the electric chair.'

Perhaps because of these experiences, or perhaps because of the qat, I had powerful dreams. I found myself entombed and forgotten in an abandoned underground railway station. Where the door should have been there was only solid brick and I woke up hammering on the wall; the man in the next room hammering back for me to shut up.

Every afternoon I was in Room 10 with Abdi and bundles of qat; in the remains of the mornings I tried to discover how I was to cross the Red Sea. I met an Italian who knew a member of parliament who put me onto another Italian who had the number of a doctor who he thought had information about boats and where they might sail from. I spent hours finding phone numbers only to hear an unanswered ringing tone. At the end of a week I was no further forward than when I arrived. I began to postpone essential calls and explore the city instead. I visited the National Museum and saw Lucy, the 3.5 million-year-old skeleton found in 1967 in the deserts of eastern Ethiopia and named after the Beatles LSD-inspired 'Lucy in the Sky with Diamonds'. On the same floor were relics of Axum, the great civilisation that appears to have started as an African colony of Sheba, the ancient Yemeni empire, then expanded to eclipse the waning mother country.

Both Yemen and Ethiopia claim the Queen of Sheba as their own but for Ethiopians the claim is perhaps more relevant to national identity: the son of the Queen and Solomon, Menelik I, is reputed to have brought the ark of the covenant back with him to Ethiopia and from Menelik I comes the great dynasty that lost power in 1974 shortly before the death of number 237, Haile Selassie.

The King of Kings always kept a good reputation in the western world. Stately homes all over England have a little signed portrait somewhere, souvenir of Selassie's tireless canvassing for support against the Italian invasion of 1935. The emperor had escaped on the railway to Djibouti. Six years later, with a combined British and Abyssinian force under Orde Wingate, he was returned to power. It was in those days of exile that the western view of Selassie began to take hold: a kindly, paternalistic, rather exotic king who was nobly struggling to modernise his nation and extirpate colonialism (extirpating colonialism was all right if it was the Italian variety). But there was another side to the emperor, one he had inherited with the position: a capacity for ruthless tyranny when opposed, combined with a willingness to use any means to cling to power. And when the young communists wanted that power from the ageing monarch, they had moved carefully, snipping away at the emperor's image and position, preparing the public for his final fall from grace. Even after his death, officially from heart failure but unofficially murdered, his power obsessed Colonel Mengistu, the communist leader. In a bizarre move, he had the dead emperor's bones buried beneath the chair in his office. Mengistu is himself now exiled in Zimbabwe.

One evening I went into the hotel bar and met a British development worker who had come on leave from Tigre. Her previous work experience had been making coathangers for Marks & Spencer's.

'Some of the aid people don't think we're doing any good,' she sighed. 'Some of them say we should just put the money in a light aircraft and fly over the countryside dropping it.'

We waited for a friend of hers who knew something about the Red Sea ports. But he never showed up and in the early hours of the morning, lying awake with qat chemicals in my brain, I decided to give up my search for information, give up the foolish desire to know anything for certain, and just go.

At the peak of the railway expansion in Europe, stations were the temples of the new age: great, booming halls and majestic facades that trumpeted their economic might. Emperor Menelik II undoubtedly wanted the same effect from his capital's communications nerve centre: a broad avenue bisects the city, rising past a monumental bronze of the Lion of Judah to the station. But there the grandeur ended: Menelik died before his railway arrived and the station buildings are no more imposing than those of any small French town. No booming halls or vast concourses greet the traveller, but signs in French, the language of the construction company, with all the petty distinctions of the period: separate exits from the ticket hall for first- and second-class passengers. Third-class passengers were not even allowed in the building.

The bronze statue with its stone pedestal bearing the face of Menelik was surrounded by the homeless and poor. On one side a small market was doing a brisk trade in oranges and cigarettes, while young boys selling little rolls of toilet paper scampered through the crowd whispering, 'Soft! Soft!' With Wubate and Abdi to help me, I walked through the quiet ticket hall, surprised to find it unnecessary to fight for a seat. Dire warnings had been given to me about the danger of thieves along the route, so I decided to take a first-class ticket, then went out onto the platform.

There is only one departure per day down the 300 miles of track to Dire Dowa but there was no jostling crowd. I strolled down to where the only train was standing, a battered three-car unit that might have once carried

Parisian commuters – not the great belching Titan of the tracks I had expected. I said goodbye to my companions and Abdi presented me with a large quantity of qat for the journey.

First class was deserted, as were second and third, and I was just regretting wasting the extra money when the side-gates were opened to let the passengers in. It appeared that I had managed to slip aboard before the official time. The platform was instantaneously filled with people carrying vast quantities of luggage. Porters in brown overcoats bent double under enormous bags labelled 'Bon Voyage', women struggling with boxes tied up with string, boys sprinting for the seats. A member of staff came striding up and called me to the barred window.

'I am arranging for a man who speaks English to sit next to you.'

The compartment aisle became jammed solid with people and bags. Three girls were marshalling an army of porters laden with plastic holdalls full of helium-filled party balloons already inflated and held down by bottles of water: presumably both balloons and helium were unavailable in Dire Dowa. Bags of paper roses and fruit were thrown up on the racks.

The member of staff struggled through to me. 'This man will sit with you. He worked with us many years ago.'

A cheerful, grey-haired gentleman of athletic build was behind him, greeting everybody with vigorous handshakes and throwing himself down beside me. 'Can we speak French? You prefer English? Oh dear, mine is rather weak, you know. Anyway, hello.' He held out his hand. 'My name is Sahle.' No sooner had we shaken than he disappeared to greet more friends, only returning a few seconds before our departure which was punctual and noisy.

The line was obviously considered as a street by the population who lived alongside it: little tin-shack shops sold cigarettes and qat, people lit fires or wandered after their cattle, and bright patches of tomatoes, aubergines and red peppers dried on the railway sleepers. The huts were often little more than benders of sticks and grass, others were more permanent with mud walls and thatched roofs gathered into little top-knots. Purple flowering creepers ran along brushwood fences and clambered up thorn trees. A prim white cat sat on a doorstep and studiously ignored us. We passed a few factories and then the city petered out into a broad high plain swaying with pale teff grass, the staple crop of the

Ethiopian highlands. To the east, in the far distance, was a ridge of serrated dark mountains. The sky was a startling blue with vast sails of white cloud moving across in stately procession and I felt a surge of pleasure to be out of the city and on my way.

'Years ago there were trees here,' said Sahle. 'Trees all the way to Dire Dowa. My grandfather used to take me to hunt kudu near the line about twenty kilometres before Dire Dowa. Now you won't find a single tree there.'

I asked if he had retired from the railway.

'These days I drive a taxi in Dire Dowa, but I did twenty-five years with the railway.'

'In Haile Selassie's time?'

'Yes. I often went on the train with him. He had his own carriages, of course, and they would go quite slowly along so he could wave to people from the rear platform and throw money for them.'

Money from heaven, I thought, remembering the development worker and the light aircraft.

'The emperor's train is still there in Addis,' Sahle added.

I nodded. In fact, I had been to visit the carriages during my morning explorations of the city. After a few hours spent chasing permission to see them, I was escorted by five guides and two armed soldiers through a double-locked gate and into a hangar a few hundred yards from the station. The first two carriages were dark and sombre with a tiny brass bedstead where the emperor slept. A connecting door allowed access to the queen's quarters – 'If she wanted,' said one of the guides. Next door was a lounge with rather formal, uncomfortable red leather chairs. All the blinds were down and the wood panelling dark. There was a feeling of claustrophobia and gloom as if the railway, symbol of light and modernity, had been joined to something more sinister.

Sahle knew the carriages well. 'They were built in Switzerland in 1934,' he told me. 'When we held a railway exhibition in Dire Dowa during Mengistu's time, we had some photographs of them there. I was chosen to show around the communist leaders at the opening ceremony and when we came to these photographs one of them said, "Ah! These must be the imperial carriages, a symbol of the decadent and corrupt regime, now owned by the people and used by the people." Of course, I was expected to agree with him, but I told the truth. I said, "In fact, they are now used by top communist officials only."' He laughed at the memory. 'You should have seen their faces.'

'Wasn't that a little foolhardy?'

Sahle's eyes twinkled. 'These dictators are always the same. An uncle of mine who was a general in Haile Selassie's army had the habit of speaking his mind and the emperor hated him for it. Of course, he was always surrounded by people who flattered and deceived. One time all the generals were called to pay homage. Each man had to crawl on his face up the hall and kiss the emperor's foot. My uncle was last and when he came to press his lips on the royal boot, it kicked him in the mouth.'

'Did he protest?'

'On the contrary, he thanked the emperor for his kindness.'

This was the other Haile Selassie, not the kindly dignitary seen on photographs in the west, but a despot surrounded by servility and corruption, behaving very much as his predecessors had done.

The first stop was the village of Akaki, the huts almost hidden behind tall grass and thorn trees. Children came running alongside with bowls of dry beans and seeds, or holding a cigarette aloft or a cup of water.

No one got on or off. In 1930 Evelyn Waugh arrived here from Dire Dowa with delegations attending the coronation of Haile Selassie and the train paused while everyone shaved and donned their uniforms. 'The Dutch Minister soon appeared at the side of the line in cocked hat and gold braid, the Egyptian in tarboosh and epaulettes, the Japanese in evening coats and white waistcoats and top hats.'

I leaned against the window bars, trying to imagine the scene and ignore the dozens of young salesmen who were leaping up at me. One, screeching 'Mastica! Mastica!', tried valiantly to shove a stick of chewing gum up my nose.

Within two minutes we were again rolling along at twenty miles an hour. I asked Sahle if the communists had been as bad as Selassie.

'Oh, worse,' he said without hesitation. 'My nephew was at secondary school in Dire Dowa and a spy informed the cadres that he was a counter-revolutionary. This was during the Red Terror. He disappeared. To this day we have never found his body or heard what happened. Then his sister, my niece, was taken, too. They shot her in the head in the street outside the house. We were not allowed to touch the body until we had paid for the bullet.'

[35]

He gazed past me at the fields of green. Two boys herding white, hump-backed cattle waved their sticks at the train.

'Some time after that I received an invitation to go and visit our Colonel Mengistu at the presidential palace in Addis Ababa.' He frowned. 'Of course, I was very afraid and I refused. Then they telephoned me and said it was an order. So I travelled up to Addis and went to see Mengistu.'

'What did he want?'

'I was ordered to play him at tennis. At that time I was in charge of the Dire Dowa tennis club and they must have got my name through that. I had to arrange for a court to be built inside the palace and then I played him. For about five years I had to keep going.'

I remembered seeing the palace from the church where Menelik II was buried: a high wall with watch-towers and machine guns surrounding a huge compound full of trees and just a glimpse of rooftops beyond. A passer-by had pointed to the gate: 'Not long ago, people who were taken in there never came out.'

I asked Sahle what Mengistu had been like.

'They were all afraid of him. The ministers would come cringing up to the tennis court if they had to interrupt. Once they were discussing something there by the drinks table and Mengistu suddenly lost his temper. He brought his fist smashing down on the table and they scattered like rabbits – even important ministers ran to hide.'

'Did you ever beat him at tennis?'

He began to chuckle.

'Did you?'

'No.'

'Could you?'

'He was a very good player.'

'But you were better?'

'Absolutely not.' His face was totally expressionless, but his eyes were sparkling. 'Look . . . ' He pointed out of the window and there were tall stands of sugar cane by the tracks. 'We are coming to Debre Zeit. You can buy sugar cane to chew.'

I rummaged in my bag. 'I've got something else actually – do you want some?' I pulled out Abdi's present.

Sahle shook his head firmly. 'No, I never take it – not any more. No qat, no cigarettes, no alcohol – nothing.'

The train pulled in past hordes of children brandishing batons of sugar cane. Once we stopped some leapt on board and began to hawk their wares down the aisles, while others tapped on the window bars. The three girls sitting in front of me were making pearl tiaras by blobbing tiny droplets of glue onto thin wires. One of them leaned over the seat and asked, with obvious distaste, 'Do you chew that stuff?'

'Yes.'

'Why? It is very bad.' She sat down again. I became aware that I was the only passenger in first class with qat, except for the man who sold Coca-Cola from an ice-box by the door. This was a third-class habit. Sahle told me that his church, a branch of American Mennonites, had banned alcohol and qat for its members. He would not, however, go so far as to condemn the leaf; there were too many fond memories of it.

I sat enjoying the views as we pulled out of Debre Zeit, chewing happily all the same, my mind running on with the beat of the rails: mennonites – mnemonites – science of memory – church of memory – mennonites – mnemonites.

The building of the Djibouti to Addis Ababa railway was dogged with disaster and despair from the very beginning in 1897. It had already taken twenty years to convince Menelik that it was not some fiendish colonial stab at the heart of his empire but there were plenty of other opponents yet to be won over.

Menelik's instincts were that the French had fewer territorial ambitions and so Djibouti was chosen as the starting point, a decision which infuriated the British. Quite correctly they surmised that this would kill their own port of Zeila stone dead.

The logistics of the construction were staggering: the sleepers weighed two hundred kilos each and there were 1,333 of them for every kilometre. The iron telegraph poles and rails were often too hot to handle and when workers survived the heat they were likely to be shot by armed gangs of Issa tribesmen who were implacably opposed to the enterprise. Thousands of camels perished bringing water to the men as the line pushed out across the southern reaches of the Danakil desert. This was a bold undertaking: the desert was one of the hottest places on earth and almost totally unexplored. The tribesmen had yet to give up the anti-social habit of castrating visitors and recent expeditions to the interior had been wiped out. Into this hellish region the Awash river disappeared, never to emerge, its course uncharted, and there were reports of the wild Sultan of Aussa whose men became warriors only on killing other men – something they would do at every opportunity, even, so it was said, ripping open the stomach of a pregnant woman in the hope of finding a male foetus. As far as these fearsome killers were concerned the railway was definitely an unwanted visitor.

Every worker on the line needed armed protection. Squads of mounted riflemen patrolled at all times. This helped reduce the killings to about one a week but the warriors still managed to pinch the telegraph wires to make jewellery. The French appealed to Menelik who ordered that anyone found with copper ornaments on their wrists would lose their hand, those bedecked on the ankle would lose a foot, and swells daring a necklace would be beheaded. He was speaking the right language; telegraph wire thefts stopped instantly and the tribesmen had to console themselves by forging spears from stolen rails.

But the most serious problem was not the savagery or the climate, it was corruption: 'One glorious scandal,' a British minister described it. Actual costs were only half what was spent. Railway officials would smash up their own track, report a raid, then demand funds from Paris to compensate local chiefs. In one case, a thousand dollars was despatched but the chief in question received only a loincloth and two bags of dates. Unsurprisingly, the money ran out soon after the line scraped across the border of French territory and into Abyssinia.

After tortuous negotiations, British capitalists agreed to help and the line limped into Dire Dowa. It had taken five years to cover 195 miles but even that hard-won distance was scarcely finished. At one point where a bridge was needed, the rails simply dipped down into the riverbed and up again. Locomotives charged at it but four attempts were often required.

For three years Menelik frustrated further work, fearing British involvement, then suddenly he changed his mind and berated the engineers for tardiness. By now the European powers, Britain, France and Italy, were squabbling over the matter. Nothing was done until 1909 when Menelik, acting on a whim, simply gave the concession to a Dr Vitalien, a medical man from Guadeloupe. Not that this added much vitality to the enterprise: the first train did not puff wearily into Addis Ababa until 1917, four years after Menelik died. After all the effort, the blood spilled and money wasted, the first cargo began to move up from the coast on a journey that would prove to be, on average, six weeks. Most of this lengthy period was taken up by inefficient bureaucracy and rampant corruption but nevertheless, as gleeful critics pointed out, the railway had managed to match precisely the time taken by its main competitor, the camel caravan.

We were now approaching the edge of the Awash valley and the landscape was changing: on twisted black rocks webbed with creepers solemn parties of baboons sat watching the train. For some miles we saw no human beings at all, then passed two small boys standing silently under a solitary acacia in a sea of white grass.

As the sun set we began the descent into the valley, the light fading through gold and purple to a soft grey twilight. Once down on the valley floor we began to pass groups of slender girls carrying water pots on their heads and children driving big-horned, big-eared cattle into thorn enclosures. The air was filled with the smoke of dung fires and under the acacias stood the pale ghostly shapes of termite mounds.

We stopped in the larger settlements, picking up passengers until the aisle was jammed with people. Every station had its speciality: oranges, guavas, samosas, and lumpy yoghurt in rusty containers of various sizes. Boys in grubby tunics came along swinging jerry cans and shouting, 'Wuha! Wuha!' An old man perched himself on a suitcase beside Sahle. I gave him some qat and he told me he was going to Awash town to find medicine for his wife who had been ill for three days.

The carriage lights flickered on, then died.

'In Dire Dowa you must be careful,' whispered Sahle. 'Do not go out at night. If possible, go directly to Harar when we arrive – it is better.'

I asked why.

'There have been some incidents: a German tourist was shot dead two weeks ago, before him a Dutchman. We don't know who did it. There are some groups. It was not robbery, nothing was taken – they just came up behind them and shot them in the head. No one knows why.'

'Is it Ittihad?'

[39]

Even in the gloom I could see his head jerk back in surprise. 'You know about Ittihad? Well, some say it is them.'

'Who are they?'

'No one knows.'

'Are they Islamic fundamentalists?'

'It is said so.'

I could no longer see the man across the aisle. The other passengers were beginning to fall asleep and Sahle's voice had dropped to an almost inaudible whisper. I asked if any local people had been killed.

'In our church there have been nine so far. There were ten who converted from Islam, now only one is left and he is in hiding. The situation is not good.'

One of the girls in front had turned and was looking at us through the gap in the seat headrests.

'She is also of our church,' said Sahle. 'Her sister is getting married.'

The two of them exchanged some words in Amharic. The train slowed and rattled across a long cantilever bridge. I could see nothing but darkness below.

'In 1983 there was an accident here,' said Sahle. 'The driver came too fast into the curve before the bridge and the two carriages broke loose and went over the side of the bridge into the river. Five hundred died.'

'Are you a believer?' asked the girl, perhaps thinking of the souls of the dead.

'I was brought up a Christian,' I said hesitantly, fearing a lecture, 'but I don't go to church now.'

'Why?'

'I suppose I don't believe in it anymore.'

Sahle pointed out the window. 'Don't tell me all this was created by chance. You'll be telling me next that it is only chance we are sitting next to each other.'

I shrugged. 'I don't know.'

'When your journey is finished, you will remember and say that this meeting was not chance.'

The girl was distracted by one of her sisters who wanted something from a bag on the luggage rack. The drinks-seller tapped Sahle on the shoulder and asked if he had any of his empty bottles. I looked outside but all I could see with my head pressed to the bars was a tiny patch of stony wayside earth rushing by in the light of the locomotive's headlamp; the rest was total blackness.

Some hours later I was woken by Sahle. Outside it was still night but there were the lights of Dire Dowa on the horizon. At five o'clock we clanked slowly into the station, the locomotive sending plaintive hoots over the silent box-like houses.

# 4

Sahle had told me not to venture beyond the station gate until daybreak and most other travellers seemed to have the same idea, laying out little camps by the deserted station offices. But no sooner had I settled down than Sahle reappeared.

'Come, quick.'

We went through an arch and out into a broad square lit by car head-lamps; beyond I could see tree-lined streets radiating outwards with all the French-style 1930s buildings shuttered up and dark. The air was hot and very still but the people were in a state of semi-suppressed frenzy: women in colourful robes herded children towards battered old Peugeot taxis, hollow-cheeked youths with wispy beards grabbed potential passengers and shoved them into buses, a wild-eyed man in a forage cap held his stomach and rocked himself, another seized my arm: 'Who shall fight the last battle? Who shall fight?' His crazed eyes glaring into mine. Sahle eased him gently aside and bundled me into a mini-bus bound for Harar.

He pushed a scrap of paper into my hand. 'If you come back to Dire Dowa, telephone me,' he said. 'There's an interesting old merchant, an Armenian, I'd like you to meet him.'

We shook hands and the mini-bus set off, driving fast out of the town and almost immediately into a narrow valley that led up the mountain. At a checkpoint we were told to leave the bus and, looking around, I saw a cluster of stunted trees, then dry rocky slopes rising into the darkness. The soldier who searched me found a few old qat leaves in my jacket pocket and said something in Amharic. The passengers all laughed.

'He says you are the first man to try and smuggle chat *into* Harar,' one explained, the town being ringed by qat-tax checkpoints for departing vehicles.

At the top of the hill we were stopped and searched even more thoroughly. The sky was paling in the east.

'What are they searching for?' I asked the English-speaking passenger who was almost invisible under a blanket, the temperature having plummeted during the ascent.

'We do not know but they did not find it.'

But another passenger grinned and mimed firing an automatic rifle.

The air was now quite damp and we ran into a mist so thick that the driver slowed to walking pace, periodically sending his assistant out to scrub the windscreen as the wipers could not remove the thick foggy cobwebs. I knew from the map that there were some small lakes nearby but we never saw anything of them.

Eventually, the road gained a bit more height and we burst out into the clear rosy light of dawn. Behind us, mountain-tops swam in a sea of white cloud and ahead, wreathed in tendrils of dewy mist, were fields of qat, small trees standing about twelve feet tall at most and planted close together. There was coffee too, about the same height but with darker, shinier leaves.

If you arrive by this road there is no welcoming view of Harar's old city, merely a gentle descent through a rich fertile land of trees and small farms. If you approach from the south-east, however, as the old camel caravans did, you are met by the sight of the walled city on a hill that greeted Richard Burton and, twenty-five years later, Arthur Rimbaud; from that direction, apart from an ugly concrete mosque, the view is relatively unchanged. If you come from the north, the road straightens itself into a grand boulevard lined with mature trees and government offices built during the Italian occupation before the Second World War, and it was at the start of this boulevard where our bus gave a sudden and sickly fart, then died. Too tired to bother walking the last mile, I took directions to a small hotel up a side road past tall stands of bamboo where weaver birds were chirruping. Here there was a pleasant courtyard with white wrought-iron chairs and tables under shady trees. I immediately slumped down in one of the chairs and was surrounded by a team of robber cats who were shooed off by a pair of waiters in cricket umpire coats. Mustering my few words of Amharic, I asked about a room but this sent them scurrying off to the kitchen, returning with a plate of sliced sausage.

For some time my waves and signals drew no response. It was rather like trying to get a sightscreen moved late in the long sleepy afternoon of a village cricket match. Finally, a third umpire was summoned who spoke English.

'I would like a room.'

'You do not like sausage?'

'Yes, I like sausage but not at the moment. I want a room.'

'Ah, you want a room!'

'Yes – with a shower if you have one.'

I was taken to a room on the end of the block with a small verandah. The bed had been slept in but I was too tired to care.

'Good – I'll take it.'

'And your sausage?'

But even as we glanced back at the table the cats were making away with the last of it and the third umpire sprinted away to retrieve what he could.

I slept until lunchtime, then went and sat under the mimosa trees. Glossy starlings were preening their iridescent feathers in the shade. Alem, the third umpire, was summoned by his colleagues and suggested I had sausage. I declined and enquired for other dishes. He suggested kutfoo: flat bread and meat. I agreed.

'You like your meat cooked or not?'

'How do you like it?'

'Not cooked – mostly we are not cooking it but foreign peoples are different.'

'Well, I'll have it not cooked.'

And as I said this, my heart went out to James Bruce, the Scottish explorer whose epic travels during the 1770s were disbelieved and ridiculed mostly because of his astonishing claim that the people of Abyssinia ate raw meat. Nothing, it seemed, rankled more with the sophisticates of London than this transparent calumny of African culinary arts.

[44]

In his book, *The Blue Nile*, Alan Moorehead quotes a popular satirist of the day:

> Nor have I been where men (what loss alas!)
> Kill half a cow and turn the rest to grass.

Bruce had the misfortune to be a pioneer and there was no independent observer to verify his outrageous claims. He withdrew to his estates in Scotland and simmered. Years later when a dinner guest cast doubt on the possibility of humans eating raw meat, Bruce went to the kitchen and prepared some raw beef, peppered and salted in the Ethiopian style, then presented the dish to the man saying: 'You will either eat that, sir, or fight me.' The man took one look at Bruce who was six feet four inches tall and ate up.

I found the meat quite tender and much better than the cooked version which I tried another day. Bruce, incidentally, was probably the first Britisher to come across qat and his artist, Luigi Balugani, made a watercolour of it, the first known image.

By the time I came to walk down to the old town my mind was already on the afternoon session, planning a few pleasant solitary hours writing up my diaries in the room.

It was a bright, blue-sky day and the long boulevard with its mature trees made a pleasant shady walk. On the left I passed the butter-coloured palace that Haile Selassie had been forced to sign over to the Dergue after his abdication. Now it is a rather lifeless café, lost in dank undergrowth, where the elite of Harar like to hold their weddings.

After this were the government buildings and various offices of political parties hung with slogans in Amharic, then the road narrowed through a crenellated archway into the old town. This is the Harar Gate, built by Ras Mekonnen, Haile Selassie's father and Governor of the city after Menelik II seized it for Ethiopia in 1887. Mekonnen was a man hated as a Christian coloniser by the Muslim Hararis – hence the damage to the inscription over the arch.

There were qat-sellers with sacks on the ground. The qat had the same reddish stems and dark green leaves as that sold by Haj Ali in his East End shop. In this region only women do the selling, for a man it would be shameful; one poor individual was even pointed out to me as the 'man who tried to sell chat!' It seemed his wife had died and, desperate to make money, he had taken up her former trade, only to have the entire market mock him. The event was more than five years old but he remained a source of great hilarity.

All of these qat-selling women were Oromo, a term given to the Muslim tribes who occupy most of the land. They have narrow faces, tall slender bodies and a love of the colour orange which they favour for headscarfs, hairnets and beaded necklaces. The main street inside the gate was crowded with them: swinging along on bare feet behind donkeys laden with firewood or else standing in the jewellers' shops gazing longingly at golden trinkets, while the Harari shopkeepers in their white skullcaps and shirts murmured words of encouragement. The few Oromo men to be seen kept themselves apart from the ladies, sauntering nonchalantly with a pencil or a comb tucked in their frizzed hair and a long-handled, small-headed axe over the shoulder, a peculiar tool-cum-weapon that is found in a narrow belt of latitude from central Africa to the shores of the Persian Gulf. They wore knee-length jellabiyas, sometimes with a sleeveless jacket. Most had put on their footwear for the visit to town, a kind of imitation pair of shoes with moulded plastic laces.

The buildings along the main street were simple one- or two-storey blocks painted in pastel shades of creamy white, butterscotch yellow or blue; one of the bars had a wooden balcony under broad eaves with flower pots along the balustrade. Inside it was partitioned into dark cubicles and large ladies swathed in white robes were ministering tiny glasses of foamy coffee to tired gentlemen. Further along the street were clothes shops featuring hand-painted murals of snappy westernised dressers, other places were selling considerable selections of china vases with plastic flowers or the latest cassettes from Ethiopian artists.

At the end of this road is a small square with the church that Menelik forced upon the resentful Muslim population after his forces finished looting. It stands on the site of the mosque over which the conquering leader urinated, rather like a dog marking his territory but also as revenge for the savage Muslim attacks led by the sixteenth-century Harari Emir, Ahmed Gragne, 'The Left-Handed One'. Like troubled areas the world over, the Harar region is plagued by long memory.

To the right of this was a cinema where, examining the billboards, I attracted a band of children screeching, 'Cuba! Cuba!' and 'Rimbaud! Rimbaud!' The poster showed two sweaty white musclemen doggedly slaughtering sallow-skinned orientals who had foolishly forgotten to bring any guns along. Pointing to one of the two Rambo-style warriors, the children assured me that he had once lived down the lane. Clearly, a new warrior-hero was being born, a man worthy of Ahmed Gragne's home town: part symbolist poet from France, part blood-crazed, body-building, action man from Hollywood.

Beside the cinema was a small qat market where women were doing a brisk trade in the shelter of colourful sun umbrellas. It was a business Menelik and his forebears would have shuddered to see so close to their church, qat being regarded as a Muslim vice in which no good Christian would ever indulge. One of the earliest references to qat in Ethiopia comes as part of a fourteenth-century threat by a Muslim king to plant qat on the Christian king's capital. So infuriating was this taunt that King Amda Sion felt obliged to 'perpetrate every enormity' against Muslims and did so with great efficiency for thirty years until his death in AD 1342. Even today Christian qat-users are often unwilling to admit the fact, the habit being shameful for them.

To escape the continued attentions of the children I wandered downhill into a warren of narrow rutted lanes, hemmed in by high whitewashed walls of mud and flinty stones.

Harar is an introverted place architecturally. The walls curve and divide and snake but never open out. Narrow alleyways lead off around secretive corners. The streets run with foul liquids but occasional glimpses through cracks in green doorways revealed clean-swept yards and cool dark entrances behind ornate carved frames.

I emerged in the main souk of the old town, a square with some modern buildings in the centre and crowds of brightly dressed Oromo women milling around piles of vegetables and the baskets for which the town is famous. Tailors were swiftly running up orders of pleated petticoats in flowery fluorescent yellows, while the waiting Oromo girls made flirtatious swipes with wooden clubs at passing youths.

Before the Harar Gate was built, this market was the commercial centre of the town, where slaves were publicly sold and merchants planned vast journeys down to Zeila on the Somali coast and then to India or Arabia. It was the jealous protection of this lucrative trade that concerned the Emir in Burton's day, the explorer noting that in good years up to a thousand men might be shipped out from Zeila. To many Victorians the whole business was abhorrent: condemnations of it came as readily as an anti-drugs message does to a contemporary politician. But Burton, typically, refrains from fashionable broadsides, perhaps knowing that the truth was complex. On the east coast of Africa the slave trade was less brutal than on the west: many slaves were willing partners in the trade, knowing that life in a rich man's house in Arabia could lead to acceptance and adoption by the family.

At a drinks stall, I fell into conversation with Abera, a student at the agricultural college. I asked him if there was a central qat market and he invited me to a bercha or qat session at his house. We strolled up towards the Harar Gate but turned left before reaching it to emerge at the side of a second gate, Baab al-Nasr. This area, known as the Christian Market, was lively with petty traders eager to sell the latest fashions in platform flip-flops or tee-shirts stamped 'High Traffic Area'. Others sold cigarettes by the carton – all smuggled via Somaliland.

We went down a few steps and into the qat market, a tiny area jammed with traders and customers.

'Make the foreigner chew well,' shouted one old woman. 'Then he'll stay forever.'

All the qat looked alike to me but Abera insisted otherwise, pulling me over to one woman's sack. 'Look – and listen.'

He selected two identical sprigs and rubbed the leaves against each other. 'Different sounds, aren't they?'

I nodded uncertainly.

'This one is yesterday's chat which she is trying to sell off, but no one will buy – only fools and beggars.'

It looked pretty good to me but I shook my head vigorously. 'No-o-o!'

'See these black spots, and how the colour is not quite so perfect? These are old stems mixed in with fresh to hide them. Look, they've been recut near the bottom. We call this bultey – yesterday's chat.'

Realising her goods were being maligned, the old woman grabbed the bundle back and screeched at us.

Abera winked at me. 'She says it is good – to keep you going all night.'

He took up another bundle. 'This is dima because it is very red in the stems and the leaves. People say this one will give you a headache. When I chew this for some days then stop I get dukak – chat nightmares – then the chat monster will come to your dream and demand to know why you didn't take chat. He sets you some impossible task – last time he poured some water in a bottle top and ordered me to swim.'

He turned back a leaf. 'Those tiny dots are a fungal infection. Not enough to stop you buying this chat but not good. Anyway we shall not buy this.'

We moved on to another seller: a thin-faced Oromo lady with a mouthful of gold teeth. Like all the sellers she carried her sack up every day from the countryside, a round trip of fourteen miles.

'Most of our words on chat are Oromo,' explained Abera. 'Because they are the farmers. Like this one is urata, the bottom of each stalk is like a nailhead, the best chat.'

I asked if everyone knew so much about qat.

'Not all. Some people are good at buying chat – they never make a mistake – but I just know what I learn in the market or at college.'

Without any bargaining, we bought two bundles and headed off to Abera's house inside the city walls. It was a simple place: a straw-covered courtyard barely large enough for a donkey to turn around in with small rooms directly off it, not one of the grand Harari houses I had peeped at through gateways. Abera's family were Guraghe who had migrated from their home region south of Addis Ababa in the traditional way: father leaving one wife behind and taking a new one in his new town – after the formality of conversion to Islam. Quite often the two wives never meet until they are widowed when their husband's funeral brings them together.

We entered a simple room furnished with grass mats and a single bed. One of Abera's sisters came and lit some incense then made coffee, roasting the beans, pounding them and serving the coffee thick and sweet in small china cups.

Abera, I soon discovered, was something of a family prodigy. Not only had he won a scholarship to study abroad but he spoke English, Amharic, Guraghe, Oromo and Harari, the last two picked up in the streets of Harar. I told him of Burton and my wish to explore Harar before retracing Burton's route to the coast. He was familiar with the man's exploits but

[49]

open-mouthed at my hope to emulate them. 'Are you insane? Burton had guns when we did not. Now we have guns and you do not. You are not Burton and this is not Burton's time. It is far more dangerous now.'

The absolute conviction of his words worried me. 'Isn't the border open with Somaliland?'

'Not for you. Didn't you hear in Addis about the shooting of the government minister?'

I shook my head.

'The border area is not good,' he insisted. 'Only smugglers use those areas. They bring things on camels – Air Camel we call it. I showed you the cigarettes that they bring but there are many other things, even televisions and videos are carried by camel. It used to be by truck but with the new EPRDF government, they are forced to be more careful. Camels can go silently on footpaths at night without lights so it is difficult to catch them. Once they get to Jigjiga on this side of the border they transfer to trucks or buses.'

He passed me a clutch of qat leaves all picked and cleaned ready to chew. 'This is aterara – a gift of chat. You must put it in your mouth in one piece.'

As the chemicals cut in, the qat seemed to unleash bolts of raw adrenaline that set my eyes watering. But as time slipped by this feeling subsided into a gentle sense of comfort and ease. Three hours on and I'd have sworn I had known Abera for years. The light faded and he lit an oil lamp. I fell into a contented silence that slowly ripened into a vague sense of melancholy. With this change, the room that had been a retreat now became oppressive.

'Let us walk,' said Abera.

We went out into the darkened alleyways. 'If they bring bright lights in the street, the people smash them,' said Abera. 'They like the darkness.'

Down one side road by a church there were dozens of crude tents made from rags and plastic bags on frames of sticks. Inside one a candle glowed and a baby was crying. A figure came lurching towards us and veered away, a man's face momentarily glimpsed.

We drank honey wine, tej, in a shack where a strange gentleman dressed as a chemist refilled the conical flasks. A large white goat strolled around lapping up spillages from the tables.

After six of these I was reeling slightly and we retraced our steps to the road.

'Wait for a taxi,' Abera instructed, but I was adamant I would walk. Thieves did not frighten me.

He laughed. 'Yes, you can do that. But it's not thieves, it's the wild animals.'

I stopped grinning. 'What wild animals?'

'Hyaenas.'

I searched back through my memories of David Attenborough documentaries, but failed to locate footage of hyaenas eating people. 'They don't eat people.'

'There have been incidents,' he said. 'A week ago a woman walking here at night. One ran up behind her and grabbed her by the leg. By good chance some men saw it and chased the animal away. But for you it is okay – they usually never attack men. And they cannot run fast downhill. Just run downhill if you see one.'

With the comforting phrase 'usually never' in mind, I started on my long walk home. There was no one else around. After a mile I took the track up to the right and left the dim light of the boulevard for the utter darkness of the backroads. I had some time to think about what Abera had said. The mental picture I had of a hyaena was with rear legs definitely shorter than the front. Surely, I reasoned, that meant going uphill would be harder? And I was now going uphill past some deep thickets of bamboo cane. Should I run up or down?

The dim pink neon tube that marked the hotel gate was in sight and with relief I strode up and hammered on it. Then I heard it: a blood-curdling howl that echoed around the valley and set all the local dogs yelping in fear, a howl more horrible than anything I had ever heard before. And one word in great blood-red letters leapt into my mind: HYAENA. No sooner had this dreadful cry ended than a huge bristling beast came loping around the corner, massive head low over the tarmac road and teeth bared in a perpetual mirthless grin.

If not for one jutting piece of iron, my record clearance of a six-foot corrugated iron gate might have had all the grace and elegance of a springbok eluding an extra tall Kalahari bushman. Only it did not. As I came down on the safe side, my tee-shirt caught on the snag. There was a sharp rip and I was dumped, half-undressed at the feet of the guard.

'Hyaena,' I gasped, winded by the fall.

[51]

He smiled and leaned on his stick. I tried to explain the reason for my extraordinary behaviour but without the necessary Amharic all I could think to do was impersonate a hyaena howl.

He laughed softly and turned to shout the news across to his fellow guard. Later, when the lights went out, I heard him come and lay a blanket in front of my door and lie down. But whether it was to keep me inside or wild animals out, I was not sure.

# 5

I slept well that night but experienced vivid dreams. In one I was walking alone through the African bush and noticed a speck, a sort of scab, in the skin between the first and second fingers of my left hand. I picked at it. There appeared to be some sort of thorn embedded. I picked a bit more. The thorn began to emerge and I got hold of the end and very carefully started to extract it. The thorn became a stick about as thick as my thumb. There was no pain. The stick was kinked after the first few inches and with its bark intact except for a series of spindly little scratches on the surface. When I finally got it all out, it was about nine inches long. A second stick came from between the next two knuckles. The cuts on my hand did not close up.

I met Abera that morning and we walked from the Christian Market down around the south side of the wall. My dream was still so vivid in my mind that I immediately told him. He listened with serious eyes.

'The meaning is clear,' he said after a pause. 'There is something you are searching for – here in Harar or on your journey – but what you are searching for is inside you.'

'Qat,' I said with a laugh. 'I'm searching for qat. I want to know if it came from Harar and when. And I'm looking for a way down to the coast.'

'That is what you tell me. Maybe that is what you tell yourself. But the truth is that there is something else.'

It was a beautiful morning. On our right tall trees rang with birdsong, on our left was the wall, crenellated and ancient, running down the descending contours like a serpent on a staircase. The track was a broad curling swathe of yellow dust, next to it ran a simple hand-dug irrigation channel. Far ahead rose range after range of mountain plateau, fading from emerald to violet.

Abera pointed through the trees to the gardens and vegetable plots below. 'Before the Dergue, the Hararis owned all the land and the Oromo paid rent and farmed it. The Hararis were very proud and very grand and called the Oromo, Gallas. Now this word is not allowed by the Oromo.'

'But does the wall still separate them. I mean, do Oromo now live inside the wall?'

'No, none. There are Gurage like myself but mostly it is Harari. When they lost their land many began to move away, to Addis or to outside, like America, but about nine thousand remain.'

We came to a huge old fig tree and next to it a gate that had obviously been reconstructed – by the Italians during their occupation, Abera said.

'It is the Witches' Gate. Fortune-tellers and so on would gather here. Even your dream of sticks – we could have asked someone here a few years ago.'

But now the gate was deserted. I wondered if the practice had become unfashionable due to fundamentalist Islam.

'Those dream-tellers and fortune-tellers are still here but they work inside the city now. In Harar those fundamentalists have not much influence. After the war some Pakistanis came and opened a school to teach their way of Islam. When it became known what they were saying the school was immediately closed and the teachers ordered to leave within twenty-four hours.'

But outside the walls, as I knew, it was less easy to control and it seemed almost as though the women had retreated to the psychological safety of the walled town, even if its defences were now full of holes.

We walked on. I was keen to see the gate through which Burton had entered the city on 3rd January 1855. He does not specifically mention the name but the old road from the coast would have led him to Argob Gate on the south-east corner of the wall. There we found a crowd of chattering Oromo women unloading firewood from their donkeys and a small market in full swing under the wall. The gates themselves were closed, blocked with a ping-pong table under which a herd of goats was sheltering from the sun. But a gap in the city defences had been bulldozed next to it, allowing a steady stream of people and animals to enter.

Outside this entrance Burton and his two companions had rested while waiting for word from the Emir. 'We sat at the foot of a round bastion, and were scrutinized, derided, and catechized by the curious of both sexes, especially by that conventionally termed the fair.' He was exultant but clear-headed enough to admit that 'many would have grudged exposing three lives to win so paltry a prize.'

After a time the new arrivals were taken up a cobbled lane to the Emir's palace, little more than a courtyard leading to a large shed. Shoeless but still armed, they were directed inside. The room was dark and decorated with matchlock rifles and polished shackles. Ahead of them on a raised wooden cot with a low railing along the back was a sickly-looking young man in a crimson, fur-trimmed robe and red conical hat. There was a brief comedy in which the visitors were manhandled into position for a kiss of the regal hand – 'bony and yellow as a kite's claw' – then Burton presented his letter from the British authorities in Aden and so gave up all pretence of disguise.

It was a nervous moment, possibly life-or-death for the explorer, but both men rose to the occasion admirably: the Emir with a gracious smile and Burton with delicious understatement: 'This smile I must own . . . was a relief.'

And that was that. With a whispered order and a sign, the Emir dismissed them. Burton was taken to a house one hundred yards away where he stayed for his entire ten days.

In those times, Harar was at a low ebb. The ancient trade routes down to the coast were unsafe; Aden was blossoming as a rival. The explorer paints a desolate picture of the town he had risked his life to reach. The men are unprepossessing, he says, riven with small-pox, eye diseases and scrofula, their voices are loud and their expression justifies the proverb 'Hard as the heart of Harar'. He admits the women are not unattractive, even though their voices are 'harsh and screaming'. Both sexes, he claims, are renowned for their laxity of morals and such freedom of manners renders a public flogging occasionally indispensable. In short, he concludes, the Somali proverb has it right: 'Harar is Paradise inhabited by asses.'

Burton's observations, unforgiving as they were, could scarcely help but be influenced by the nature of his reception. He was kept virtually a prisoner, with little chance to wander and study in the way he loved to do. For ten days he and his companions lived on a knife-edge, knowing that their lives depended on the caprice of a cruel despot whose prisons were said to be living charnel houses from which no one ever emerged. One senses his frustration: he has reached his impossible goal only to have any possibility of benefiting from it snatched from his grasp. In Somaliland his curiosity turned up all sorts of information. He even extended his prodigious knowledge of human sexuality with data on the preferred love-making habits of Somali women. But in Harar such succulent titbits were singularly lacking. 'How melancholy a thing is success,' he wrote later.

From Burton's scant indications it is impossible to guess the location of the house where he was held, but the description of the layout tallies with what is now the Emir's House Museum. A flight of steps led us up to a small courtyard and on the left of this is a doorway into a traditional Harari house and the type of room where Burton and his party were held.

It was a cool space, without windows, and decorated with hundreds of round flat baskets. A small chubby guide was waiting. 'You are welcome,' he said, clicking immediately into his patter. 'The house you are looking at is traditional of the Harari. Notice the stone floor where you stand leads to side rooms, symmetrical, and in front is wide stone benches set at levels – two. First level and lower is for less important visitors. The second around the first on three sides is for the Emir or important man of the house with his important guests alongside himself. Over there,' he indicated another separate platform on the right of the door, 'is for servants.'

On the highest ledge of his prison, Burton had sat and reflected on his situation: 'I was under the roof of a bigoted prince whose least word was death; amongst a people who detest foreigners; the only European that had ever passed over their inhospitable threshhold, and the fated instrument of their future downfall.'

'Please,' said the guide, holding out a hand. I handed him some coins and we continued through to a side area where a bed was placed. 'In honeymoon time, for three days this bed was closed off and food passed through this hole.' It looked one of the less comfortable ways to spend three days. The bed was especially unyielding and on it lay a thin leather cushion as solid as stone. The guide saw my doubtful look. 'And that is the cushion to resting head upon.'

I heard Abera in the main room stifle a laugh. The guide moved briskly on. After he had finished I asked a few questions but his knowledge soon ran short. He had not heard of Burton. 'You must speak to Abdulsatar,' he said. 'This is one old man who is knowing more things on many subjects – more than anyone else in Harar.' He gave some vague directions to a house near the 'Arab' mosque.

Out in the street Abera gave me the truth about the cushion. 'It is not for the head. Those rich men liked to marry very fat girls and sometimes it caused difficulties on wedding night to find the correct spot. So the cushion was to raise the buttocks and improve the target.'

The great explorer and collector of sexual customs would, I am sure, have appreciated that.

That two of the most notable Europeans of their age should be inextricably connected with the remote Ethiopian city of Harar is a quirk of fate. Not only that but both Arthur Rimbaud and Richard Burton were men who seemed to be trapped in a period that was slow, if not unable, to understand their genius. Looking back, a century later, they appear as men who were able to rise above the moral climate of the times but also as men whose restless need to travel had an almost diabolic intensity. When Burton was asked why he travelled, his answer was simply, 'The Devil drives!' And by coincidence, Rimbaud was born in France on 20th October 1854, at the same time as Burton completed his preparations to leave Aden for Harar.

Burton lived much of his life under a figleaf of suspicion: as a young staff officer in the Bombay Army he had been sent by Sir Charles Napier to investigate disturbing reports that fine upstanding British soldiers were being corrupted by the homosexual brothels of Karachi. He did so on the understanding that the report would never be circulated, but when Napier left it got out – apparently circulated by an enemy Burton had made. The scandalous implication was that Burton, the under-cover agent, could not have penetrated such establishments without compromises. The episode ended any hopes for Burton's army career, but not his ability to find controversy. In later life this was most notably demonstrated by his translations of eastern erotica.

At about the same time as he was in Harar, Parliament was debating the Obscene Publications Act, a draconian law that demonised sex in the way that western powers now reserve for drugs. Victorian Britain was in the grip of a hysterical, knees-together, buttoned-up big freeze when it came to the human body. A favourite tale of Burton's was the newly-wed wife chloroformed on the bed with a note pinned to the pillow saying: 'Mama says you are to do what you will with me.' They were illiberal times and Burton set out to tackle them. His *Arabian Nights* carried a set of footnotes that amounted to a salacious catalogue of human sexual behaviour, or depravity as it was then known. Ironically, Burton's modern academic reputation has suffered because he tended to exaggerate the erotic content of the tales – something like being caught spiking the curry, with curry powder.

It is the capacity for dispassionate observation that attracts the modern reader to Burton. Whether it be slavery, sex or drugs, he catalogues and describes, but he does not prejudge. There are no sweeping assertions or lofty criticism. On 'al-Kat', he limits himself to historical and geographical comments that contrast sharply with those of the lesser individuals who followed him.

The bedrock of his reputation was the journeys but he had missed out on the source of the Nile and that dispassionate description of human behaviour was always threatening to do damage. His foolish wife set out to remedy matters on his death, burning his translation of *The Perfumed Garden* after he painfully achieved his ambition of completing it the day before he died. His journals and notebooks received the same treatment. But her attempts to protect his fame only diminished him. Unfortunately for the Burton legend, he had not died on a litter somewhere in Africa after failing to convert the locals to the Church of England, but had lived to write a clutch of lively travel books, translated thousands of pages of important eastern books and improved upon the twenty-seven languages he knew, while forgetting the thirteen or so he had no more use for.

Arthur Rimbaud's reputation, on the other hand, seems unstoppable. A Frenchman described the poet to me as 'the nineteenth century's answer to Jim Morrison'.

He had abandoned Europe and poetry at the age of twenty, apparently determined to annihilate his previous life and disappear without trace. The poems, all written before that sudden departure had resonated with images

of distant shores and wanderings as though his life, like an afternoon on
qat, has time all tangled:

> In a magnificent house encircled by the Orient entire,
> I brought my life to completion, and I passed my illustrious
>     retirement.
> I have drunk my own blood. My task has been lifted from me . . .
> No longer must I even think of it . . .
>                                         I am actually beyond the grave.

But when he did travel east there was precious little that was poetic in it.
He had come to Harar in December 1880, a would-be trader with developing passions for self-enrichment and scientific exploration who found
nothing to commend his fiefdom in the green hills of Africa. Letters home
were often mere lists of complaints: of crushing boredom and discomfort,
of the postal services, of the weather and lazy natives. He is a petty bour-
geois expatriate dreaming of the pot of gold which will take him away
from it all. It was as though the butterfly, after its day in the sun, had turned
into a caterpillar.

He wrote to his mother: 'I send caravans to the coast with local products: gold, musk, ivory, coffee etc . . . half the profits go to me.' But in April
1884 his company was liquidated and, returning to Aden, he ended up in
league with Pierre Labatut and Paul Soleillet who ran caravans into Shoa,
central Abyssinia. The plan was to buy secondhand rifles in Europe and
ship them up the Gulf of Tadjoura to the town of the same name, a lifeless hole newly acquired by the French. From there Rimbaud would take
them up to Menelik.

At Tadjoura he waited for the guns, carefully counting how much he
would make and how many trips would buy him comfortable retirement.
Months went by, Labatut died, Soleillet died. The guns arrived and were
taken up to Menelik who squeezed Rimbaud till he squealed. All was lost.
Rimbaud gave an account to the Vice-Consul in Aden: 'Menelik confis-
cated all the merchandise and forced me to sell to him at reduced prices.'
With characteristic modesty he fails to mention his own generosity in
dealing with his partners' creditors.

The Vice-Consul replied loftily that Rimbaud might have lost less if he had been able to adapt to the 'particular methods of those places and their rulers'.

Rimbaud returned to Harar and by February 1891 he was complaining more than usual, this time of pains in his leg. He had been in Harar, on and off, for more than ten years but time had run out. A nightmare journey to Zeila followed with Rimbaud on a litter, unable to walk. When he reached Aden he was sent to Marseilles where he arrived in May and almost immediately had his right leg amputated. Four months later he was desperately ill and trying to arrange passage on a boat to Suez when he died. He was thirty-seven.

Rimbaud's Harar house is one of the town's few tourist attractions and it was by chance that, after leaving the museum, Abera and I found ourselves outside the building in a quiet lane no more than one donkey wide. We had bought qat and were looking for Abdulsatar, but without much success.

Not everyone accepts that Rimbaud's House was Rimbaud's house. There are well-founded rumours it was built by an Indian merchant after the poet had died and the real house in Mekonnen Square is gone. We first visited the caretaker, a lady of middle age wrapped in purple cloth whose family used to lodge in the place until the French government decided to pay for renovation and she was evicted. Having lost the house, she makes a few birr by letting tourists peruse her film script – a gift from the makers of a French feature film about the poet.

I asked if she knew why Rimbaud was famous.

She shrugged. 'Because he was a Frenchman and he lived in Harar when there were no other Frenchmen in Harar.'

The house was a grand structure of colonial style rather than Harari. A courtyard led to some steps and the front door of a two-storeyed building with tin roof. It reminded me of the Chinese shophouses in the Far East, symmetrical with simple central spaces giving off to smaller side rooms. The main feature was that the whole upper floor had been turned into a gallery looking down through an oval space to the lower floor. It is gloomy and inward-looking, like Harar – exactly what one imagines for a tortured ex-poet.

From the windows were views south-east across the Arab market to the routes that once led out to Zeila and civilisation. On the ceiling were some faded naive paintings of tropical scenes.

'Rimbaud painted these,' said the caretaker.

'He should have stuck to poetry.' I muttered. This was no Gauguin, but then I saw a man in there, painting, for whatever reason – to brighten his dim prison cell, to record memories, or to express a longing to escape that could no longer be expressed in words. Whether it was Rimbaud or a nameless Indian merchant hardly mattered. On one was a tropical island scene: palms and a beach. The view was from the sea, as if painted from a departing boat, and there in the trees was a ragged white man in straw hat looking back, a Robinson Crusoe who has just turned his rescuers away.


It took some time to locate Abdulsatar's house. Abera did not know the area around the Arab mosque very well, an area of particularly high featureless walls and narrow lanes that curved and split and turned back and stopped dead. A youth eventually took us to a gate up a short dog-leg of a cul-de-sac.

A woman, probably a servant, came to answer. She told us that Abdulsatar was sick and had been taken to see a traditional doctor for some medicine. Abera asked her to tell her master that a British man had come and would like to talk to him about Harar and its history. Then we left.

Abera had arranged an afternoon qat session that day with a well-respected group of merchants who met regularly to discuss religious and social matters. Similar groups meet all over the town, some with a common love of poetry and literature, others to talk about football and girlfriends. For the men and youths of Harar, this is the mainstay of social life, and they drift in and out of groups as their interests change and develop.

In honour of the occasion it was deemed appropriate by Abera that I should treat us all to the best qat in town. For this we had to visit Nabiha, a lady who had a successful business supplying to the wealthier qat fiends of Harar. We found her shop in the Christian Market and the lady herself, vast and cheerful, ringed like Saturn, first with green leaves then with customers. Among the more traditional young men, Abera told me, Nabiha was admired as much for her great girth as her good qat. He winked: 'Remember the cushion!'

The secret of Nabiha's business success was an uncanny talent for selecting the best qat despite, she confessed, never having tried the stuff because of 'the disgusting smell'. Her method was to assess the trees in advance and buy up hundreds of the most promising for a whole year ahead. For this Nabiha Quality Assurance guarantee her customers were prepared to pay a premium over and above the prices demanded by off-the-ground sellers at the Harar Gate. Smartly-dressed government officials and managers in suits and ties were stopping by; some regulars had their leaf ready and waiting in a plastic bag beside Nabiha's ample backside.

It was good stuff. Bright supple leaves with shoots that were almost all eatable. As we inspected various bunches, more were arriving wrapped in shawls on the heads of Oromo ladies. We took bundles for six people.

'Is she married?' I asked as we walked away.

He shook his head. 'No. These days the young men want girls who look American. It is too old-fashioned to want the big one.'

'But she must be rich, too.'

'Oh, yes. The qat trade has made her one of the richest women in Harar.'

'You seemed to like her . . . '

He drew himself up, laughing scornfully, and trying to look sophisticated. 'Me!? I like the modern girl – Whitney Houston – that type.'

There was a pause as we threaded our way through the crowded lane. Gangs of donkeys, having brought loads of firewood into market, were now setting off home in high spirits, pushing through the people like unruly schoolboys.

'One hundred years ago, she would have been the most beautiful woman in town,' I said when Abera managed to rejoin me.

'There are some who still prefer the traditional type,' he admitted. 'They say she is very desirable. Of course, for me – no.' And yet he could not help adding, with a dreamy smile, 'But it's true, she is so very, very fat.'

The house where we were to spend the afternoon was down a short alleyway near the main street. We knocked at a wooden gate and were greeted by Omar Ibrahim, the householder and owner of a couple of gold shops. He was a small smiling man with light brown skin and rounded features – an Arabian ancestry softened in the African melting pot; certainly he would have looked absolutely at home in the souks of Aden, Muscat or Zanzibar. Like other Harari shopkeepers he wore an embroidered skullcap, white shirt, checked futa and sandals.

I greeted him loudly in Arabic and he smiled even more.

'And upon thee be peace and blessings and the mercy of God.'

'God give you life.'

'God give life to he who comes!' And laughing he turned to Abera. 'He has brought qat – is he one of us?'

'Praise be to God. He takes chat like a Harari – I think he *is* Harari.'

'By God! This is a wonder.'

Across the courtyard I could see an open doorway leading to a traditional Harari room with its cool green walls and broad ledges at various heights. Omar Ibrahim took me to the door and pointed out the round baskets on the walls.

'These are for marriage ceremonies. The girl must learn how to make these so that the man knows she is knowledgeable in home-making skills.'

There were recessed shelves on the rear wall and stacks of china cups and saucers. 'When the marriage takes place,' he said, 'the family must not borrow any cups or plates, as that would be shameful. That is why you will see Harari houses always full of these things.'

I had hoped we would take qat in such surroundings but it was not to be: instead he led me to one side and to a second doorway. This room was rather more humble: a simple rectangle without furnishings except for narrow oriental rugs along the back and sides, some hard cushion backs and bolsters for the elbow. Already seated with piles of qat in front of them were eight men, some along the back wall and some in the middle of the room on the bare floor. I greeted them and shook hands with each.

'Ahlan wa sahlan!' said a venerable old man with a kindly face. 'Come and sit here beside me.'

This man, I soon discovered, was Sheikh Muhammad, sheikh being a title of respect from those who knew him. On his right was Ali, another goldsmith, and next to him, in the corner, Omar Ibrahim. To his right were two more merchants. In front of these great personages sat the workers, servants and messengers, men dressed in grubby trousers rather than clean checked futas and without the dignified kuffiya or skullcap, although one had a pink silk jockey's cap. Not having the benefit of a thick carpet and cushion against the wall, they tended to slouch over their bolsters and somehow sink lower. In this way, I realised, the social arrangement laid down in the ledges next door had been scrupulously preserved.

[63]

There were differences in behaviour, too: the men in front were louder, more given to raised voices and jokes, while Sheikh Muhammad was the opposite, all dignity and poise.

The first thing to do was give the qat and a whisper from Abera told me to hand it to Sheikh Muhammad. He laid it in front of him and rocking gently began to recite the Fatiha, the first chapter of the Koran. The men assumed a kneeling position with palms upward, quietly following his words.

'In the name of God the compassionate and the merciful. Praise be to God, Lord of the Universe . . . '

When this was over he took a small handful of sticks and threw them across to one of the men in front of him. This portion was then carried off to the women. Further small portions went to the other servants, workers and messengers, the larger divisions kept for Omar Ibrahim and Ali – Abera and I had kept our bundles separate. Sheikh Muhammad himself was not taking qat. The man who had gone out returned with a tray of coffee, thick sweet drops of it in tiny china cups.

'Is there chat in your country?' asked the man in the pink cap.

'Yes,' I said. 'It comes from Harar.'

There was surprise from some of them while others nodded.

'They fly it from Dire Dowa,' said Omar Ibrahim. 'Not just to London but to other countries too.'

'Well, our qat is the best in the world – like our coffee.'

I asked if he knew the origin of qat.

'There are trees here that are five hundred years old, so it is said. But all we have about the origin of chat is legends.'

This was obviously something they had little time for and no amount of persuasion could get anyone actually to tell me one of those legends. Only one of them said, quite perceptively: 'In all our legends there is nothing about qat being brought here from other places – such as Yemen – but in their legends, qat is always brought from Harar.'

Sheikh Muhammad turned to me. 'For this question and other historical matters you should try to meet Haj Abdulsatar. He lives near the Arab mosque.'

The others nodded and murmured in agreement. 'He is an expert.'

'In the old days people took very little qat – maybe just this much,' said

Ali, the second goldsmith, holding up three sprigs. He was dressed exactly like Omar Ibrahim in white skullcap, white shirt and checked futa, but had a thinner more Arab face. 'They used it to help concentration when they were copying the Koran by hand.'

Sheikh Muhammad picked up a book that was beside him and showed me it. 'This was copied by hand in that way.' He pointed out a note scrawled on the frontispiece. 'It says it was paid for with twelve she-camels.' I took the volume carefully, the black leather binding was loose and the pages full of borer insect holes.

'I have read of scholars doing the same work in Yemen,' I said. 'Also sometimes writing poetry.'

Sheikh Muhammad nodded. 'The ancestors of many people here came from Yemen, particularly the Hadhramaut. Haj Abdulsatar is from Yemen originally: a mountainous place called Yafa – do you know it?'

I shook my head.

'The men would come to be merchants,' he continued. 'Then they would marry women from Harar and stay. This was in Islamic times, of course. Before that we only have legend, but it is said that the Queen of Sheba was also Queen of Harar.'

He took the Koran from me and looked through until he found the verse on Sheba, then read:

> For the natives of Sheba there was indeed a sign in their dwelling-place: a garden on their right and a garden on their left. We said to them: Eat of what your Lord has given you and render thanks to Him. Pleasant is your land and forgiving is your Lord.
>
> But they gave no heed. So we let loose upon them the waters of the dam and replaced their gardens by two others bearing bitter fruit, tamarisks and a few nettle shrubs.

I realised he had chosen the passage dealing with the dispersal of the Sabaeans following the collapse of the ancient Marib dam in Yemen, a cat-astrophe that is reputed to have happened in the same year as the birth of the prophet Muhammad, AD 570. Marib was once an important way-station on the incense route that began on the southern coast of Arabia then, skirting the Empty Quarter desert, ran northwards up to Gaza. The combination of hefty customs duties and productive irrigated gardens made it one of the most pleasant and wealthy of ancient cities. 'It is said that they [the houses] have numerous gold and silver columns, and the doors of their houses are decked with ornaments and jewels,' wrote Agatharchides, a second-century BC Alexandrian scholar. It was certainly wealthy enough to attract the Romans on one of their most disastrous forays in 24 BC. By the sixth century Marib was economically declining but the collapse of the dam finished it and when I had visited in 1987 the land was still barren. Since then Sheikh Zayid of Abu Dhabi, whose family were reputed to have fled with the flood, has paid for a new dam and Marib is flourishing as a man-made oasis once again.

Sheikh Muhammad finished the verse and closed the book. 'But the Hararis do not know their own origin in detail. Think of all the peoples who have been here, governed here, and all the places Hararis have been. Those are the origins: some are Yemeni, some Syrian, some Turkish or Egyptian. Even the British ruled us here.'

One of the servants cut in. 'The British gave us nothing. The Italians left machinery and other things but when the British left they took it all.'

I tried to look apologetic.

The man next to him, a thick-set African, said: 'That's not true. They did give us something. Do you remember when King George and Queen Elizabeth had a baby? They gave us all sweets at school.'

The servant nodded. 'Oh, and they gave us bombs. When the Italians were here, the British came and bombed the town.'

'Sorry about the bombs,' I said and they all burst out laughing. One serious old messenger man leaned across and touched my knee.

'British okay – good mens.'

The others had broken away into Harari. The qat had stoked them up and now the talk was unstoppable. Suddenly the room was full of languages: Harari mainly but with Arabic, Oromo and Amharic too. English provided a few handy exclamations, 'Very Good!', 'Astonishing!' and 'Good Heavens!' Their faces were animated and discussions raged with a seriousness that occasionally seemed hostile, only to burst into laughter and smiles. The light fell on their faces from the open doorway. Coffee was brought again and little china cups pressed to the lips. The air filled with incense smoke pothering from a stone crucible. The old messenger rested his head on his neighbour's shoulder, eyes open. Ali smiled, gold teeth glinting, and passed me a bouquet of picked leaves.

At sunset Sheikh Muhammad rose to go, saying goodbye quietly and not shaking hands – a departure done without fuss, lest the mood be disturbed. Omar Ibrahim was mostly silent now, still smiling but not listening. A golden glow of light climbed the wall opposite the door, fading to red and violet. Even the garrulous servants began to feel the night drawing closer and fell to signs and whispers.

Almost as soon as that moment of quiet contemplation and calm arrives it is tinged with sadness. The kayf, the state of contentment, was described by Burton in his *A Pilgrimage to el-Medinah and Meccah*:

And this is the Arab's *kayf*. The savouring of animal existence; the passive enjoyment of mere senses; the pleasant languor, the dreamy tranquillity, the airy castle-building . . . In the East man wants but rest and shade; upon the banks of a bubbling stream or under the cool shelter of a perfumed tree, he is perfectly happy, smoking a pipe, or sipping a cup of coffee or drinking a glass of sherbet, but above all things deranging body and mind as little as possible, the trouble of conversations, the displeasures of memory, and the vanity of thought being the most unpleasant interruptions to his *kayf*. No wonder *kayf* is a word untranslateable into our mother tongue.'

When we left the room, Omar Ibrahim came to show us the door. 'We are here every day, taking chat, and you are welcome.'

We said goodbye and I resisted Abera's wish to drink tej. The qat was taking me down and I wanted to sit alone in the garden at the hotel. Sometimes it does that: brings a weight upon you, a great sighing melancholia for something you cannot quite put a name to. Then your face becomes inert and emotionless as though the nerves have been cut, but your thoughts drift on. The qat has stirred the mind and stilled the body until the moorings have slipped and the one has sailed free from the other.

I went to my room. A dribble of soapy water in the cracked basin made me jump. I put up the bedspread as a curtain and lying down began to listen to the hum of mosquitoes.

# 6

A few days later Abera and I set off down into the labyrinth around Abdulsatar's house.

The same servant came to the gate and smiled in recognition. 'Yes, I told him about you and he wants to see you, but this morning he had bad news from San'a in Yemen. His sister has died.'

She and Abera talked for a while and a telephone number was written down.

As we walked away he turned to me. 'Now this lady has died in the very place you are wanting to reach.'

'Why do you say that?'

'Did you dream again?'

'No,' I said truthfully, 'I can't remember anything from last night.'

He looked doubtful. 'You told me that San'a is like a paradise in your mind and you wish to go back to it.'

We stopped in the shade of a doorway over which a bright sprig of bougainvillaea was surging. 'When you want to reach something but must do a hard and difficult journey first, that is like a Muslim hajj, isn't it?'

I nodded. 'It could be.'

'What do you call it in English?'

'A pilgrimage.'

'But San'a is not a paradise. Sheikh Muhammad told us yesterday that it was destroyed by water and only nettles remain.'

'That was Marib,' I protested, 'not San'a.'

He was looking very seriously at the ground. 'Did you dream of the sticks again?'

'No.'

'You said there were signs on those sticks, like writing. Was it in Arabic or Amharic?'

The conversation was quite mystifying. 'Neither of them. It was more like heiroglyphics or perhaps the ancient South Arabian letters.'

'From those we get our Amharic letters,' he said. 'Could you copy out what you saw?'

This stopped me for a moment. I hadn't thought of trying. All I could recall was some scratched symbols: I wanted to tell him they were more like the Dancing Men in the Sherlock Holmes tale but it seemed unlikely he would know the story. Now he was playing the detective, suggesting that those random scratches might be semaphoring something to me, something I should know.

'I'm absolutely sure I cannot,' I said and he grinned; I think he thought I was unsettled by the very idea.

'We listen to our dreams here,' he said. 'I just wondered. Last night we received news that my grandfather had died.' He paused, watching my face. 'At our place in Guraghe. He wanted me to marry a local girl, the daughter of his friend, now I have escaped that fate.'

I understood then that he had hoped I might have some power of foretelling with dreams.

A cheeky smile stole across his face. 'Everyone you meet – someone in the family dies. You are a dangerous man.'

I gave a nervous laugh and tried to stop this worrying line of conversation by setting off up the lane again. 'I think I'm going out to that aid agency office you told me about to ask if they travel down to Djibouti or Somaliland.'

'That is fine,' he said. 'Today I have to take qat with my family and neighbours because of my grandfather. We will try to find Abdulsatar again tomorrow. Don't worry,' he added when he saw my doubtful face, 'we will find him one day.'

I was not so sure myself. The days had been slipping past and I was eager to continue with my journey. After walking out of town for about two miles, I found the aid office but it was deserted. As I left a huge luxurious

Landcruiser of the sort usually seen outside Harar's restaurants and better hotels came skidding alongside.

'You looking for somebody?' An Ethiopian with quiffed hair, sunglasses and black leather jacket leaned out the driver's window, looking like an African Elvis.

'I was looking for the director.'

'That's me.'

'Right. I wanted to ask about the Somaliland border – if you go there – if it can be crossed?'

He shrugged. 'We ain't never been there, man. We just heard to watch out for Dire Dowa.'

'Why's that?'

'Beats me – something happened I guess.'

He shoved the gear stick. 'Take a plane.' He let the clutch in and sped off towards town. I walked.

Coming back through the souk, I stepped around a man sleeping in the sun covered in flies, his limbs blackened and bloated. Gangs of children were chanting: 'Cuba! Cuba!', a relic of the fifteen thousand Cuban advisors who helped in the 1977 Ogaden War. One boy with a pinched aggressive face was screeching, 'I love you!' By the time I reached Harar Gate I was ready to take a swing at the next person who spoke to me. I bought qat and rode in an ancient clanking Peugeot taxi to the hotel. As soon as I was settled on the bed with the leaves rustling and picked and moving mouthwards, the cares vanished. I felt at ease and relaxed. When Alem, the waiter, came in with soda water we began to chat in a quiet and companionable way. The qat was beginning to rule my emotions: mornings were hours of frazzled irritation, afternoons were at peace. Without the qat I wouldn't get the peace.

Alem was a slim, fit-looking man with a gleaming bald pate and remnants of frizzy hair – a sort of fire-damaged Bobby Charlton. He had a sad story to tell of his wasted life. As a boy in Gondar he had run away from home only to be conscripted into the army and find himself fighting in the tank battles of the Ogaden War against Somalia. Then an officer took pity and sent him to military accountancy school and after three years he was drafted to the Eritrean front. Over the next few years he witnessed the steady encroachment of the rebels.

'The officers knew nothing of fighting in that place but the rebels knew everything. At the end the officers would tell us, "Go there!" and we would refuse because it was crazy and we knew we would die. Sometimes if the officer insisted we go, we shot him.'

Captured by the EPRDF advance, he had been held prisoner, then sent to Harar where some men from his unit would vouch that he was not a war criminal.

'Now I am here. I cannot go home because I know no one there, and here I know no one. Do you know what Karl Marx said? "It is not the living who suffer but the dead." That is very true.'

At breakfast the following morning, Abera arrived bursting with news of a plan he had hatched.

'Abdulsatar will spend the next two days mourning and then it is Friday when he'll be in the mosque so it is probably impossible to see him before Saturday.'

I sighed. 'Saturday – inshallah.'

'Okay. Now listen. To help him feel in your favour you can do something. His sister died and so his friends and relatives will all be visiting him for three days to sit with him. This is Harari custom. Also people take presents of food to help feed the guests who come to stay. You should send a present too, and then he will feel he cannot refuse to see you.'

'But he's sick. I'm sure if he could see me, he would.'

'Yes, but this will help.'

I agreed and handed over what seemed like a large sum of money just to buy coffee and sugar as gifts. In fact I felt as though I had been handing out rather a lot of money to Abera: for qat, for tej, for meals, for everything. I was beginning to feel like the goose that laid the golden egg and wished he would offer to pay, just once, so I could tell myself I wasn't being taken for a ride.

I didn't see him again that morning and convinced myself that the coffee and sugar gifts were a ruse to get qat-money. When I met him later, he immediately invited me to lunch at his house, apologising for not having the money to pay at a restaurant. I protested that I had not even noticed and felt doubly ashamed for the earlier doubts and now the lie.

[71]

'I have a good place for you to take chat today,' said Abera whose own mood was perpetual cheerfulness. 'Really, with very interesting people.'

We went out by the Witches' Gate and followed the track up towards the Christian Market but before we reached it, turned away from the city and took a footpath down to a small group of houses in a thickly wooded area.

'It is a good friend of mine,' he said, shouting a greeting as we passed through the gate. Inside the compound we went to a separate block where there was a padlocked door. A servant came and opened it for us.

The room was modern but on traditional lines. Beyond a narrow, lino-covered entrance was a raised area set out for qat sessions with rugs and cushions. Behind the cushion backs was a set of 1960s-style living room sofas with black leatherette armrests and tweedy orange covers. When needed these could be shoved forward to make a passable pastiche of a European lounge. On the walls were some old black and white family photographs: one showed a young man in suit and tie about to make a call with an old two-piece telephone. Next to this was a poster showing the phases of the moon above the entire text of the Koran in tiny lettering. Opposite was a rug of the Kaaba at Mecca.

I made myself comfortable in one corner, opening up my qat and starting to pick shoots. Almost immediately all the paranoia and irritability evaporated; I could not believe I had entertained such thoughts. The qat was rearranging my day for me, pushing all things negative, all my hates and suspicions, into the morning; afternoons were all things bright and beautiful. As with most drugs, the pleasure of having it had become the pleasure in ending the lack of it.

A woman came in with a censer, insisting that I should waft a few draughts into my lungs.

'Without incense, chat is nothing,' she said, quoting a Harari proverb. Abera gave her some qat and a couple of cigarettes.

Now Nasr the host arrived, greeting us warmly in Harari, 'Amanta khu?'

He was a tall thin young man with a slow, almost languid, way of moving but with quick intelligent eyes. No sooner had he changed into a futa and taken his place than a second individual arrived, an older man with chubby cheerful features and an engaging manner. Abera was very respectful towards him.

Once we were all comfortably seated, we made polite conversation: I told them about my trip and how it was proving difficult to catch Abdulsatar.

'Oh, but he is the man to speak to,' said Muhyadin, the second man, 'but very old now and in poor health – may God strengthen him!'

Soda water and coffee were brought. Nasr asked me about Northern Ireland, a conflict he had studied in relation to Ethiopia's own problems. Muhyadin put it in a philosophical context, referring to Bertrand Russell and Karl Marx.

'Have you read Burton?' he asked. 'His *Ten Days at Harar*? We had a tele-vised debate once, after the EPRDF victory, about how the province of Hararge would develop politically. You see some people here want auton-omy, some want independence, some want to join bits of Somalia and be independent. I quoted Burton to them: "He who controls Berbera holds the beard of Harar". You know Berbera is on the Somali coast so Burton means we must live together, we cannot be independent when we are inter-dependent.'

'And did people know who you were talking about?'

'Burton? Yes, of course – in Harar they know him. Some years ago there was a quiz show on Harari radio and one question was "Which gate did Burton enter Harar by?" because you know in his book he does not mention this by name.'

'Argob Beri?'

'That's right. Ten points. Ha! He came in from the valley below. He describes sitting and sketching before riding up through orchards. From this we know it must be Argob Gate.'

I asked what his opinion was of the man.

'Here in Harar we have people who know very much about this place but what did these men write? Where are their books and their papers? In just a few days, Burton discovered and wrote more than all these others. His description of the language is still valid. Some say his book was used in order to colonise us but I think Burton was interested only in knowl-edge. He learnt more in that short period than some do in a lifetime. We can all learn from such a man.'

Nasr and Abera were nodding. Muhyadin's face shone and he scooped a large handful of qat to pass across to me. 'Try this – really – very good qat. Do you have it in Britain?'

[73]

'It's imported as "Yemeni salad".'

They laughed. I asked if he thought it a good thing and he nodded. 'Qat has two characteristics: first it gives you energy to work, especially intellectually. I myself would never have passed my exams without it. When I began to chew I discovered I could read more, even memorise large sections very quickly.'

I was to hear this claim made regularly and, if confirmed, it would revolutionise the university bookshop: 'Modern languages? I'd recommend a light, low altitude Yemeni qat. We do a starter pack with textbook and tapes for 9.99.'

Muhyadin took some sticks and passed them to Abera.

'The second thing is that it can bring depression and reduces sexual energy. But all useful medicines have side-effects. Look at alcohol, it can kill. And then qat is sociable – would we be sitting here talking like this if not for qat? When I was in Canada I didn't find anything like it and I saw that the people were not drawn together by anything in its place. Not alcohol, a qat session is nothing like standing in a bar. People in bars don't often discuss serious issues or ideas and they have no other place for such conversation. On balance it is good thing we have it – although in future we may do without it.

'There is a story that people tell here of its discovery,' he continued. 'A legend. They say there was an Emir of Harar called Awzulkarnein and he had two horns on his head. These horns gave him magical powers but none of the people knew as he kept them hidden under his turban. One morning, a man who wanted to see the Emir came early to the palace. He was very early and the gate was closed but he looked through a crack in the wood and there he saw the Emir coming from his room without his turban. Of course, he saw the horns.

'He ran from the palace, scared out of his mind. 'Oh God, the Emir has two horns but if I tell anyone he will find out and punish me.' He ran out of the city, desperate to tell someone the news, but afraid. So it built up inside him. This knowledge made his stomach bulge. At first just a little, but then more and more until he was in agony his stomach was so huge – like a pregnant woman!

'It was too bad. He went to the forest and dug a hole. Then he bent over it and whispered: "The Emir has two horns." Immediately, whatever was

[74]

inside came out – straight into the hole. He covered it up and went away. His stomach was normal again. But in the spot where he had dug the hole a tree began to grow with two long straight stems.

'One day some musicians were walking through the forest searching for branches to make drumsticks. They came to this place and found the tree with its two straight branches – perfect for what they needed. They cut the sticks and went to the qabr – the tomb of a saint – where there was to be a big ceremony. But before it could begin the drumsticks jumped up, by themselves, and began to play the drums and the drums sang "The Emir has two horns! The Emir has two horns!"

'So now everyone knew he had two horns and that is a sign of magical power. They went to him begging, "Please, your majesty, we are very tired and cannot work. Please give us something to keep us awake and strong." The Emir went and prayed to God for this and God was merciful. He sent down from paradise a tree whose leaves would help the people work hard and concentrate well. And the Emir told the people to go into the forest and find this tree and cultivate it. So they went to the place where the musicians had cut their sticks and found a beautiful tree growing there and this tree was the qat tree. That is why they say it is the tree of paradise.'

He sat back, tucking his legs under himself. 'As a boy I can remember people would say a prayer thanking God for the qat before every bercha and there was one line, "Let blessings be upon Awzulkarnein."'

The name was not new to me. Dhu al-Qarnain appears in the Koran and builds a great wall of iron and brass to hold out Gog and Magog. The name means 'The Two-Horned One' and is thought to have been derived from ancient Greek coins that show Alexander the Great with two horns. Whether Awzulkarnein is also Alexander is open to conjecture but the double-horned god was certainly no innovation.

In Yemen there are legends that Dhu al-Qarnain brought qat and from there it was brought to Harar. This might imply an origin outside Ethiopia or Yemen. One of the earliest known references to qat is in an eleventh-century work by the Arab al-Biruni, where he states that qat comes from Turkestan. Another reference, disputed by some scholars, comes in a pharmacopœia of AD 1222 written in Samarkand and recommending the drug for relieving depression. Perhaps most obscure but intriguing is the heiroglyphic inscription on the wall of the Temple of Isis at Philae in Egypt. Isis was the goddess of the fruits of the earth, double-horned like Alexander in Greek sculpture, and much-beloved of the Roman Empire in its decline. The inscription forbids the priests from using a substance identified with the symbols for k and d. As the priests were known to have used their dreams in divination, the substance was presumably banned for preventing sleep. Whatever that mysterious substance was, and qat can only be a remote possibility, it must be one of the first to be prohibited.

Nasr had gone outside for a while and when he returned the conversation moved to politics, his favourite subject. Then Muhyadin asked me my plans. I told him about Burton's route and the long slow approach to San'a.

He nodded in understanding. 'You will take the long cut rather than the short.' He began to quote from Byron, 'There is a pleasure in the pathless woods, There is a rapture on the lonely shore.'

Abera grinned, proud of his friend's learning. 'When all the exiles came back after the Dergue were defeated, most brought TVs, videos, cars – those things they bought in the United States or Europe. But Muhyadin brought only books.'

Muhyadin smiled. 'When I left Ethiopia because of that party of butchers, we took that way east. We walked to the coast by night. But when I came back – I was fifteen years in exile – we flew direct from Canada. Sometimes I wish it had been the other way around. I should have flown out and walked back – yes, really. I was returning to a place full of memories, terrible memories, but also my home. That is not the same as going somewhere new, it is like approaching a sleeping lion: if you must do it, then you do it carefully and slowly. So you are right to proceed with caution.'

'And is it possible, that route?'

'I don't think it's a good idea at this time,' he said. 'Zeila is nothing now – you'll have to go to Djibouti for a boat, even if you do manage to cross the border into Somaliland. Remember that Burton was using the main port of his time, you should do the same. After all the two are only a few miles apart; it is just that there is a border between.'

I pressed them for information on the situation. Had they heard about the German tourist shot dead in Dire Dowa? Who were Ittihad? Were borders open? Was there fighting? They shook their heads; no one was prepared to speculate for my benefit. Abera said: 'Information – it is all very vague. Nothing is certain.'

Later, as darkness fell, Abera made a sign that we should go.

At eleven in the morning next day I went alone to Abdulsatar's gate and this time the servant girl let me in. There was a broad paved courtyard, freshly swept, with a pomegranate tree shading the middle. I crossed to an open doorway that led into a traditional Harari room. Beyond the threshold was a stone bench in two levels, the higher seat enclosing the lower on three sides. A door to the right led into the rest of the house and beside were some herbs hung up to dry. In the left rear corner was a small bookcase filled with great leather-bound tomes and stacks of dusty papers; on the wall above was an astronomical chart. Beside the bookcase sat Abdulsatar, an elderly Arab gentleman dressed in white with a pale complexion and one rheumy eye closed with the years. Behind him were photographs of himself as a younger, stronger man, dressed as a judge and on the rug in front of him was a glass of bright, green qat tea with a spoon in it.

We greeted each other and shook hands.

'I am sorry we have not met properly,' he said in a frail voice. 'And today I am unwell again.'

I explained that I would have to leave.

'Next time you come then, we will sit and talk. Do you take qat? You do? Oh, very surprising.' He stirred his glass but did not drink from it. 'Unfortunately, I can only manage qat tea now.'

'Is it useful?'

He chuckled. 'Useful? Naturally, I think it useful. One's mind benefits. Memory is improved. Ideas come. If only it had similar effects on the ageing body. But what was it you wanted to ask me?'

'I'm interested in qat and its history, and Harar too – as the first European visitor was British.'

His good eye gleamed with interest. 'Yes, Burton. Many years ago Father Emile sent me a copy of Burton's monograph on the Harari language. I examined it and checked it thoroughly and found it to be excellent. There were only two mistakes which were regarding the phrases for opening and closing doors. This was because at the time of Burton's visit, doors were secured with leather ties. When metal locks arrived the words changed. Otherwise his description of our language was precise and correct and still useful for modern times.'

The speech had obviously tired him and I made movements to leave, secretly hoping he might suggest I stay.

'Yes, you will have to leave,' he said with a rueful smile. 'You came for information from me but I get all my information from your own country. My habit is to listen to the midday news on the BBC World Service. I have listened to it for forty-six years without missing a single day. Perhaps we all believe truth can only be found far away.'

We shook hands and I stepped back out into the light. When I was halfway across the courtyard I glanced back, Abdulsatar was sitting with his ear to a small transistor radio while sipping his qat tea.

# 7

Abera and I went to see Muhyadin to say goodbye, then I bought a little qat for the afternoon and climbed aboard a mini-bus bound for Dire Dowa. I had accepted that the precise route Burton had taken was impossible but I was determined to make it to the coast, continuing my journey by railway. That would take me north-east across the Danakil desert to Djibouti. I was beginning to feel that Djibouti was unavoidable, that the seedy, decaying port was dragging me down towards its hot black mouth. I had been there a decade before and I did not want to go back. But the only other route was further north, through Eritrea, and I had no visa to take me there.

The return to Dire Dowa was quite a different journey in the sunshine: the red roadside earth, the brilliant green of the trees and pale blue sky – all cut with startling clarity. A few miles down the plateau was Awodei, main packing centre for most exported qat, including that which is sold in Haj Ali's shop in London's East End. The huts and shacks were tatty with few signs of the wealth that the tree brings.

Further along were two small lakes and near them the burned-out remnants of an armoured column. 'Oromo Liberation Front,' explained the driver. 'Fight with EPRDF for Oromo independence after communists finished.'

'Still fighting?'

He made a face. 'What can they do? They must fight.'

Shortly before we reached the edge of the plateau we stopped; a large bundle of qat was taken out and tucked somewhere under the vehicle.

Around the next corner we pulled up at a checkpoint where various cars and buses were being searched. A youth carrying a shawl stuffed with qat got out and sauntered away unnoticed before a tough-looking female officer came across and ordered everyone else out of the vehicle. An old woman moaned in pain and was allowed to stay. Bags were searched, nothing found. This was the tax checkpoint for qat, notoriously poor at finding anything but always well-supplied with leaves for the afternoon.

We drove down the hill a short distance, picked up the youth with the shawl and retrieved the bundle from below. The old woman grinned, grunted and gave birth to a large plastic wrapper full of qat that had been up her skirt.

Heading down the hill, we passed the boundary between qat-growing upland and qat-free lowland, a boundary that was marching downhill with the assistance of water pumps. Normally the tree grows only between about 3,500–8,000 feet in frost-free conditions and with good water supplies. Until recently this would have kept the product to the highlands beyond the edge of the plateau but now it was creeping downwards, taking up more land. Abera had told me how he had been involved in a project to stop Oromo farmers growing qat. The plan was to teach them modern agricultural methods that would increase yields on food crops and so increase their profitability.

'Why? I asked. 'If the farmer gets good cash from qat – what's the problem?'

'We need food. If they all grow chat, food prices will increase.'

'Then qat prices will fall and the food-growers will be better off.'

But this ignored the obvious fact, a fact staring me in the face as we passed poverty-stricken non-qat-growing farms: they did not have nice tin roofs like the houses in Awodei, the children were dressed in rags and the women were forced to walk miles collecting firewood to sell.

Close to the bottom of the hill we went through the same procedure of hiding qat, being searched and picking up the youth with the shawl. The countryside here was parched; camels browsed on thorn trees or carried loads of firewood. As soon as we rounded the last bald foothill we hit Dire Dowa.

The town is built at the point where a large dry watercourse, a wadi, emerges from the hills. On the north side is the railway and a town laid out in neat blocks with broad boulevards where the tree-trunks are painted white up to head height. Blue Peugeot taxis, not one under thirty years old, were laid up in the shade, all four doors wide open and cardboard sheets over the windscreens. The bus roared through this area and turned across a long bridge over the dry riverbed into the poorer side of town. Here the buildings were less well kept, some clinging to scraps of colonial stucco, all blotched and scuffed with yellow distemper and trapped in tangles of wiring. The people, too, had seen hard times: young Somali boys dressed in filthy rags with mean little faces were hanging around the bus stop like hungry jackals.

I set off to walk back towards the station. There were some cheap hotels in the streets near by and it would save time if there were a train next morning.

It was on the bridge that it first occurred to me that something was wrong. I had stopped in the middle to look down the watercourse at people foraging amongst the sun-bleached boulders. By chance I glanced back and noticed two men who had passed me just a few seconds before. They had stopped too and were looking at me, whispering to each other. I turned away and began to walk.

I was used to people staring – it is not unusual in such places – but this was different: no one shouted 'Cuba!' or 'Firenje!' and ran away laughing. Once over the bridge I headed down a long straight road to the railway station, passing a café on my right where men were taking black coffee in tiny glasses. A waiter in a grubby white jacket and carrying an aluminium tray spotted me and froze, a glass halfway to a customer. They all watched me go past. I began to mutter.

'Yes, hello, I'm a white man – remember me? Built the railway, didn't mix much.'

Ahead were some traffic lights and a traffic policeman. The buildings had not changed in fifty years: slatted shutters, dingy interiors with dusty ceiling fans stirring the overheated air. A car had stopped at the lights which now changed to green, unnoticed by the driver and his passenger who were busy discussing me. I crossed over the road and went up a few steps into the Continental Hotel.

There was a dilapidated lobby where a few idle gents were sitting on a sofa of chrome tubing and red leatherette. Then there was a cake display without cake and a Gaggia coffee machine without coffee. On the far side was a doorway and beside that a botched attempt at a reception desk where a thin girl sat motionless, like a lizard waiting for flies. I dumped my bag on the floor. The room had gone silent. I wanted someone to whistle the theme to *The Good, the Bad and the Ugly*, then we could all laugh and the normal hum of conversation begin again. But no one did.

The receptionist waited.

'Hello. Do you speak English?'

She nodded.

'Do you have a room?'

She smiled. 'Hello. How-are-you?'

'Yes, I'm fine, thanks. I was wondering if you had a room?'

'I-am-fine-and-you?'

'Yes, I'm fine. Thank you. I want a room – *room*.'

'What-is-your-name?'

'Kevin – what's yours?'

'What-is-your-name-pee-pee?'

'No – Kevin. My name is Kevin.'

'No-pee-pee? I want your pee-pee.'

Her hand was held out expectantly but not, as I correctly guessed, for a urine sample. I took my passport out and she began laboriously to copy my name into a vast ledger. I tried again. 'Er . . . can I see a room. *Room*.' Hand signal of a square, then mime sleep.

She took a key from a drawer and I followed her through the doorway into an open courtyard around which all the rooms were arranged. In the centre was the ruin of a thatched hut and some dishevelled banana and papaya trees. Thirty years before it must have been a pleasant place to stay. We went to a door and she pushed it open.

'Bed-room.'

'Thank you.'

'Give-me-money-now. Ten birr.'

I nodded and pointed to the entrance. 'I'll come soon.'

It was a spartan dwelling. There was a single bed with matchwood cabinet beside it, a similar wardrobe, a basin, and a window without shutters or glass, just two ragged curtains. The only personal touch was the packet of three condoms placed thoughtfully on the bedside cabinet.

[82]

I put my bags under the bed and went back outside into the deserted courtyard. The door, I noticed, had at one time been kicked in, the wood around the lock crudely repaired with a couple of short nails leaving the latch a few millimetres short of the doorjamb. It could not be locked but I made a great pretence of doing so.

In the lobby there was a payphone next to the gang on the sofa. No one had moved. They watched me while I rang Sahle, the man I had sat next to on the train from Addis Ababa. Fortunately, he was at home.

'Kevin! Are you in Dire Dowa? Really! Okay, I'm coming to see you now – just wait in your room and don't go out. What number room is it? And don't go out. Wait inside the room.'

I paid the girl and returned to the room. It was time to start on the qat but, as Sahle was coming and did not approve, I decided to wait. Within five minutes I saw him hurrying across the courtyard, dressed in smart white trousers and canary yellow polo shirt.

We shook hands warmly but his smile did not last long.

'Have you heard the news?'

'No.'

'About the Frenchman? He was shot dead yesterday on the bridge in broad daylight.'

'On the bridge! I've just come over it. Who was he?'

'A tourist, I think, he didn't live here. They came up behind him and shot him in the back of the head. There was no robbery or anything like that – just killed him. First the Dutchman, then the German, now this – we cannot believe it.'

'Who did it?'

He closed the door. 'Look it is very important now that you stay inside. They have taken all the expatriates out by plane to Addis. You are the only one here now. It's very dangerous. These people are saying they will kill any foreigner they can find. Even we are afraid.'

'But isn't there lots of army around or police? A security operation?'

He shook his head. 'Nothing. No one knows why. Nothing is happening. They simply arrested everyone at the scene of the murder. The Frenchman was with a friend, a Yemeni youth, and he was shot too, but only injured. They arrested him and his family. That's all – nothing else has happened.'

[83]

I sat down on the bed. 'Is this place safe? The door doesn't lock and anyone can stroll in off the street. I walked here so loads of people saw me arrive.' I was remembering now the faces and it seemed that they had looked at me as if I was already dead. 'Maybe I should move to another hotel.'

'There is no point. Even the Ras Hotel, the most expensive, was bombed by them recently. Better to stay here, then you have only a short walk to the station in the morning.'

I gave him a grim smile. 'Something to look forward to. But is there a train?'

He moved towards the door. 'Yes, it will leave at 6 a.m. I have to go now, but I will come back later and we can buy a ticket.'

'What about the merchant – the old man you told me about?'

'Voskan? You better not.'

'Just tell me where I can find him – I'll get back before dark.'

He thought for a moment. 'If you really want to go, I will take you there. Maybe Voskan will bring you back. Be ready at four o'clock.' He went out and shut the door behind him.

That afternoon I sat with my qat on the bed, writing my name and address into my notebooks and looking up nervously every time there was a noise from outside. Shortly before Sahle returned I washed and changed. There was a small five-inch long knife in my bag that I had bought years before in Sudan. It had a neat snakeskin sheath with a plaited leather thong to fit around your upper arm. For the first time since buying it, I actually put it on, then threw it down on the bed. Unless the blade happened to stop a bullet, it was unlikely to do anything but cast suspicion if I were searched.

Sahle walked me quickly to his taxi and we drove at regulation Dire Dowa pace – about twenty miles an hour – along the boulevards. The stunning white heat of midday had passed and now the shadows crept out from under the trees and stretched themselves lazily across the street. A few ladies ambled along wearing colourful flowery chiffon in the Somali style, a particularly ineffective form of dress that requires constant hitching up and adjusting of what appears to be several hundred yards of loosely-draped material.

We stopped at the station and picked up a first-class ticket, then went on

Bab al-Nasri, one of the five original gates to the walled city of Harar, known in Burton's day as Asmadim Bari.

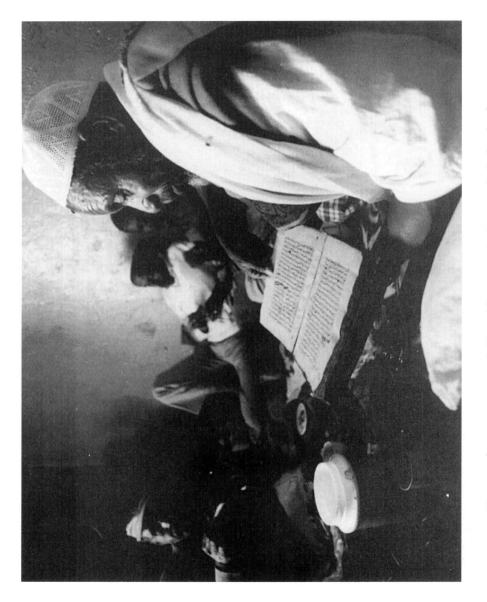

Koran reading at a qat session in Harar. The connection between the leaf and sufism, established in the 13th and 14th centuries, continues to this day.

Al-Gisayr's dhow in the Gulf of Tadjoura off Djibouti. Sails are no longer used but the design of the boat has altered little in accommodating marine engines.

Mokha. A ruined minaret stands alone in the desolation of the once great coffee port. In the background stands the tomb and mosque of the mystic, Sheikh Shadhili.

Qat farmer picking leaves on Jebel Saber. Both individual leaves and long sprigs are harvested, the latter usually command higher prices.

The mosque of the sufi Ahmed ibn Alwan with a spur of Jebel Saber in the background.

A mosque in a Yafa village. The corner 'fangs' on the neighbouring house are typical of the region.

Wadi Bana on the northern edge of Yafa.
Camels remain a popular form of transport in areas where roads have yet to penetrate.

to Voskan's shop. It was in a side street near the bridge. Hefty iron doors had been flung back to reveal a space surrounded on three sides by a simple counter. Shelves behind held a few items of electrical machinery. In the customer area was a table and two chairs where a short, stocky European of about sixty was sitting gazing out into the street.

Sahle introduced me and then made his excuses – a tennis lesson he was giving. We shook hands and I thanked him for all his help. He jogged back to the car, every inch the keen club member on the lawns, trying to squeeze another game in between the first thunder-clap and the coming of the rain.

When he had gone, Voskan waved me to the chair. 'Please, take your seat. And, please, don't tell me you have come to ask about history and trade and so on because poor Eric sat there only yesterday and asked such questions.'

He spoke English well, with a slight French accent. An Ethiopian boy behind the counter came forward and passed me two business cards. One for Voskan and one for Eric the Frenchman.

'He left here about four o'clock – this time – and walked to the bridge with his companion, a Yemeni man who had been born here. Somewhere along there two men came up behind them and without warning shot Eric in the back of the head.'

He shook his head sadly. 'This is a terrible thing. And now you come – when all the expatriates have gone. Well, that is only the French teachers at the Alliance Française. But it is a bad time to come. They only shoot tourists.'

I would remember that line during the hours that followed.

'But what about you?'

He laughed. 'Me? I am here. Where will I go? This is my home and I am too old to go anywhere else. But we are shocked. These killings in Dire Dowa. I can remember when there was nothing, anyone could walk the street. I myself have walked to my shop every day of my working life until today – my wife insisted I drive. Will you take tea? I always have tea at this time.'

He got up and fetched a tray off the counter set with a flask full of hot water and china cups and saucers. Across the top of each cup he placed a square of pale blue toilet tissue then took a pinch of tea from a jam jar and placed it on the paper. Hot water was poured over it and then the paper was screwed up and dropped under the table.

'Take as much sugar as you like – the Somalis take five.'

The cup chuckled as I stirred. It was white with little pink flowers on it.

'You've come down from Harar I suppose?' said Voskan. 'Well, it's a nice place but quiet now. I can remember in the 'fifties, when the French used to visit from Djibouti for weekend trips, the town was full of life: parties and dinners and noise.'

He reminisced about those days when Dire Dowa must have seemed like the future of Africa: organised, colourful and multi-racial with Europeans on top of the economic pile. I wondered how his family had found their way to such a place, and when.

'Let me tell you – a long time ago. My parents were Armenian and my father fought for the Russian Imperial Army against the Turks in 1915. You know they were trying to solve the Armenian question by slaughtering people. He met my mother fleeing north and they fell in love and got married. First they lived in Bulgaria, then in Russia until the revolution. They tried Cairo for a year – my mother's uncle had a house there – but it was hopeless, so they sailed up the Red Sea and landed at Djibouti. They had no passports in those days, no visas or anything like that. It was not necessary.'

'My father's ambition was to start a shoe factory and they went up to Addis Ababa and opened what was the first shoe factory in Ethiopia. When the Italians invaded in 1935, the place was looted and burnt down, so they had nothing. Fortunately, at that time the French railway company were giving land away very cheaply here in Dire Dowa. It was a cosmopolitan place – full of French and Greeks and Arabs – over one hundred Armenians too, so they moved and started again. Now there are two only Armenians left.'

I sipped my tea, which was very welcome: I had not eaten or drunk anything since breakfast time. 'So you were brought up here?'

'Yes, but not all the time. During the Second World War I was sent to Venice for schooling. Imagine! I was in the most beautiful city in the world and unable to enjoy it. Then afterwards, in the 'fifties, I went to work for Antonin Besse in Aden. Do you know his name?'

I had heard of the man. Besse was the stuff trading legend is made of.

Having started as a clerk in Aden, he had branched out on his own and amassed a fleet of dhows and steamers that ran to almost every port on the Indian Ocean coast. In the Port of Aden annual for 1960 I once found an advertisement for his trading group which conjured up a lost world of British imperialists: Austin motor cars, Old Spice aftershave, Gilbey's gin and BSA sporting rifles. Besse is best remembered in Britain for endowing St Antony's College, Oxford.

'Besse lost a lot when nationalisation came here,' said Voskan. 'But of course they had sold up plenty and got out all right – we are still going on.'

A tall, very thin man draped in filthy rags with his hair standing up like black flames and clutching a solitary scrap of newspaper, stopped in the doorway and stared.

Voskan shouted something in Amharic, then in Somali. The man scowled and in English replied. 'I am not a beggar, sir. So do not admonish me as such.' And slowly he shuffled off.

'There are some I give to,' Voskan explained. 'But if you give to all, then they all come – hundreds of them.'

We sat drinking our tea.

'Who are the big merchants?'

'Well, the Hadhramis from Yemen are great merchants and many were here, some still remain. People say they are descended from the Phoenicians which would explain their skill at trade. But legitimate trading is bad now – everything is smuggled. They bring it along the old Zeila road by camel and donkey – camels for the desert, donkeys in the mountains. Machine parts, televisions, clothes, cigarettes, everything comes that route. And they smuggle out too. A few years ago the army caught a convoy of five hundred donkeys carrying coffee.

'Of the Ethiopians, the Guraghe are merchant people but their operations tend to be small-scale. The Hadhramis and the Greeks were the big-time.'

We were interrupted by the arrival of two Ethiopians: one a tall solemn man in his thirties, wearing a cream Harrington jacket and matching cap; the other, a grizzled old man who smiled a lot but did not speak. They sat down and accepted tea.

'Why are you questioning our friend?' asked the younger man. 'Have you research interests in Dire Dowa?'

'Not in the academic sense. I'm just travelling through to Yemen.'

This obviously failed to impress him, so I added, 'Of course, I may write something about my journey.'

'Have you reported yourself to the relevant authorities?'

My face froze in a smile. 'I'm just passing through.'

'To write anything should require a declaration – for your own protection.' He had a strange way of talking to a spot three feet to the left of me with little sinuous movements of his neck as though he were swallowing a hair. 'And with these current uncertainties you must also register your presence with the British Embassy and local police.'

I didn't like what I was hearing, so I asked what his own interests were. This got me a long lecture on the topic of his doctoral thesis, only cut short when he mentioned Harar and I diverted the conversation back to Voskan. 'When did Harar start to decline? It used to be a big trade route down to Zeila, didn't it?'

'Oh yes, but the railway ended all that. Before the railway they would go by camel to Zeila and then by boat. Besse had many boats, of course, seven large ships when I was working there and many smaller dhows – sambuks the Arabs call them.'

'What is your homebase?' asked the persistent and inquisitive young man. 'I mean your institution.'

'I don't have one.' His eyes narrowed in suspicion. 'I'm working for myself.'

'Ah, for materialistic purposes.'

The older man looked at me and said cryptically, 'Leith Docks.'

I smiled at him and we fell silent for a while, as though ruminating on the significance of this contribution. More tea cups were brought and the blue toilet paper put into service. Voskan dealt with some customers asking about generator spare parts and a party of beggars who were on his regular payroll. When he came and sat down again, he asked if I had tried qat in Harar.

'I never liked it myself, but in Aden the coolies would work for two days non-stop when they were chewing it. Then on the third day they were good for nothing. But if it's true that it gives you stamina, what do you think of all these athletes? Do they test for qat at the Olympics? They should. Once we had a request from a French company to send samples. It was in the 'fifties. We prepared them as they instructed and despatched the samples. Two weeks later they requested some more as the first lot had not been good. After the second lot we never heard anything. I think that the active chemicals degrade very quickly and perhaps they could not find what they wanted.'

The young man was staring at me all this time, but now he spoke, his eyes shifting off to the left. 'They made tea from it – in Victorian times.'

The older man was smiling at me. 'Glasgow,' he said.

'Did you know Eric?' asked the young man. 'He was here, you know, here in this room, sitting in that chair where you are now. Danger here is multiform. Where are you staying?'

'Near the station.' Suddenly I didn't want anyone to know where I was staying.

'Registration is a necessary step. If you are the next one, how will your relatives be informed?'

'It's kind of you to think of it.'

The story of the Frenchman's death was gone over again and we finished our tea.

Voskan stood up. 'Well, it is time for us to go – before it is dark. I will take you in the car.'

He called instructions to the boy about locking up and we shook hands with the two other visitors.

'Dundee, Clyde, Lerwick,' said the older man, in a sort of frenzy of good will.

'He was a sailor,' explained Voskan. 'He went to Scotland a lot.'

'Ah!' I nodded, trying to think of something encouraging to say but all I managed was, 'Greenock.'

He let out a shout of recognition, overjoyed at this and shook my hand vigorously.

Voskan and I got into his car, a VW jeep with canvas roof and no windows. On his own admission he had not driven for some years and we now set off in first gear at a steady walking pace.

He waved at the buildings alongside his shop. 'This block – all of it – belonged to me. Then they nationalised it, the communists I mean. You were allowed to choose one place for yourself, so I kept the shop and my wife kept the house. All this went to them.'

Most of it appeared to be in virtual ruins, held together by scraps of old political posters.

'Will you ever get it back?'

He shrugged. 'Does the snake give back its dinner?'

He pulled up at a corner. 'If you walk down here, in a few minutes you come to your hotel.' We shook hands and I got out and watched him drive away. After all the talk of danger, I felt a bit irritated that he had dumped me with a walk ahead. But then, I reflected, he lived here: there might be all sorts of other factors. I was simply a stranger.

He was right about the few minutes, but they were long minutes. Previously in Ethiopia the problem had been to ward people off, every street kid and every con-man wanted to speak to me. Now I was left alone: the light fading fast, the streets all in shadows, and a few dim bulbs gleaming behind closed shutters. Striding quickly up the hotel steps, I found the doors open and the lobby deserted. The courtyard was quiet. I scanned around for other guests but only two or three rooms were occupied, voices coming from inside. When I was sure there was no one about, I pushed my own door open and entered. There was a bang. I leapt sideways. Something black shot out from under the bed, hit my shoe, ricocheted off the wall and sped out across the yard. A rat. I gave a dramatic screech, fell on the bed and felt my ears go whoosh. I remembered to breathe. I remembered to get up and close the door. Ever since I woke up in a Sudanese prison to find one on my chest, I have been prone to dramatic screeches when touched by rats.

I blocked up the gap under the door with stones from outside, shifted the wardrobe against the door, and moved the bed into the far corner away from the window.

The city was soon quiet. I lay down and by eight I could no longer hear any cars moving along the street outside. A breeze picked up and rustled through the trees. At every noise, four thousand bolts of adrenaline would light me up like the condemned man's last cigarette and I crept across the room to peep from the curtain, my brain consumed with nightmares of violence. But each time it was only the watchman, shuffling towards the stinking toilets, slapping his stick against the wall and chuntering to himself.

I did not sleep. The hours passed slowly.

At 4.30 next morning I dressed, packed my bags and wrapped an Arab headscarf very thoroughly around my head. I had arrived as an Englishman, but would leave as an Arab – the opposite of Burton. The hotel was quiet, the watchman asleep as I let myself out onto the steps. A few hundred yards away down the darkened street, I could see the station building and a crowd of people.

I began to hurry along. 'Firenje!' shouted a youth who was standing behind a tree. He grinned and I relaxed. The disguise was obviously a failure and so I threw the scarf back.

Dire Dowa station was lit by a sickly yellow light, a large French colonial building on which was written 'Chemin de Fer Djibouto-Ethiopien'. The iron gates were locked and in front was a large crowd of people, most sitting quietly on their luggage, of which there were vast quantities. I picked my way through the boxes tied up with string, the baskets full of food, the great green cones of qat, the plastic water tubs, the mattresses and the enamel flasks of tea. These were travellers ready for a long journey, even if the man at the ticket office insisted that it would take only ten hours, 'God willing'.

Porters in blue overalls were energetically keeping order with the help of bits of stick torn from packing crates. One took me to the wall next to the main entrance and placed me on my bag, back to the wall, facing the crowd. Pointing to his eye and then me, he promised to keep watch for which I was ridiculously grateful, but I never took my eyes off the crowd.

Before long I noticed someone coming towards me, a big black man, not tall but very very wide with powerful shoulders that supported a crew-cut boulder of a head. In his hand was a small roll bag and when he was still three yards away, he suddenly flung it down next to me. It landed with a thud. Then, baring a fine set of white teeth in a grin, he shouted what sounded like: 'Yo ma bro.'

He bent down, grabbed my hand and began to crush the smaller bones inside, all the time bellowing with laughter and shouting, 'God walks! Man, He walks!' Then with a sigh he dropped himself heavily onto my bag next to me. I had met Cedric. And, if I had known anything about him at that moment, I would have walked smartly back up the road and checked in to the Continental Hotel for two more nights.

Cedric claimed to be Nigerian and spoke improbable but comprehensible English in staccato bursts of machine gun fire. When he talked, people listened but they looked at his hands; he waved them about a lot: they were an inch and a half thick, as wide as they were long, and hammer-hard.

I told him about the killings in the town and he showed surprise. 'What is happening in this country? Why are they not protecting we visiting folks? If I had known this miss-rable info-mation, I am telling you, I would not have stayed one minute. No way.'

It was hard to imagine anyone being foolish enough to attempt an assassination of Cedric and I had the feeling Cedric was quite aware of this fact, too. We talked for at least half an hour as we waited, but at the end of this, all I had learnt was that he was Nigerian, named Cedric and on his way to Djibouti. He was too old to be a student, certainly not a diplomat, a businessman or an ambitious trainspotter; he was dressed in jeans, denim jacket and tee-shirt; he smiled a lot and laughed at every opportunity, and when he learned I had a first-class ticket, he immediately went and upgraded his own so we could travel together. There would be plenty of time to discover more.

At 5.30 the gate was opened and passengers struggled through with their bags. The first class was dominated by enormous leather-faced women who barged everyone aside and marshalled armies of porters to fill up the luggage racks. Mattresses were unfurled on the floor, greasy billy-cans of goat meat sampled; they spat out the windows and chain-smoked. Cedric was beside himself, guffawing with appalled delight at such behaviour. 'Look at these people. God walks! Rea-lly. Look at those but-tocks. What have they got in there? We are in danger from these women. Hon-est-ly. What bacteria are they producing? We are goin' to contract some graaave illnesses, I am telling you.'

But we did not move from our central position; it was all too entertain-ing. At the first paling of the eastern horizon the locomotive grumbled into life and we began our journey. The fat ladies celebrated with an orgy of hawking and spitting, while Cedric kept up a steady commentary on all he saw.

The line followed a wadi and after only a few miles the land became quite green, puckering into low hills on either side of the snaking valley. Hornbills glided away in hooting undulations, tiny deer under acacia trees sprang into zig-zag sprints, a family of warthogs trundled down into a gulch choked with pink flowers, their tails held up like tank aerials. Cedric was excited by the sight of guinea fowl scattering wildly with their gorgeous plumage, wattled necks and beady eyes.

'Very good that one! Very tasty. Eggs, too.'

Iridescent blue rollers launched themselves from the telegraph wires, along with doves and woodpeckers. In a little clearing lay a rusting yellow armoured car, the gun pointing at the sky, but apart from this and the railway there appeared to be no other sign of humanity.

Cedric had remembered some slight he had suffered at the Nigerian Embassy. 'They ask me why I want to go to Djibouti. Ha! I said to that fellow. "It is not your business. Shall I show you my father? Do you want to know how I fuck my wife? Shall I show you how I will break your numbskull, you roguish fellow!" Then he was very nice with me.' He whacked his knees at the memory, roaring with laughter. The other passengers had begun to notice him, some small children crept in and peered over the seat in front in frank astonishment. The Coca-Cola-seller asked where he was from.

'South Africa, my good friend.'

He turned to me. 'Always you better confuse these people. There are many obstacles in life, believe me, and it is better to confuse such characters.'

The sun was well up when we reached the first village: a collection of huts made from mud, rush mats and flattened UNHCR food tins. Most of the villagers were waiting by the tracks with various simple things to sell. The men were toughened by sun and wind with thin sinewy legs, bare feet and flame-red beards dyed with henna. I reached down and bought some samosas, gritty and filled with hard brown seeds, but I was glad of anything.

At the next place the men rushed forward holding goat legs aloft. Three times a week the train comes through and they slaughter the animals when they see it approaching. Not one managed to sell anything, though Cedric was impressed. 'If I lived in Djibouti I would come every day for fresh goat meat.'

'But where do you live? In Nigeria?'

He laughed. 'No, in Kenya.'

'You have a business there?'

'Impot – I am doing impot.'

[93]

'Oh, really. What sorts of things do you import?'

But at this he just laughed and laughed, and I gave up.

The landscape was steadily drying out as we jogged along for hour after hour. Villages clustered around their water tower in the centre of vast barren circular deserts that the flocks had created. Slim figures in brown cloth could be seen walking towards the far-off smear of pale green, the spume at the edge of this wave of destruction where a few thorn bushes clung to life and herds of black-headed Somali sheep foraged. A squirrel dashed under a dwarf thorn tree and a brace of partridge whirred away to safety.

Then there were no more trees, even stunted ones, just endless termite pillars standing all the way to the horizon like remnants of a lost civilisation inhabited only by white vultures. The wind began to howl through the compartment, carrying clouds of dust, but no one moved to shut the windows that had been jammed open with empty cans – the heat would soon have been too much.

The termite mounds came to an end and we passed a white tent in the middle of nothing, the sky white and the sand white, just two men scorched black by the sun waving at us, animated shadows in a shadowless noonday sun. If they were track-layers, then there was no track to lay, no tools I could see, only a small fence of thorn sticks around their lonely dwelling where the sand was banking up on the leeward side. Along here every telegraph pole had a burn of vulture droppings around its base and the track was lined with the bones of camels, undisturbed in the century since they had died carrying water to the railway navvies.

I dozed for an hour or two and woke, the landscape as unremittingly stony as before, though there were occasional signs of rain: pans of dried mud with footprints of men and sheep in them. Far across this desolate place I spotted a hut made of grass and children playing outside; further on there was a man, whiplash thin with an Afar dagger in his belt – the notorious scrotum-snatching jile.

'These people are most dangerous,' Cedric told me. 'When I travelled on this train two years ago, one rogue – a soldier – he searched my bag and found some money. It was a mistake to allow him to find that money. He was holding it up and showing the carriage. "Look at this man's money." Rea-lly I was afraid of robbery. I did not sleep, not even a single wink.'

'Was it a lot of money?'

'Believe me, it was significant: forty-five thousand American dollars in cash notes. But sometimes I carry three hundred thousand. That would have been death for me.'

I was impressed. Why do you take so much?'

'I do not like this plastic. I use cash. I have my bank account, of course. I have many bank accounts. One is in Knightsbridge – National Westminster. You know that one?'

'You were going to Djibouti that time?'

'We were going to Addis. I left my car in Djibouti and went on this train. Now I want my car and I am going back for it.'

'But that was two years ago?'

'I left my car with a friend and now I am going to take it from him.'

'After two years? Maybe he won't want to give it up.'

'What are you saying? It is my car – how can he retain it for himself?'

'You import to Djibouti?'

'No, Kenya – these electronic things.'

He told me about televisions, calculators, videos, computer games and so on. How he bought them in Hong Kong. It was all very convincing.

The locomotive was now hooting loudly and we pulled into a station called Aicha, where there were a few stone buildings, a church and a large water tower, then the long stony plain to a low ridge. Next to a pile of rocks a camel sat dying, its head desperately lifting, then falling back to the ground. The village idiot came and stood staring at the locomotive while masturbating – much to Cedric's amusement. He lay back in his seat and cried with laughter. 'Get me an instrument to record this moment! Bring me video apparatus! I cannot believe it – I never saw such frivolity, I am telling you.'

But the lunatic lost interest when the engine was switched off and sauntered away down the track. Word passed along the carriage that we were here for a long time as the line was blocked.

'I am very hungry,' Cedric announced. 'Let us purchase some foods from these people.'

We clambered over the sleeping passengers in the aisle and jumped down. Aicha was proving slow to cash in on this unexpected windfall of several hundred trapped customers. In fact, the only people showing any

entrepreneurial skills were a gang of uniformed men who were busily confiscating qat for their afternoon session. A needling, gritty wind scoured
the village and even the telegraph poles looked forlorn without the cheery
decoration of vulture shit.

Cedric and I explored the high street. At the front of the crude single-
room buildings, little thatched shades leaned heavily on crooked poles; one
or two had fallen down. People lay inside, passing the hours by groaning
or picking at something septic; our greetings were met with either hideous
cackles of laughter or dismissive grunts. Halfway along there were two
shops and we discovered why Aicha was passing up this golden opportunity for self-enrichment: there was almost nothing to sell. Each shop had
identical stock: a few soap cakes, three or four dusty Coca-Cola bottles
which were empty and some Abu Walad biscuits from Yemen. I felt a deep
sense of depression coming over me – the prospect of a night spent here
was utterly horrible.

Cedric was approaching things more practically. 'I could eat a goat,' he
said, dragging me into a shack where he had spotted a woman cooking.
'Look, let us buy a goat and they will cook it for us.'

The people seemed quite unabashed by our rude entry, not smiling or
showing any particular interest as Cedric explored the cooking facilities.
'Hon-es-ly. I am famished. Let us buy a goat. Do you have a goat, my
woman?'

The woman of the house, who could not be expected to have the least
idea what he wanted, gazed gently back from her stool with the great
dignity that comes of a life full of indignity. She was the first thing I had
seen in Aicha that was not old, ugly or broken.

'They must have goats,' cried Cedric, examining an empty cooking pot
in disbelief. 'If they have one thing, believe me, it is that creature. How else
are they survivin' in this god-forsaken desert?' He tried shouting the word
'goat' very loudly and often, but this failed.

'Come on, Cedric,' I protested. 'Let's go.'

It was as though he had not heard me. 'You are right – what am I talking
about? One goat is no good – we need two. I can eat one myself immediately and whatever you cannot swallow we will take for our supper.'

He marched through the back door to where there was a thorn-roof
shelter and I heard a whoop of delight.

'God walks! Look at this. Two goats. Let us purchase and do something with this hunger.'

With a sinking feeling I went and looked, and sure enough there was a small herd of goats waiting to be eaten by Cedric.

'Cedric . . . ' .

He whipped round on me, jabbing a stubby finger into his chest. 'Look at me. I am a man, am I not? And this is my stomach.' He grabbed his tee-shirt and lifted it up, revealing an impressive belly and huge pectoral muscles. A kind of fury had possessed him and it was impossible to know if it was real or feigned. 'Tell me how I am to survive if I am not feedin' myself? You are a thin man and have no need for so much feedin' but, believe me, I can eat one goat right here and now. Do not get between me and my goat.'

I went back out and tried to speak Arabic with the woman, but she answered in Somali.

'Cedric, what are you going to do – kill the goat and offer money? You'll start a war.'

He stamped out the house. 'Pah! These people are fillin' themselves with chat. I am telling you it is abnormal. They eat that stuff and believe they are on top of the world. Here! Can you imagine? It must be a wonderful leaf to make this hell into heaven!' He shook his head in disbelief. 'God is a mysterious character, I am tellin' you.' His temper had gone as fast as it had come but I would not forget the tiny tremor of fear when he had faced me.

We went back to the train and I sat on the ground fifty yards away in the shade of a stone wall, hoping Cedric would not join me. I was irritable and fed up, but I had plenty of time to get over it. Two hours passed. A man walked off into the empty desolation towards the ridge, his ragged tunic flapping in the super-heated wind. The camel went on dying. Passengers squatted to relieve themselves. My mind drifted to school days and summer afternoons in sleepy English lessons with Mr Medley, 'Deadly Medley' we called him, dozing after a nip from his hip flask and a bumble bee buzzing at the window while we read 'Adlestrop'.

> Yes. I remember Adlestrop -
> The name, because one afternoon

Of heat the express-train drew up there
Unwontedly. It was late June.

The steam hissed. Someone cleared his throat.
No one left and no one came
On the bare platform. What I saw
Was Adlestrop – only the name

How I had ached to escape the somnolent emptiness of the classroom
for the thrilling excitement of travel in Africa.

Two more hours passed. Then, just as I thought we were condemned to
spend the night in Aicha, the driver reappeared and climbed into his cab.
The blockage had been shifted.

I ran back to the carriage to find Cedric ranting to himself. 'Look at
these women. They have not moved in ten hours. We are facin' a miasma.'

Unfortunately, it was true. The stench in the compartment was nause-
ating and only became bearable once we were moving and airflow re-estab-
lished. I accepted a few qat leaves from the drinks salesman. 'What are you
doin' to yourself,' Cedric burst out, 'indulgin' in this frivolity?'

But at least it was an activity, the hand going slowly from lap to mouth,
something to remind oneself that time existed in this awesome emptiness. To the west, about fifty miles away, lay Lake Abbé, where the Awash
river ends its journey from the highlands around Addis Ababa, a fact that
remained the last great mystery of African geography until as late as
1934, when Wilfred Thesiger reached its shores. His guides had shown
him the remains of a previous expedition under the Swiss, Werner
Munziger, which had been wiped out by the Afars in the customary
manner.

As the sun set, the land wrinkled upward a little and the railway found a
small wadi to wind along, a pale ribbon of sand edged with green below
the grey stony hills. Darkness fell. There were no carriage lights. After an
hour I saw a light up ahead and we pulled into Dewelle, the Ethiopian side
of the border.

Before the train came to a halt, youths were jumping off and disappearing into the darkness with large bundles over their shoulders. When
we pulled up, the carriage lights flickered on and a mean-faced official in

ragged uniform came clumsy-footed over the sleeping passengers, shout-ing, 'Vaccination certificates – yellow fever vaccination certificates.'

I looked in my camera bag. I looked in my pockets. The women had already got theirs prepared and he was quickly on to Cedric and myself. Cedric handed over the yellow document.

'You!' shouted the official.

I began to explain. 'Your embassy in London actually did say that it was no longer . . . '

Cedric leapt to his feet. 'It's here, in his bag.' He pointed at my holdall on the rack above. 'But difficult to find – don't worry, my friend, he has it.'

The officer, dwarfed by the immense Nigerian, scowled. 'It is forbidden to travel in Ethiopia without this vaccination. I am coming back to you and, if you do not have this certificate, you will get off this train and return to Addis Ababa.' He tossed his head and marched to the next row of seats.

I sat in stunned silence. This was too awful a fate to consider – another night in Dire Dowa. Cedric seemed quite happy now the man had gone, but if he came back, what then?

'Cedric, your certificate – I mean, you have an English name and he won't remember it. Lend me yours and I'll show it to him.'

He was surprisingly reluctant to indulge in this minor deception. I had to persist before he handed the little book over. I glanced at the cover. The name written there was not Cedric, it was Arthur.

I suppose he saw me read it. 'There are obstacles in this world,' he explained. 'These people will create so many obstacles. So you must make arrangements. I make arrangements. If a beautiful girl tells me, "Oh, you are a pretty handsome fellow." Is it nice? Yes. But is it true? For me, no. I am big and I am ugly. But I like to hear it, believe me, even if I know she is lying with her jaw. That is an arrangement. I make arrangements.'

He took my silence as 'not yet convinced' and drew closer to whisper. 'Look at this obstacle they are making – this stupid border. They make their visa, their passport. This is an obstacle. I am a man. Can I not walk in my own world? Who are you to prevent my passin'?' He was getting carried away again. 'Is this my world or not? Who are you to make this obstacle against your fellow human being? So I carry my passport and if I need another one I show him another one.'

'You have more than one passport?'

He roared with laughter and slapped his knees. 'God walks!'

'Where from?'

'Kenya, South Africa, Zambia, Zaire, from every country I am needin' a passport – this time I am Nigerian.'

'But how do you get so many?'

'By arrangements, that is all. I have a house in South Africa. I have a house in Nigeria, another in Kenya. I need to move. I need these passports.'

'For your electronics importing business?'

His knees took another pummelling. 'Electronics! That's right. Ain't life a mysterious business?!'

There was a bump and the carriages lurched. I was praying we might head off before the vaccination man returned. A team of smarter, well-organised immigration men now came along stamping passports. It crossed my mind that the ragged uniform of the official revealed something about his standing, or lack of it: the vaccination certificate might just be a ruse dreamt up by a discredited official to extort money. Nevertheless, it was a relief when the train began to roll and he had not appeared.

We moved gently out of Dewelle into the darkness and stopped. Out of the blackness appeared a swarm of figures carrying large bundles and heading for the third-class carriages. Then, with a last hoot, we moved away across the three-mile belt of no-man's-land toward the Djiboutian customs post.

'This one is very special,' laughed Cedric, 'Believe me. I never saw a border post like this.'

Before we reached it the driver stopped to allow off any passengers who preferred to detour the tiresome formalities, then we arrived.

On our left up a long steep bank was what appeared to be a roofed cattle pen. Beside this was a well-lit office around which people were moving like moths, never entering but not leaving. Gangs of thin men in green uniforms were waiting by the tracks tapping batons against their boots. There was a burst of activity in the carriage as bags were sorted and documents arranged; faces that had grinned through the Ethiopian border were pinched and nervous.

The train had not come to a halt before they were on board, shoving their way through and screaming orders. They had a white-green foam around their lips, their eyes were like thick brown glass, their hands grabbed and shoved. The women screamed abuse, men bellowed, arms jerking out, faces clenched like fists in fury. I had never seen it before, never thought it possible, but here it was: we had been invaded by men crazed with qat. Lack of sleep, no food, too little water, too little qat – or too much – crushing boredom: these were customs officials determined to find drugs, who really needed to find drugs, who would keep the drugs to make life bearable. Set a thief to catch a thief.

Everyone was forced off the train, then herded towards the pen. A raised baton was enough to encourage most, but Cedric stood his ground and I hovered next to him.

'No. I am not going in that cage. I am not an animal.'

Five soldiers were around us instantly and one stood close, an officer, demanding in French that we follow the others.

Cedric began to crack his knuckles. 'I am tellin' you. I will not enter that cage intended for animals. If I am treated like an animal, there is a danger for you that I may behave as one.'

Whether the officer spoke English or not, he understood. An impressive order was given that we must stay where we were. Our passports were taken. Over by the office I noticed a group of people squatting in a tight circle, a soldier ran at them with raised stick and they bent like grass before a wind. Several of them were hit.

The train was now being subjected to an intimate body search. Men climbed on the roof. Others poked wires into dark spaces underneath. Toilets were searched. Bags emptied. A woman had a spectacular epileptic fit by the track while her relatives panicked. I called a soldier over and asked him to fetch a doctor. He shrugged. 'There is no doctor here.'

'Then what shall we do?'

He stared blankly at me. 'Do?'

'She may die.'

He shrugged. 'It is true, she may die, but I think she will not.'

I went to fetch another officer but no one would come.

Half an hour passed. A few lucky passengers had got out the pen but most stood, hands hooked through the wire staring down at us. Our passports were returned and we reboarded. The train hooted.

Just as it began to move, they opened the pen gates. There was a stampede, people falling over one another, people tumbling down the bank, women falling over their robes, young men sprinting ahead. Not everyone made it, even when we paused to pick up the shy, retiring types who had trudged around with their bundles. With the carriage lights failing yet again, we rolled on towards Djibouti city, still two hours away.

A tiny country by African standards, Djibouti is centred on the Gulf of Tadjoura, a hot little crack in the dried out hide of the continent where the Rift Valley, exhausted and dessicated after the Danakil desert, with not even as much as one teardrop left to leak into the warm salty sea, dies quietly a few yards short of the water and five hundred feet below it, protected from inundation by a narrow bund of lifeless stone. The land is a stony desert strip, sixty miles wide with few reliable sources of drinking water and a climate of almost unrelieved staggering heat. There are no manufacturing industries to speak of, no agricultural products besides a few goats, there are no cool mountain resorts, no parks, no forests. But there are two tribes and they fight over it, occasional dusty little conflicts, unreported much. The land was once a series of petty sultanates along the coast with a tribal interior. Then in 1857, Henri Lambert, an enterprising French consul in Aden, bought Obock on the northern side of the Gulf for ten thousand silver dollars. The French flag was hoisted, but the place forgotten until the 1880s.

It was a decade in which the scramble for colonial possessions became feverish, and with the Italians and British carving out fiefdoms to the north and south, the French moved to consolidate. An ambitious twenty-four-year-old officer, Léonce Lagarde, stole the sultanate of Tadjoura from under the British noses just one day before the British planned to annexe it themselves. Then the French grabbed land on the southern side of the gulf up to Loyada, the present border with Somaliland. High hopes were held for the territory to rival Aden, but Obock was hemmed in by mountains and without a natural harbour, so in 1892 it was abandoned for Djibouti.

One can only marvel at the optimism of such men. It's true they had the examples of Captain Haines at Aden or Sir Stamford Raffles in Singapore, but Raffles had tried once before at Bencoolen in Sumatra and who remembers Bencoolen? Djibouti was a barren coral flat with sandbars washed over at high tide. According to one source, the French arrived to find that its sole inhabitant was 'a jackal dying of hunger under a thorn tree'. Others thought this presented too rosy a picture.

The French are still there, though the military presence has been reduced from 34,000 men to around 3,000 since the communist threat from Ethiopia and South Yemen disappeared. Djibouti has independence, a president from the Issa tribe and an increasingly disgruntled Afar community.

There were few lights to show the size of the city ahead: a line of orange dots strung out to the port, a cluster of pin-pricks at each end fighting back the darkness; the country had been having serious electricity shortages and during the summer people had died from heat when the fans stopped turning.

The central station has none of the charm of Addis Ababa's, but my judgement was coloured by thirst, hunger and total exhaustion. We struggled along the platform among the crowds of men bearing green rolls on their shoulders: eight feet long, bouncing and bending as if inside might be a captive Princess Jasmine. All the way from the border the men who were unable or unwilling to try dodging around the customs checks on foot had been busy unscrewing the panels of the train, retrieving their qat from secret hiding places and reparcelling it ready for market. Now here they were, stepping out briskly to sell, even though it was one o'clock in the morning.

Outside in the forecourt a howling mob was waiting – not taxi-drivers, not would-be guides or anxious relatives, but qat addicts. Emaciated, ragged people with the eyes of insomniacs hung about in dark corners, while the well-to-do, no less desperate, jammed the street with parked cars and hurried over to the sellers. These were all women, many sitting on chairs with what an unwitting observer might have taken for homely knitting bags in their laps ready to click away like some African Madame Desfarges under the guillotine. Others had it on old tea chests, covered in damp bedsheets or hessian.

But water, not qat, was what we needed. Nothing more than two bottles of Coke had passed my lips since Voskan's tea. I pushed my way into the mob to where there was a stall and demanded water. A plastic bottle of French mineral water was produced and a large quantity of Ethiopian currency accepted. I drank. Cedric took one for himself and drank the two litres in about half a minute before the astonished proprietor.

With this need satisfied, next was sleep. Bus men and taxi drivers were grabbing at us, yelling in French. Cedric went one way, I went the other. I was bundled into a mini-bus, pushed out. Cedric appeared. I was man-handled into another bus. A man in a white suit punched the driver through the open window. Two youths dragged him away. The driver disappeared clutching his bloody nose, another man got in.

'Where is this bus going?'

I was trying to remember the French words but Arabic was coming out. 'Illa fain hadha?'

Men shouting in my face. A mad staring eye presses close and pulls back. Bag? Where's my bag. Cedric pushing through has the bag. Can you speak French? I can't remember it, can you? Yes, but not now, I can't think. The bus jerks and roars and goes ten yards. They are bawling place names and I'm shouting 'Centre de ville' and no one is listening. We both get out and in another. We move a little but a car smashes into the back. A man is being dragged away from a qat-stall and beaten. The crowd closes around the bus. The driver gets out, another gets in. We move out and drive.

Cedric could not remember anything about the town. I told him it was ten years since I had visited and I didn't expect to recall anything. Everywhere was in darkness, the air foetid with rotting vegetable matter, a sickly heat gripping the throat. We passed into streets of crumbling colonnaded shops with pale facades where the stucco grapes and vine leaves were falling off as though too tired to hang there any longer. Under the archways, in front of the darkened shops, were the huddled shapes of sleeping people wrapped in sheets. Then we passed a place that was all lit up and smart. A pair of swing doors swung open to reveal a red light on the brute face of a French military policeman as he came swaggering out.

We dropped into an open area, obviously a market by day but now empty. On one corner was the ghostly white stump of a minaret like a lighthouse without light and the only thing that looked clean and well-kept in all the mess of tin roofs, packing crate shacks, and piles of stinking refuse. Cedric thought he knew this place and, with less certainty, so did I. We paid the driver and walked endlessly in squalid back streets: he could not recognise the hotel he wanted, but would not give up searching. I could not understand why it had to be that particular hotel, but he insisted. There were no inhabitants to be seen, only soldiers and police slouching on every corner. Finally, we picked another hotel, a Somali-run place with a safe-looking gate, a courtyard and a guard who we woke after plenty of shouting. It was still fantastically overpriced, so we had to share a room in which there was nothing more than two single beds, one pair of flip-flops for the shared bathroom and a grumbling air-con unit. I threw myself down, filthy and too tired to care, chuntering about African squalor at Parisian prices as I fell, blissfully, into a deep sleep.

# 8

Djibouti did not appear quite so insane by light of day. Cedric and I were out early, woken by hunger pangs. We walked through the shanty town where pools of foul yellow liquids shone beneath a pure blue sky and people sat in doorways chatting to passers-by. Someone shouted, 'Journalist!'

Sandwiched between this poverty-stricken area and the crumbling French colonial architecture of the offices and shops was a market where we found breakfast. It was a simple white-painted weatherboard shack run by Yemenis who had come from Aden when the British cleared out in 1967. One of them remembered Cedric from his last visit and sat down to chat, or rather start on a long list of complaints and grievances about Djibouti's serious decline in fortunes. He had smooth Afro-Arab skin and a mouth full of gold teeth. Like all the men he was wearing a futa, loose shirt and skullcap, not the flat woven saucer of Egypt and Sudan but the raised oval dish of Aden and Zanzibar which allows air circulation.

'Since the French built their own bars and restaurants at their base, the place has died. Then last year the government had a war against the Afars in the north which took lots of money. Now the place is dead – you won't believe what you see.'

He swished his hand at the hordes of small flies on the table and they gave tired sluggish jumps, then fell back again, lapping desperately at patches of spilled water. Already sweat was pouring down my face, dripping into the white enamel tea mug when I drank.

'Behind here is the Ethiopian shanty town full of poor people who came here hoping for a better life. Now they have nothing and they are angry. At night you'll see the soldiers all around it – they fear that place. Don't go in yourselves, it's full of thieves.'

We did not mention that we had walked through twice already. Breakfast came: fried slivers of liver with onions and warm fresh baguettes. It was delicious, although there was a certain degree of skill required to eat the food and not the flies. Cedric managed three platefuls before declaring himself ready to find his car. 'Then I can take you to the port for asking about boats to Yemen. Then we can visit a beach.'

That sounded like a very good idea, given the temperature: with the clock past ten many residents were taking the chance to have a short lie down to recover from the folly of getting up in the first place. We strolled out of the market and down a long street lined with crumbly concrete walls and scraggy ornamental trees. On one side was a Djiboutian military barracks, on the other a secondary school. Crossing a sleepy road junction, we found our way into a residential area of smart villas, most of them hidden behind high walls or thick hedges of bougainvillaea, hibiscus and jasmine. Guards at every gate looked on us suspiciously; in such places, walking was a sure sign of either criminal intentions or insanity.

Cedric finally picked out the house, a white single-storey villa behind heavy iron gates which we pushed open. A gravel courtyard for parking took up the entire garden with double car shelters flanking the house, both of them empty.

Cedric strode over, arms held wide. 'Where is my car? It was in this place. What has that fellow done with my car?'

A maid came meekly from the fly door but she spoke only Somali and it appeared we would have to walk to the man's office. This took us back into the colonial colonnades of the shopping and business district where we had seen the French military policeman the previous night. Built on a grid-iron plan, the two-storey buildings have survived, if only just; those that have not yet fallen down remain better than anything put up since. The paint may be peeling, rubbish piling up, the squiggles of stucco looking more like wormcasts than decoration, but the slatted shutters of the upper windows and cool arcades beneath are more bearable than the few modern banks and supermarkets that have been thrust into any vacant lots. Walk into these air-conditioned monsters and the sweat on your forehead forms an ice cap. Not that getting in is always easy: large crowds of beggars, many disabled or crippled in some way, block the route, while youths with little open and shut home-made cardboard cases importune any European with eclectic offers of postcards, cigarettes and jars of muscle embrocation.

We left these banks and their attendant nuisances behind, going along one shady colonnade into a quiet side street of flaky paintwork and arriving at an unremarkable open doorway.

'It is here,' said Cedric, indicating the entrance. 'But let us look . . . '

He went up to the next street and glanced down it.

'My car!'

It was a beige four-wheel-drive pick-up with raised suspension, mag wheels and a rear cab over the back. Inside I could see that it had a CD player and plush interior but externally it was in poor condition: the paintwork had blistered in places and webs of fine cracks were breaking out all over.

Cedric ran around, looking inside and underneath. 'What is this rogue doin' drivin' my car? How has he gained admission?'

'You didn't leave him the key?'

'What are you saying? Of course I did not. And this car is very special, believe me, it has two safety alarms. If you try to drive it, the fuel will cut out and an alarm come on. How has he done this? Look at this bodywork. It is disgraceful.'

I wanted to say, Well, if you leave it for two years without a word, what do you expect?

Cedric was peering inside. 'And he has his things in there, but my things are not around. In *my car!* I had this car built for me specially in South Africa – not for him to go taking his girlfriends around and behavin' like he is the Lord God Almighty. This car cost thirty-five thousand dollars in cash to have built how I liked. I don't want any car like anybody has – and I don't want anybody drivin' it except me.'

I was not really paying much attention to this tirade: the car was certainly an upmarket Japanese model, but as for individuality, all it had was a dowdy beige colour that no one in their right mind would pick. It was a little longer than normal perhaps, but that scarcely registered in my mind at the time.

Cedric slapped his hands and stood back. 'Let us visit this fellow and collect the key.'

All the way to the door he raged about people misusing other people's possessions without permission. 'What is this world coming to, I ask you? I pray for Lord Jesus to come and clean up this mess, I really do.'

We went inside, along a short corridor, then through a second door and into a large modern office, all cleverly arranged and divided with screens and potted plants. The air was cold. This was the large office of a successful enterprise although there was no indication of how the money was made. The men were all in dark ties, white shirts, black trousers and patent leather shoes, while the women dressed as ladies in *haute couture* advertisements from the 1950s: stylish blouses and skirts with elegant hair. Most had the sheer, silky brown skin of the Somali, but there were other racial types too: Ethiopians, Arabs, Egyptians and Indians. One of the latter came towards us clutching what appeared to be an elephant gun.

'Where is Daud?' demanded Cedric, and we were taken to wait next to a cashier's glass window.

A smooth urbane chap in tortoiseshell-rim spectacles came hurrying over, hand extended, face wreathed in smiles.

'Cedric! Cedric! Oh my God, where have you been? We were so worried – I thought you were dead or something. I even started driving your car because I was worried it would rot if no one used the engine. Really, come and sit down. How wonderful to see you again, my friend. You look in good health – how is your health? Where are you staying? Nasser's hotel is now a school, you know. He went back to Somaliland. And the Comoro boy is gone and – what was her name, Lulu – I never saw her in more than two years. It's four since I saw you, isn't it?!'

Cedric was quite charming himself. If I had expected recriminations, I was dead wrong. He smiled and smiled and shook Daud's beautifully manicured hand and introduced me as 'a close friend and colleague' – an unexpected promotion. And the car was hardly mentioned. They talked about nothing very much: Daud waxed lyrical on Djibouti's economic prosperity and mentioned his trips to Egypt and Paris; Cedric mentioned Taiwan and India.

'Yes, Nasser just disappeared,' said Daud pleasantly. 'The commissioner of police came to me one evening and asked if I was the man's friend and

I said, "Not really, but I know him." And would you believe that very next day the hotel is closed and I hear that Nasser has been picked up and deported to Somaliland. Political, I suppose.'

He was very French and charming, but I decided that seeing Cedric had been about as welcome as a visit from the Black Death. They chatted for a few more minutes, then, as we were about to leave, almost as an after-thought, Cedric mentioned the car keys. 'I would like to take the car now, Daud.'

Daud's smile was unbreakable. 'Of course, if you must. It's just that I have a friend arriving at the airport tonight – could you collect it tomor-row? It would be so helpful.'

'What are you saying?'

Daud's face, for an instant, lost its composure, his eyes widened and the smile fell faster than a synchronised swimmer in shark-infested waters. Then Cedric snapped back to being Mister Nice Guy: his face broke into a smile and his arms were held out in generosity. 'What-are-you-sayin'? Of course, take the car tonight. There is no problem, believe me. I am just very happy to find you, Daud. Do not worry yourself about this car.'

We were soon back in the shattering sunlight and I led the way into a cool arcade, then towards the sea. I wanted to visit the port and discover if it was going to be feasible to take a dhow to Yemen. It seemed as if years had passed since I had first asked Haj Ali about the crossing. Possible complications and revised plans were running chaotically through my head. I had no knowledge of any European ever having achieved the voyage recently, no knowledge if there were dhows or how often such boats might be expected. There was the grim, inescapable possibility that I could be in for a long wait.

Cedric, however, had his mind on other things and I became aware of his grumbles. 'What is this man telling me these things for? "My friend the commissioner of police." That is bullshit. And the Comoro boy gone away – why would he leave here? I will try and find him. I must find him. At least that boy is not a gigantic liar. Nasser was Daud's friend, too. And he is tellin' me that business is good – what total bullshit. Do I not have eyes in my head? Can I not see what is happenin' here?'

This was all too evident. This was the centre of the business area and, though it had always had a run-down, neglected appearance, there had been a bustling vibrancy to it. One street I remembered had been a place for money-changers, the people spilling out all over the street, men listening on little transistor radios for the BBC business news reports, shouts of exchange rates for a myriad of currencies – Saudi rials, central African francs, Kenyan shillings, and the all-powerful dollar. But no longer. The money men were almost all gone and the packed bars where you could drink cognac with your breakfast croissants were either closed up or empty. On the wall a sign called for freedom for political prisoners but there was hardly anyone around to read it.

'Where shall we go now?' asked Cedric.

I told him about the port and he nodded. 'Good. I will come with you as I know that place and can help you.'

It seemed a lot to expect and I wasn't sure I wanted his help but there was no choice, he absolutely insisted.

From the waterfront we took a long black road with lagoons on both sides. Far off was a shimmering collection of wooden boats and a second road apparently running across the sea to where stacks of freight containers stood rusting under silent cranes. The sun drilled down on us mercilessly.

At the junction of the second road a man in a futa was standing on one leg, holding up a large tuna fish for passing cars to see. No one stopped. The harbour did not look at all hopeful, most of the boats were wrecks, showing just a few spars of blackened timber above the motionless water. There were none of the smartly painted big old dhows I had hoped for, just two sun-scarred tubs with packing-case cabins.

I greeted some men and spoke to them in Arabic.

'Yemen?' they asked, incredulously, 'by sambuk – why not by plane? You have money.'

Eventually they directed us to another port, pointing vaguely towards the stacks of containers. We retraced our steps to the junction where the tuna-seller was waiting and headed for the other port. The road went past the soft drinks bottling plant and into an area of scabby concrete office blocks, all algae stains and crusty corners like enormous chunks of coral thrown up on a beach. At the end was a red and white pole across the road and a swarm of men in uniform. We tried strolling nonchalantly past them, but one grabbed my arm.

'Lex pass! Votre pass!'

Cedric turned him aside with smiles and soft words. A paper came from his pocket and this seemed to make everything all right. We walked on along a tarmac road with two steel rails down the middle on which a loco-motive was moving some empty cattle trucks around. A car sped by with a French soldier in the back wearing the kepi of the Foreign Legion. We aimed towards a long grey building which seemed to be the quayside ware-house.

'What did you show the soldier?' I asked.

Cedric laughed. 'There are so many obstacles, my friend. That one is the identity book for a Polish seaman. I told him we were going to our ship. Always you make them confused, do not let them think, make them believe you are stupid and keep moving.'

'Where did you learn that?'

'Nigeria. That is one very good country, believe me. You learn to walk in Nigeria, you can walk anywhere.'

'On the train I thought that maybe you were smuggling something – I don't know, drugs maybe – heroin.' I could hardly believe that with no wit-nesses around I had just accused him of being a drugs smuggler. Cedric did not mind in the slightest. He found it very amusing. 'And why not? I will smuggle that stuff if I need to, but I do not need to. And if they are catchin' you, the punishment is too significant. There are other ways to make your path in this world, my friend – only make them believe you are stupid, confuse them. I am telling you, you have to move fast.'

'Like with Daud?'

'Daud is not stupid, but he thinks he is cleverer than me – that is very stupid, believe me. He does not know half of the business we play, but he thinks to trick me.'

'You're business partners?'

He scowled. 'Not exactly. We did some business together. I paid for him to take a holiday in Egypt – now he is tellin' me about it to impress me what a big man he has become. Does he not remember where the money came from? And who the money came from? Of course not. I am tellin' you I am a peaceable man, I do not like violence. One time a man owed me five thousand dollars and he thought he could escape from me. I catched him and very soon, believe me, he changed that bad attitude of his and gave me the money. I did not need to kill anybody.'

'You think Daud will try and keep the car?'

This flicked a switch inside him, his face darkened and his fists clenched. 'What are you sayin'? That is my car. I have many cars. I have BMs in Zambia, Toyotas in South Africa, trucks in Zaire, but I do not make a present of this car to Daud.'

I dropped the subject.

We came to the end of the grey building and a view down the quay-side opened out before us like a scene from a painting by Hieronymus Bosch: hundreds of skinny sweating coolies dressed only in grimy futas were slaving to shift several hundred tons of cargo out of three dhows that were tied up between a French naval patrol ship and streak-sided Liberian freighter. Men with sticks ripped from crates were running among the workers, damping down fights with hefty whacks. But, like bush fires, no sooner had one been quashed than another leapt to life and in they went, sticks flailing. Other coolies lay exhausted on scraps of cardboard in the shade of stacked milk cartons, fruit juice containers and biscuit boxes, while yet more were besieging the foreman, obviously desperate to be hired. From the upper decks of the warship French sailors in tight shorts and tee-shirts viewed the whole scene with good-humoured contempt.

Examining the dhows, I realised that two were flying Yemeni flags and my heart leapt. The first was a simple affair: the broad-beamed workhorse of Arab shipyards with a crude shelter rigged up aft and a mast that could be utilised should the engine fail. This boat was empty, its cargo of bottled mineral water already on the quayside and the captain, or nakhoda, loung-ing in the shade. I stepped aboard and greeted him.

He had a narrow mean face with three gold teeth in his mouth and a gold thread in his skullcap. As commanding officer he wore a shirt outside a checked futa and sandals made of car tyres; his men were barefoot and bare-chested, covered only by filthy futas tied up with string.

'How is Djibouti?' he asked.

'Praise be to God, Djibouti is Djibouti and Yemen is Yemen,' I answered.

'You want to go to Yemen?'

I nodded. 'When do you leave?'

'Now.'

'Oh, too soon for me.' He was a man I would not have chosen to trust with my life and I was glad that I wasn't going to have to.

'Try that boat,' he said. 'But al-Gisayr, the nakhoda, he is no good.'

I disembarked and walked along.

This second ship was immediately more to my liking. It had a big blue-painted stern rising in stout curves through three decks to a wheelhouse with strong wooden rails and a massive old rudder, creaking gently. On one side was a wooden box overhanging the sea, the thunder box, and there were neatly lashed barrels and boxes, flaps of sail and a rakish mast leaning forward as if itching to get out in the swell. The sides were freshly painted in gold, red and green with pale blue for decks and white for the captain's cabin below the wheelhouse. The hold was half full of milk cartons from Yemen and an enormous, heaving crowd of coolies was manhandling the boxes across the quayside into the shade. In the centre of this seething throng was a small, elderly Yemeni directing operations from the gun-whale.

I pushed through and looked up at him. He wore a neat white shirt outside his checked futa and a skullcap, but whereas the first captain's face had inspired misgivings, this man inspired trust. His eyes twinkled with good humour, his thick white beard and weathered skin denoted long experience and his voice was firm, barking orders that were instantly obeyed by his crew, if not the coolies.

We shook hands.

'Ahlan wa sahlan,' he shouted. 'Look at us. Ten thousand cases of milk to unload and at this speed we will never leave. God help Djibouti.'

I asked his name. 'Muhammad Ahmed, but no one here will know it. Say al-Gisayr, they will know who I am in Djibouti, Aden, New York, every-where.'

The crowd laughed appreciatively. Naturally, a crowd had gathered, curious to hear what we were talking about.

'Inshallah we will leave for Mokha tomorrow,' he said. 'And you can come with us, if you wish it. Have you a visa for Yemen? But I think it will not be tomorrow – you should come here to check.'

'Do any sambuks go from here to Aden?'

'Very few. You will wait a long time. Now there are none.'

The press of bodies was threatening to tip me down between the boat and the wall so I wriggled out to where Cedric was waiting in the shade. Everything was going perfectly: the dhow trade existed and the chance to travel was there. All I had to do was wait a day or two and I would be Yemen-bound. Mokha as an alternative to Aden did not disappoint me: the ancient port has long been claimed as the point by which both coffee and qat entered Arabia. I would be following those mystics with their bundles of leaves and powders through the Bab al-Mandab, the Gate of Tears, the treacherous narrows that guard the Red Sea, and on into the cool highlands of Arabia.

By the time we made it back to the town, the place was lying stricken beneath the heat and the cool highlands of Arabia seemed very remote indeed. Men lay asleep under the arches, stretched out where they had fallen, as though victims of a sudden cholera epidemic. All offices were closed; the only sign of activity was around the umbrellas on street corners where ladies were selling qat.

This was chewing to survive: the small leaves a moribund yellow and dotted with black, only kept alive by the wet sheets laid on top. Nearby, in corners, ragged men with sun-blackened skin and whitish-green scum on their lips were slumped over a few hard leaves, caressing them gently. Other customers grabbed me, shouting with manic intensity: 'Chat! Chat! C'est la salade!' and thrusting bundles to my mouth.

I found a relatively quiet corner to buy some. Prices were inflexible: the qat-importing business to Djibouti is largely controlled by one company which sets the rates.

After lunch at the hotel the manager approached me smiling: 'Ah, very good! Very good. Please – you can take your qat on the roof with the others. The boy will bring anything you want – tea, coffee, soft drinks or cigarettes.'

Cedric was uninterested in such frivolities and disappeared, saying he was going to look for someone he knew.

On the roof I found a large white washed room, open on two sides to a terrace. The walls were lined with rugs and cushions where four men were already comfortably seated in their vests and futas. Some shirts and trousers hung on the pegs by the door.

I greeted them and took a place where there was a small wooden stool for an armrest. The men were eagerly reading a Somali newspaper and discussing current affairs in a curious mix of Somali, English and Arabic; one of them had a small transistor radio pressed to his ear. There was a pleasant sense of calm and tranquillity after the streets, and I sat there quietly, glad to be left alone with my thoughts and notebook.

The news that Aden was difficult to reach by sea was not totally unexpected. What had been one of the world's greatest ports thirty years before was now inaccessible by boat and showing no sign of arresting the decline I had witnessed in 1994. That had been just after the attempted secession of the south had been put down.

North and South Yemen had united, somewhat improbably, in 1990. The North was, and still is, a tribal democratic alliance; the South had been a pariah state of ultra-orthodox Marxism. Economics had driven the communists to accept unification, but four years later, as the Socialist Party, they attempted to blast their way to independence. It failed miserably. Aden, their one-time capital and stronghold, was besieged and overrun by northern troops and tribesmen. There was an orgy of looting, and when I arrived a fortnight later, the city was dead in the water.

Now, I had expected to arrive at Steamer Point like millions of others had once done, including Burton and Rimbaud. I had even written to a friend there and announced my visit. But it would have to be by the back door – the road from Mokha.

A bead of sweat splashed down onto my notebook, smudging the ink. The relief at sitting out of the sun had made the room pleasant at first, but now I felt my body still gripped by the heat: it seemed to rise in waves from my throat like the shimmering haze from a car bonnet on a hot day. I tried to think about San'a, 'The City of Divine and Earthly Joy' and the paradise of long, quiet qat sessions in its ancient houses at the end of this journey. Should I attempt to arrange a 'perfect' San'a qat session, I wondered, or should I leave it to fate? But the voice of the radio disturbed me. Odd words of English thrown into the stream of Somali: 'The Public Guidance Committee . . . executive body . . . United Nations special envoy . . .' And in my subconscious a powerful deep current began to shift and form. I was listening to the radio and I was thinking about Cedric.

The more I thought about Cedric, the more I began to worry.

There was a car. He had bought it – custom-built – in South Africa to move it to Djibouti by sea for a month's holiday, only to leave it for a long

time (two to four years, depending on who you believed). Now he was back
to reclaim the vehicle and his friend, who had so kindly looked after it, was
sending signals to scare him off – 'my friend the commissioner of police',
'how is your health?', one friend deported and another 'disappeared'. This
was not logical; if Cedric's actions had been eccentric then his friend's were
doubly so. A man leaves his car with you and you get good use from it for
a year or two, then on his return, instead of thanking him, you start an
offensive to keep the car as your own on the grounds that 'I thought you
were dead'.

My initial doubts about Cedric had been allayed somewhat when he had
mentioned electronics imports, but that was before I had found out about
the false passports and documents. Now all those doubts came back. His
denial about drug smuggling did not impress me. As someone once said
of Lillian Hellman, 'Every word she says is a lie – including "and" and
"but".'

I pushed some more qat sprigs into my mouth and took a long long
draught of the cool mountain water: Yemeni Shamlan mineral water, probably off al-Gisayr's neighbour's boat, and so sweet when taken with qat. In
the torpid, deadening heat that water was like a mirage, a promise held out
from across the Red Sea, an escape from the cloying vapid air and the
stench of decay, this hell made habitable by the green lifeline from Harar.
'In another dream I had a chlorophyll habit,' wrote William Burroughs. 'Me
and five other chlorophyll addicts waiting to score . . . We are turning into
plants.'

I picked up my notebook and wrote: 'The man who carries seven passports, a Polish seaman's papers and a vaccination certificate called Arthur
is a useful man indeed. So far I've benefited, or almost benefited, from two
of them – what next?'

We all make little compromises, we all tell lies or take avoiding action,
but I was benefiting from Cedric doing so with more organisation. Born,
by chance, in a western country, you are entitled to a nice gleaming passport that opens up all sorts of possibilities. Born in the developing world,
you get a little book that closes more doors than it opens. What can a poor
boy do? The borders were drawn by powers beyond his control without
any regard for him or his kind, lines on maps to suit the convenience of
nineteenth-century grandees in London, Paris and Rome. But if a man has

to, he crosses, whichever way he can – and in the end all borders have to be crossed sometime by someone. Cedric was a man for whom borders had no use: at best they could be ignored, at worst circumvented. It was a rational response to an irrational world. If he needed to smuggle heroin to survive, he would. The fact, or presumed fact, that he did not was because he might be caught, not because heroin was evil. There was no thin white line marking the end of what was possible: here we have nicotine, here we have alcohol, over there is heroin and cocaine. Cedric was a man who saw no limits and did what was necessary. That was what was worrying me: he was capable of anything and I hadn't the least idea what he was up to – except that I was, for some unknown reason, being sucked into it.

I picked up my notebook and, crossing out the words 'What next?', I wrote, 'Why is Cedric helping me? What does he want?' Then I sat and looked at it for a long time.

The three men had become bored with their newspaper and were quiet. I was sure that a European in the room was a rare occurrence, but no one stared or even looked at me. They were aware of my presence: a drinking glass appeared when I needed it and cigarettes were offered. Eventually, one of them, an old man with white grizzled chin and bony brown cheeks, asked where I was travelling to and I told him my plans.

'Choose your ship carefully,' he advised. 'These Arab boats are always breaking down – then they can drift for a month before anyone finds them – if anyone finds them.'

He asked how I knew about qat and soon was telling me about the Djiboutian operation.

'Qat comes mostly by plane,' he said. 'Around eight tonnes per day. I know because my son works up at the airport. There's a private company called Société Générale pour l'Importation de Chat and they bring it from Dire Dowa. Tax is a thousand Djibouti francs per kilo. That's why you find the qat here is all eatable – no waste. First it costs more to fly it and then it costs more in tax. The old land smuggling routes are finished – except for the train – because the Ethiopians are much stricter now.'

I asked them about the economy and they all sighed. A younger man said he was a trader from Hargeisa and had been in Djibouti for most of the summer. 'There were two months without electricity – the hottest months with temperatures reaching fifty degrees. Can you imagine?

Everything here is broken or old. When the French reduced their bases, there was no money around. The Saudis gave the government a few billion but on condition that all bars were closed. That suited them because the Brothers [he meant Muslim fundamentalists] needed to be kept quiet. But look at it now. The restaurants are empty. Bars are shut. Ships don't want to come here any more. They wasted most of that Saudi money fighting themselves up in the north and managed to destroy the only water bottling plant. There is nothing here – they even import the water!'

He became involved in a side discussion with the man next to him, slipping into Somali. I asked the man with the radio if he agreed. 'Yes, it's all true. We are just waiting for something to happen. There are people waiting – underground movements – and we wait to see what they will do. It will be worse before it is better.'

Despite such grim warnings, the atmosphere was relaxed. Beyond the terrace, the sky turned a pale violet as the sun sank into the dust. When life was so uncertain, to come here and unwind was a necessary luxury. In the serenity that qat brings, talking over problems that were close to you was like gazing down a long telescope at a far-off country. And with this detachment came the sensible realisation that what will be will be. Better not worry, better take your qat and let it all happen.


In the evening Cedric and I walked towards the market. This was the most pleasant time of day, when the day's heat had gone and the breeze had yet to die. The simple shack restaurants had all opened and neat white tablecloths were on the tables with water jugs and flowers and folded cloth napkins. But there were precious few diners to enjoy the experience. A solitary French girl sat at a table staring into space, everyone else remained out in the street strolling. Most were girls: previously Djibouti had been famous for them – the bars were full of them – but since the Saudi money had arrived they had nowhere to wait for their Beau Geste to arrive and were forced to saunter endlessly in the streets. Some wore jeans and tight tee-shirts or other western clothes but most offered more oriental delights. Wrapped in white flowery robes, teetering on platform sandals with enormous fake white carnations tied in their hair, they were the geishas of the Red Sea coast, smirking and whispering in an indecent commingling of

[119]

languages, 'Hey, askari! askari Firengi! L'amour? Come to me – for love, Habibi!'

In the market, under the sign saying 'One sex act can give you AIDS', the qat-sellers were doing brisk business. For the other traders who had to rely on clothes or cheap watches, business was not so good. Youths bearing half-a-dozen shirts on coathangers walked backwards in front of me, shaking their wares like eager young bullfighters hoping for a rush of blood to the head in their quarry. We ate outside the same restaurant where we had taken breakfast but the hawkers did not give up, standing around the table shimmying their shirts to catch the eye or pushing a fistful of watches between mouth and plate. There was a sort of unwritten hierarchy amongst them: first came the shirts as they were usually younger and stronger, then the postcard, cigarette and embrocation men, then the watches, and finally those who had nothing, the beggars. When the man at the next table looked away from his plate for a moment, he turned back to find his dinner gone and a boy dressed in a cobweb of rags sprinting away.

On our way back we were waylaid by an unsavoury-looking man of about thirty. 'Go jig-a-jig,' he insisted. 'Come on, sailor boys – I show you good girls for jig-a-jig.'

Every greedy geisha eye for fifty yards was on us now. Shawls were tightened, false flowers in the hair fluffed up.

'What ship you from, boys, the Indian freighter?'

'That's right,' said Cedric. 'We're Indian.'

'Hey, that captain of yours with the wife on board and a bitch here in town – some guy. I found that bitch for him – what you say – plenty more where she came from.'

This, unfortunately, was all too true. 'Which you want Somali or Ethiopian – Ethiopian make like this . . . ' He gave a hideous mime of the sex act as performed by different races and some of the girls started to cackle at him. 'Or maybe you want French girl – look.' We were passing the restaurant where the solitary French girl was staring into space. 'One hundred dollar a night that one.'

'Will she marry me?' asked Cedric smoothly. 'I'm from Ghana.'

The pimp was a little taken aback. 'She . . . I don't know . . . jig-a-jig she will do for you.'

'I want her to have my babies.'

He began to put a few extra feet between himself and Cedric. 'You . . . you got special demands, maybe talk to her, I don't know.'

Suddenly Cedric was barrelling towards the pimp, fists clenched, silent and terrifying.

The pimp turned and ran. He ran as fast as he possibly could and never stopped. Cedric turned back to me, laughing. 'That guy! I did not want him to know our hotel. Can you imagine? What is this world comin' to. Lord Jesus, my good man, I am askin' you, come and save us!'

# 9

Our first call the following morning was on Daud at his office.

'I am sick this morning,' he told us weakly. 'Really, I feel terrible.'

Cedric was very concerned and the two of them went into a discussion without me, Cedric talking, while Daud shot me worried glances. The keys were handed over and the meeting ended.

'I made many repairs, you know,' Daud said, showing us to the back door when they had finished. 'The tyres were useless from all the sun and then the whole fuel system had to be replaced.'

Cedric murmured his gratitude. 'That is wonderful, my friend. Don't worry – I'm sure the car is fine.'

But when we were outside, he was less polite. 'What rubbish he is talkin'. That fuel system had to be replaced because he did not understand it had two alarms fitted.'

The car was round the corner in the same place as the previous day and, once inside, he sat searching through the glove compartment and other pockets. 'What has he done here?' He dragged out some cheap CDs of zouk music, some not in cases, and threw them on the back seat. 'What is this? Look how he is treating his own possessions – so how has he treated my own? Where are my CDs? What has this rogue done with Demis Roussos?'

The engine started first time and with a roar we shot out into the street and accelerated hard towards a shuffling group of pedestrians.

Cedric was snarling incoherently, not watching the road but still rummaging in the footwell. The pedestrians suddenly realised that the car was not going to stop like all the others and flung themselves aside. I wasn't sure if we had missed them all. Someone shouted. I sank down in my seat and tried to hide behind the cover of one of Daud's discs while holding onto the crunch bar above the glove compartment. It was zouk versions of unforgettable hits like 'Tie a Yellow Ribbon'. Cedric took a right then a left on the wrong side and powered towards the market. Ahead was a slow-moving sleepy wall of people: old men with hennaed-red beards bent double under the weight of a few bananas, crippled beggars dragging themselves along on pads of cardboard – even the young men shambled out into the street without a backward glance, comfortable in the sure knowledge that Djiboutian cars never move at more than a stroll.

'I had ten CDs here. My private collection – not rubbish from any shopping outlet – Demis and Abba and Julio and Tina Charles.'

A face appeared at the side window, twelve inches from my own, the bewildered eyes wide, then it was gone. We clipped him, not hard, just a bruise. I saw his donkey plunge headlong into a shop display of handicrafts and heard voices raised in anger.

Cedric turned and grabbed the zouk discs and started throwing them about in his lap. Out of one case fell a Demis Roussos disc.

'I am an angry man!' he bellowed. The wall of people parted like the Red Sea and we took a left curve down to the mosque at terrifying speed, jinked smartly to avoid an oncoming camel and accelerated out on a straight road. Demis was slapped into the machine and started to wail: 'Ever and ever and ever, I'll be . . . I'll be . . . I'll be . . .' Cedric began to pound his fist on the dashboard.

'That is music and look what he has done! Look what this rubbish has done! He is a murderer, I am tellin' you! He has killed Demis Roussos!'

We took a right, then did a U-turn, smack over the concrete kerb of the central reservation. There was a strangled yelp from the CD player and silence. We were now on the coast road.

'This is very bad for Mister Daud. Where are my things? Where is the bag I left in here?'

We were soon out of the city, and when the last of the fishermen's shacks gave out there was only a gravelly, bush-covered flat between road and sea. After twenty minutes we took a right onto a dirt track that ended at a beach, skidded into a pile of sand and stopped. Out in the motionless water a solitary old man sat up to his neck with his back to us, waiting for fish to come to his net. He did not turn round. Nothing moved.

Cedric got out and went round the car. I could hear him tapping underneath, then he opened the rear doors and began to search every inch of the floor, ripping up carpets to examine the metalwork. It was quite obvious to me that Demis was not skulking in there, but I kept quiet and went for a stroll to the water's edge. The sea was as still as bathwater, unable to even summon ripple in the deadly heat.

Cedric kept the search going for half an hour, then came over to me, a little calmer. I suggested the CDs were so obviously valuable that Daud would have taken them and the bag out for safe-keeping. This cheered him up considerably, enough to offer me a lift to the port.

The return journey through town was not quite so terrifying and on the long hot road across the harbour I was glad of the car. We pulled up at the entrance to the port, parking so as to block the gate. No one stopped him.

'We will collect our pass for the car,' he announced, leading me up two flights of stairs inside the dingy building. We came to a dark office where a fan was hanging from the ceiling by two bits of wire and a man had his feet on a filing cabinet. Everywhere stacks of yellowing paper waved gently in the breeze. Cedric had a blue passport this time and a story of some cargo. I found myself gazing at a torn poster. 'These men are wanted by Interpol.' Twenty or so faces stared back from above little biographical summaries and details of their crimes – mostly fraud and money-laundering. I found myself looking for Cedric among them, but he was not there.

The pass was soon obtained and we drove into the port to the quayside. I saw immediately that al-Gisayr's sambuk would not be moving that day: hordes of coolies were still swarming around while al-Gisayr gazed on with the resigned look Arab sea captains must have worn for centuries in chaotic fly-blown ports the world over.

'Tomorrow,' he said. 'Inshallah.'

Back in town, Cedric decided to visit a friend who worked in a car showroom. We parked on a pavement, much to the annoyance of a policeman who Cedric laughed at; I had the impression the policeman was not familiar with such treatment.

The car showroom was air-conditioned but not too cold and we sat leafing through brochures until Cedric's friend had dealt with a customer. Then we were all shaking hands and laughing and saying how long it had been.

'This is David, my friend and colleague,' said Cedric. 'Also South African.' I smiled and the tall balding black man was smiling and said: 'Welcome to Djibouti, Mister David.' And I realised with horror that I was David the South African, not him.

We sat and had tea. The phone kept ringing, interrupting their talk of old times, until at last the man leaned forward furtively, with a glance at me, and whispered: 'Are you still in business?'

Cedric grinned. 'Oh, yes – let us discuss it another time. I just came by to say hello. I have not seen you for such a long time.'

But the man had something to say. I feigned lack of interest, examining a car brochure cover.

'Have you brought your detector?' he said.

'We can talk about that on another occasion.'

Sitting there, staring at some sixteen-valve engine that was all new and all wonderful, I still had no idea what game we were playing, only that I was a part of it.

That afternoon Cedric wanted me to go with him to Daud's house to ask about the bag. I refused. I had my qat to consider. He pleaded with me.

'I need you to be there. What if he sees me alone? I am one man and he thought I was two. He will think you have deserted me. He will think I am weak.'

This shed some new light on my role. I was good for his image. A white South African made him seem like a big player: he had a team, he had extra muscle, he had a mysterious man who said nothing (out of ignorance, but they didn't know that). No wonder Daud had been casting nervous glances my way. I was the wild card. I was the one who might gently lean forward with a pleasant smile and say, 'Okay, Daud, hand over the Demis Roussos tapes or Cedric breaks your legs in four places.'

I did not want to visit Daud's house. But Cedric simply changed the time: 'No problem. We will go at sunset.'

The prospect hung over me during the qat session and my mind kept coming back to the bag and what might be inside. It was clearly valuable, but why had he left it sitting inside the car for two or more years? Had he left in a hurry?

My fellow qat fiends that afternoon were a dedicated group, taciturn in the extreme, with only the leaf paid any attention. I discovered that I had hurt a tooth on the left side of my mouth, thus forcing me to chew on the right which I did not like. Most Yemenis store the qat in the left cheek: some say because that is where your right hand naturally places it, others that only women chew on the right.

As the sun set, the other men went to pray and Cedric appeared. 'My friend, let us go.'

I couldn't think of an adequate excuse and so, reluctantly, got up and went with him. The suburb of up-market villas was even more visibly well-heeled by night: I caught glimpses of large Mercedes and brand-new Landcruisers in driveways, while in one upstairs window a dinner party of French expatriates was proceeding gaily with champagne glasses being passed round by a black servant.

Daud was sitting in his front verandah watching a Djiboutian television extravaganza called 'How Moulds Grow'. He was wearing a sloppy tee-shirt and jogging trousers covered in Disney characters. We accepted his offer of tea and he disappeared for a long time, missing the end of 'How Moulds Grow' and the start of a public service broadcast on the dangers of washing machines. When he returned, he flicked it over to CNN News and made an excuse for not seeing Cedric that afternoon. Apparently Cedric had been to the house but not found him.

'I was asleep,' he explained.

'But the maid went to shout you,' said Cedric equably.

'She is useless that one.'

There was the usual preamble but Cedric cut it shorter. 'The car is good, Daud,' he said. 'I am so pleased to find this car workin', I cannot tell you.'

Daud began to explain to me how much trouble it had all cost him – how he had had to sell his own car to pay for the repairs and now he was having to walk to work. Cedric let him ramble a bit, then stopped him.

'But there were some items, some precious items in that car. Where are my CDs, Daud? My Demis Roussos and Abba CDs?'

There was a warning there for the wary, a slight drop in tone, a slight lowering of the chin, and a clenched fist bigger than a steam iron. Distressingly, Daud chose to ignore these signs.

'Oh, those old discs. My God, they were twenty years out of date.'

I felt like running over and slapping him: You crazy fool. Stop now! Repent! There's still time.

'No one is listening to that music these days,' continued Mister Sophistication, attempting to share a little chuckle with me at the expense of our neanderthal friend. 'You should try zouk – it's the in-thing.'

There was a lisping, infantile quality to the way Cedric repeated that word, 'zouk'. Then he dropped the china tea cup to shatter on the tiled floor. Daud let out a little whinny of apprehension.

'I am so sorry,' said Cedric, 'I really do not know how that happened.' Very slowly he pushed the bits aside with his naked foot. 'There was a bag too, Daud. Do you remember the bag?' He spun the saucer on the edge of the table and we watched it as though in a trance as it slowed, and slowed, and wobbled and . . . Daud remembered the bag. Cedric caught the saucer in his paw. It seemed that maybe Daud had not seen the bag recently. Perhaps it was in the store cupboard. He went to look but came back empty-handed. Possibly the mechanic who had done the fuel system had taken it out.

'We can go and talk to him.'

They agreed to go the next morning at nine.

With a somewhat diminished level of friendliness the two men said goodnight.

Cedric drove initially out of town then turned and headed back. 'I need to find that Comoro boy,' he said. 'Or Lulu. They know something: why else does this rogue want to tell me they have gone?'

By night these long outskirts were almost pitch dark. Occasionally there would be a candle or a lamp in a shack doorway, lighting a group of idle bystanders waiting for something. We turned up some side streets but each time the headlights revealed our way blocked with rubble and thorn. Cedric kept saying, 'I need to think. I need to think.'

And I knew he wanted to talk, but I would need the right question to start him off. In the end he pulled up by the roadside next to a wall. A few old trucks went by, their headlamps in the dust as if a thick fog was rolling in from the sea. And I found the key: a perfectly simple and obvious question.

'How did you start in this business?'

As if I had it all worked out and there was no use hiding any more.

'In Zaire,' he said. 'We had a truck built for us, a very special truck, then we drove in from Zambia. It was a dangerous thing we were doing – bringing ivory out to send for Japan. That truck could carry five hundred kilos but you would never find it without a cutting torch.'

'Do you still do ivory?'

'No. That was how I started.'

I took a deep breath. 'So what was in the bag – the bag in the car?'

'Some papers.'

I waited. I think he was deciding then how much he would have to tell me, balancing up with how much he might need me.

'Some papers for cars in Zambia,' he went on. 'And something else – some stones.'

'Stones?'

'Amethyst or tourmaline, I do not remember – nothing much – maybe two thousand dollars' worth.'

For a man who carried three hundred thousand dollars on occasion that did not sound a lot and I was immediately doubtful of this explanation.

'Maybe Daud took them?'

'They were nothing: he knows that. The papers are more important. Those cars are BMs and they are stuck in Zambian customs. Without the papers, I cannot get the cars.'

We sat staring into the darkness. At the far end of the road there was the entrance to a French military base and I hoped they had not seen us.

'What does your detector do?'

He laughed. 'You are listenin' to everything, aren't you?'

But he would say no more, and it seemed my question had been too direct for he started the car and we headed back into town. He parked up outside the hotel and told the guard to watch the vehicle carefully. He went through into the room while I had a shower. Halfway through the power went off.

I found Cedric sitting staring at a candle in the room. The heat was already terrific.

'It is what I do,' he said.

'What is?'

'Stones. No electronics. Just stones. The detector works on a light which tells you if the stone is zircon or diamond.'

'You buy them here?'

'What can you buy here? In Djibouti there is only flies.'

He sat thinking for a while before speaking again.

'Do you know that fellow Jonas Savimbi?'

'I've heard of him.'

'He is chief of this rebel UNITA group in Angola. That is one place I get the stones. Sometimes we come through the Zaire side or there is a German pilot, Tomas, he has a light airplane. We go through Namibia and to South Africa.'

Now he had started to tell me, the words came tumbling out and it had the ring of truth about it. How stones came illicitly from the South African mines or were bought in Taiwan, then taken on to Antwerp, Tel Aviv or Baroda for resale at a minimum of eight times profit. (Baroda, coincidentally, had been Richard Burton's first posting in India when he joined the Bombay Army.) The Djibouti connection was for finding large piles of cash without raising suspicions – that was Daud's job.

'So how do you smuggle them?'

He began to laugh. I suppose it did seem a mug's question. 'Smuggling is survival. One time, in my early days, I had stones in my hand luggage and I gave it to a customs official at Heathrow Airport to look after while I got my duty free shopping! I am telling you, smuggling is survival. But nowadays I am always clean. I never carry the goods myself.'

'But you carry the money.'

'Sometimes you do it. But I never take money to the man. These are bad people we are dealing with. They will just pull out a gun and take everything. That is why I have to think. I need to think. Sometimes you have to be careful, even though I am a strong man and frightened of nobody.'

It was a jolt. I suddenly realised he was at work right now, and I was with him, whether I liked it or not. The hotel staff, all his contacts – they all saw me as his business partner.

'I walk with God,' he said. 'I never hurt no man but sometimes I frighten them a bit. It is bad people we are dealing with. You cannot mess up.' He grabbed a towel and rubbed his face. 'It is a good business for money. You could do it. I need someone here and you could help. We will walk together. What are you thinkin' of this idea?'

I tried to be non-commital. He was not a man I wanted to turn down too sharply. 'Well . . . I haven't much experience in that sort of thing.'

'You don't need anything. What you need is a mind in your skull. You have that. The situation now is that I need someone to watch me. We must go somewhere.' He was in deadly earnest, leaning forward with his elbows on his knees, face already covered in sweat once more. 'There is a job, a cuttin' job. We need to buy some tools and go out to the beach. You will keep watch for me. There is somethin' in the car.'

It was as though the electricity had come on and lit the place with clear bright light. At last I understood, and I wanted to jump up with a Eureka! and tell him so. The car from South Africa, home of diamonds, brought for a 'holiday', the car that was custom built and needed cutting now, and all the other cars around Africa – it was perfectly obvious – they were all dedicated to moving jewels out coastwards, to places like Djibouti. But two years ago something had gone wrong and he had been forced to leave the car carrying the diamonds and now he didn't know if Daud had found them or not. I had the feeling you get when a difficult anagram falls into place.

But, just as he had taught me, I played stupid. 'There's something hidden inside the car? Demis Roussos CDs?'

He did not laugh and I could see from his face he had decided I knew enough. Instead he began to talk about Daud again, and about the difficulties of doing a job like this alone when Daud could probably arrange for him to be locked up at any moment if he chose to.

A soft knock at the door startled us and the voice of the guard.

'Go away,' shouted Cedric. 'We are talkin' here. Why are you disturbin' honest citizens at this hour of the night?'

The man shuffled away.

'We must go now,' insisted Cedric. 'We will borrow tools from here or a garage. It is a simple matter. Believe me.'

'Let's do it tomorrow,' I said. 'It's too dark now.' Tomorrow I would need a better excuse than that.

He shook his head. 'Now – we must go now. Okay, there is something more in the car – you will see.'

[130]

But I didn't want to see because then I would know for sure, I would have crossed the line to becoming an accomplice rather than a dim-witted dupe. The guard had returned and was knocking again. Cedric went outside and I heard them go off down the corridor. I grabbed my notebook and started scribbling down what he had said about taking diamonds from Angola to Baroda and the eight times . . . there was an ear-splitting crash of a fist hitting the door which burst open, the pen shot up off the top of the page, a polygraph hitting paydirt, and Cedric was towering over me his eyes seeing the notebook and his mouth shouting: 'I am going to kill! I am going to kill!'

Then he stopped. In the silence I heard the guard scuttling away down the hall. A woman called out from over the back wall. Cedric's breath came in thick short gusts. My mouth was absolutely bone dry. I slid the notebook away from me under a tee-shirt that was lying on the bed. Cedric was staring directly through me.

'What are you writin' in that book?'

I ignored the question. 'What . . . what's happened?'

He shook his head. 'I am going to kill this bullshit bastard. Mister Daud – dead man Daud. You bastard bullshittin' rogue. What has he done? *What has he done?*' He began to pace the room, a monstrous black shadow skewing around from door to window behind him as he passed the candle. 'He has stolen the car. The guard saw a man with glasses, a smart man in a suit, open the car with a key and drive away. He ran here but we did not listen. It is he. I know it is he. He has stolen my car. Now I will kill him.'

The air was thicker than glue and sweat poured down him.

'You won't find him now, Cedric, he won't go home and where else can you look? Wait. His office in the morning – he's bound to go there eventually.'

But Cedric was no longer hearing me. He paced the room until after one o'clock when I lay down exhausted and fell asleep with the sound of his padding feet in my head and my notebook tucked inside my shorts.


I woke soon after dawn. The electricity had come back on and the room was cool and full of soft pink light from the red walls of the courtyard

[131]

outside. The bed on the other side of the room was empty. Cedric was gone.

In the courtyard I drank some tea and wondered what to do. There was a sort of fascination in the story unfolding: I wanted to know what was going to happen next, even though it might be unwise to do so. At nine I set out to walk to Daud's villa.

Even from a hundred yards away I knew what I was going to find. The gates were locked with a chain and through a gap in the fence I saw that the house was all shut up. You would have thought no one had lived there for months.

I walked briskly back into town and went to his office. They seemed surprised to see me since Daud was not there, he had not been there all morning and neither had my friend the black man from South Africa. I got out as fast as I could without running. It was imperative now that I left the hotel – I could think of nothing else.

Coming back along the open shadeless street I could hear the pitiless voice of the prosecution counsel: 'And then the accused, my Lord, having played accomplice to the theft of a motor car laden with stolen diamonds and finally to murder, attempted to establish an alibi with a visit to the deceased's office. An act, I might say, of such stunning naïveté that a child could see through it.' Except it would all be in French and I would understand almost nothing. The alternative ending was that Cedric would not kill Daud but frighten him enough for Daud to run to his friends in the police and arrange for Cedric's arrest – that would certainly mean I would be picked up too. Right from the start the warning had been there in what Daud had said but in my ignorance I had missed it.

At the hotel I hastily packed my bag. Cedric's holdall stood on the floor at the end of his bed and when I was finished I sat and stared at it, wondering what might be inside. All that was required was to unzip the top; it would take seconds only. There might be stacks of cash, papers revealing new angles, a weapon – it was indeed a tempting chance to add to the stock of information. What stopped me was not so much the thought that Cedric could suddenly arrive, although that did cross my mind, but the taint of betrayal. For all his faults, Cedric would never have searched my bag, I am sure of that. And he would not have walked out on a friend as I was doing, from simple fear of crossing the line between legal and illegal. If he did ever come back to find me gone, he would see this as betrayal.

Then I saw the paper. It was lying on his bed, neatly folded into quarters. Without thinking, I reached across and took it. It was a receipt from Zambian customs for two BMW cars which they had in storage on behalf of a certain Mister Dudley. Cedric had told the truth.

I sprang up and grabbed my bag. It was time to leave. The reception was crowded with people arriving and leaving.

'The Kenyan will pay his own half,' I explained, adding unnecessarily, 'he's just someone I met on the train from Dire Dowa. We just shared a room to save money.'

But before I could get out someone called me.

'Kevin!'

I looked across the room at a face, somehow familiar, but beyond recollection.

'You forgotten me? Ramzi? From the night club in Aden?'

There was a flash of memory to a wild night three years before with Syrian belly dancers and catamite waiters and dancing on a stage with some Hungarians; and in the band that night, a band of astonishing professionalism considering the behaviour of their audience, was Ramzi. It had been the golden decadent heyday of Aden between unification of North and South Yemen in 1990 and the civil conflict of 1994 when, like Weimar Berlin, Aden saw Judgement Day coming and held a party.

We shook hands and then I recognised other members of the band, all here for a concert. My eye kept drifting to the gate, dreading the arrival of a uniform. The bizarre coincidence of the meeting was too much for me at that moment.

'I'm in a bit of a hurry,' I said. 'I'm leaving now for Yemen.'

'If you come to Aden, come and see us. We play the restaurant next to Pizza Hut in Crater every night.'

I did not even stop to consider the staggering news that Pizza Hut had opened in Aden, I simply promised to make it and rushed out to grab a taxi. Drifting along through the town at ten miles per hour, I kept a sharp watch for familiar faces but saw nothing.

Approaching the port gate, I began to wonder how I was going to get inside without my master con-man friend to help. The best course of action, I decided, was to stay in the taxi and bluff at the barrier.

We pulled up and a rat-faced soldier thrust his head in the open window and scowled.

'Lex Pass!'

I pointed Napoleonically forward. 'Mon bateau!'

The taxi driver let the clutch in and we started under the pole. This drew a screech from the soldier who pushed himself half inside the window, head in front of my face, hands grabbing at my jacket. He had foul black teeth and his eyeballs were a mottled greasy yellow. His cry attracted other uniforms until a whole vulturous flock of them were flapping after us. We managed about forty yards with the soldiers' legs waving in the air before the driver turned belly up and stopped.

Now the doors were flung open, bags thrown out, and all the time they were screeching, 'LexpassLexpassLexpass!' and I was pointing forward, with diminishing confidence, 'Mon bateau!'

But what had, at first, seemed to be a disastrous situation began to resolve itself because the vultures were fighting over me. Eventually, two particularly horrible specimens succeeded in beating the rest off. Bags were reclaimed, doors slammed and they turned leering to me, 'Monsieur, mille francs.'

'Non.'

We haggled and finally agreed I would pay five hundred Djiboutian francs, if I reached the boat and it was leaving. The driver was told to head for the quayside.

A quite different scene to the previous day presented itself when we turned onto the wharf. Two new dhows were tied up; the French warship was gone and al-Gisayr's boat was high in the water and no longer covered in piles of boxes and swarms of coolies. The nakhoda and his men were lounging in the shade on the quarter deck that tapered elegantly upward and around the captain's cabin. When they spotted me, they waved me aboard.

A short ladder had been set against the gunwhale to cope with the extra height of the empty boat above the quay. When I got up on the side I realised just how large a dhow this was. In the centre was the engine house and the hold around it had been covered with removable wooden deck sections. Further forward, as the boat narrowed and curved upward, was a winch house almost buried under coils of rope, then finally a long prow, reaching twenty feet out above the water.

I clambered towards the stern, stepping around the ship's ribs on a beam lashed to the inside of the hull. One of the sailors jumped down, bare feet thumping on the deck, to help heave my bags over the carved wooden rail on the leading edge of the half deck. Here was the galley, a large box containing pots and pans and a charcoal stove next to an oil barrel filled with water.

From the rail sternwards, the view was a lesson in the Arab shipmaker's art. There was not a straight line to be seen: all was flowing curves, hand-built from a drawing held only in the craftsman's mind. And in each curve there was knowledge of how water moves, how the power of waves can be broken with a few pieces of timber. The half deck was held in the horseshoe of the quarter deck above and in the spaces created below each sailor had his locker. On the starboard extremity of this horseshoe was a ladder up to the poop and wheelhouse; on the port was the thunder box, a four foot tall blue-painted box cantilevered over the waves with a door and a hole in its bottom.

The two quarter decks extended back and up, divided by the nakhoda's cabin, then meeting behind it in the triangular space created by the massive sternpost and the chains that controlled the rudder. With the cabin between these two sides of the deck, and the roof formed by the poop, there was always shade to be found and the crew were on the landward side. I shook hands with them all, very pleased to see their bright honest faces.

'Hayyak Allah.'

'Allah yuhayyikum. Kayf haalkum?'

'Bi-khayr al hamdu li-llah. Praise be to God, we are ready to leave today.'

I handed my passport over to al-Gisayr and he wrote my name on the passenger list. There were three others.

'Who are these men?' he asked pointing to the taxi which had not left. The two soldiers were making ugly faces at us.

'They want some corruption money,' I said. 'They say if I don't pay they will take me off the sambuk.'

His eyes sparkled. 'On the sambuk, I am king and no one will take you.'

I felt like hugging him. 'But,' he added, 'it is better you speak to them and they go.'

I climbed down onto dry land and went over to the car.

'Give us one thousand,' said the rat-faced one in a green uniform.

'I said five hundred.'

'Five for me, five for him, one thousand.'

With a great flourish, I took out a five hundred franc note and threw it into the car. I think I had some notion of shaming them; I may as well put up an advertisement for free money because before I even got back to the boat, a greasy character in torn khaki pounced on me. 'The man at the gate wants his five hundred.'

'What man?'

'The gate man – you must give me.'

I said something extremely rude in Arabic but he got hold of my sleeve with a claw. 'I will take you to the town. Where is your Lex Pass?'

I shoved him aside and got up the ladder.

'I gave it to the other man. Ask him.'

This confused him and he trailed away in search of easier prey. But I was not so easily rid of the next one. He came beetling up the quay fifteen minutes later, looking for me, his paratroop boots laceless and desert camouflage uniform torn and stained. When he got up onto the deck I saw he had only one eye and one tooth.

'You!' he croaked in Arabic, perching on the rail like a hideous crow. 'What tribe are you?'

'Hashed,' I said, to amuse the crew, this being a Yemeni tribal group.

The laughter irritated him. 'Nationality. What nationality? Give me your passport.'

After some discussion, al-Gisayr handed it over and he began to leaf through with a triumphant gleam in his eye. 'Oh, you go to India? And Thailand, Indonesia, Malaysia? You are a journalist, aren't you?'

'A teacher.' I was trying to think how Cedric would have handled this. Up the quayside, the coolies were fighting to unload a Yemeni dhow carrying water bottles and I half expected to see the great con-man himself come motoring through them: 'Kevin! Why are you desertin' me? Who is this character? Go to the Devil, you rogue.' Or was it, 'Here take five hundred for your trouble.' If there was an art to bribery, then it was knowing who to bribe and who to thumb your nose at. The loathsome crow squatting on the rail did not appear to be a man with much power but he did have my passport and with a sinking heart, I watched as he flicked through and hit the jackpot: an Eritrean visa from two years before. He began to grin. 'You went to Eritrea! You are a dangerous man, yes, a very dangerous man.'

Unfortunately, Eritrea had recently fought over disputed territory, first with Djibouti and then Yemen. Tension was still high on the borders. Loathsome Crow was almost drooling with delight. He tucked my passport in a pocket and stood up. 'This is serious. You will come to visit the police in the town, my friend.'

Given the situation I had left behind me in the town, I would rather have used Loathsome Crow's toothbrush. And he saw my face fall which only redoubled his glee. I had no choice but to follow my passport off the boat and down the quay. But as we approached the swarm of coolies, a smartly-dressed police officer came striding up to us.

'Où allez-vous avec cette askari?'

I took the bit between my teeth.

'Il demande l'argent. Mon passeport, c'est dans la poche . . . huna.' I could not keep the French up for long and ended up in Arabic. 'Je . . . shaseer ila Yemen ma'a assambuk hadha.'

'You have visas for Djibouti and Yemen?' This was in English.

I nodded.

The officer demanded the passport from Loathsome Crow who emitted a sort of spiteful hissing noise as he handed it over.

'If you have the visas, it is okay. Take your passport and wait on the quayside, not the boat.'

I skipped back to the sambuk and explained the situation.

'By God, these men are thieves,' said al-Gisayr. 'Give me your passport and wait over there by the shop. And don't let these soldiers see you. Next time there will be no honest policeman and they will get money from you, or stop you leaving. We will call you when it is time.'

Once again, I handed him my passport, then went over to the shop, actually a kiosk between two warehouses. As the coolies finished work they would come padding over and flop down exhausted, then for a few francs shovel some spaghetti down and drink a cup of water before heading back.

The simple diet and hard physical labour had given them smooth skin and supple bodies, without an ounce of spare flesh. But the faces told another story: here were the lines and cracks and scars, broken teeth, jaundiced eyes and anxious frowns – the real marks of their hard lives. They argued and wrangled constantly, sometimes breaking out into childish slaps backed up with vicious insults. A radio in the kiosk played a Somali version of 'Hit the road, Jack'.

Swaggering through these men came a small boy of about eight or nine, elbows out, chin up, dressed in nothing but a futa long since stained brown with the shark oil that is rubbed into the sides of a sambuk. He was Yemeni, though physically similar to the men, and too short to see over the counter. He held his money up and bellowed, 'One Coke for Muhammad Hassan.'

Someone said something and he whipped around.

'What's with you? Son of seventy-seven whores!'

Then off he strode with his bottle of Coke, Kipling's Kim come to life on the shores of Africa.

The problem with waiting next to this kiosk was one of visibility. Every few minutes Loathsome Crow came shambling along, obviously searching for someone, and I had a nasty suspicion it was me. I saw him stop and ask at the sambuk but they gave him that expressive turn of the hands, palms up and fingers open, which is a Yemeni shrug. I pulled my Arab headscarf round my face and kept low.

For an hour I was living on my wits, hiding from every uniformed man who hove into sight, fearing both Loathsome Crow and men seeking Cedric's business partner. But then I heard someone calling to me from above.

'Ya akhi! O my brother! Up here.'

Between the kiosk and the warehouse was a sloping corrugated iron roof covering a narrow alleyway. Boxes full of mineral water bottles had been stacked on one side and two Somali youths had rearranged them to form a nice little hideaway where they were starting on a vast pile of qat. I climbed up and joined them.

'You are going to Yemen with al-Gisayr? So are we.'

'Where did you buy qat?'

'You don't have?' They shouted down to someone and I handed over

[138]

some money. 'Don't worry, he can leave the port without problem. He will bring it.'

They were sailors, they said, though they looked more like city slickers to me. Both were dressed in bright polo shirts, pleated trousers and loafers, each carrying a liberal amount of gold in their various chains, bracelets, rings and watches. Never beyond arm's reach were two leather attaché cases. Like me, they were heading for Aden via Mokha, having failed to find a dhow going direct.

The man returned with my qat but I did not start. I was too nervous, my insides all twisted with tension. Instead, when the youths had lost interest in me, I lay and watched the tug *Arthur Rimbaud* manoeuvring a rusty Indian freighter into position, the bows of the freighter fitting neatly over the stern of al-Gisayr's sambuk. I regretted missing what would have made a good photograph but I dared not cross the quay to get my camera.

This was a fortunate decision because a jeep came motoring up the quayside. There were three men inside. They passed the sambuk and I saw them looking around. I got well down and made a viewing slit between two boxes. After a couple of minutes the car returned and this time stopped next to al-Gisayr's sambuk. One man got out and held a shouted conversation with the nakhoda and his bosun. I saw their hands give that expressive gesture again and a finger point somewhere down the quay. The man jumped back in the car and it sped away. Al-Gisayr glanced across at me and made a downward gesture with his hand.

It was two o'clock before anything happened. I saw al-Gisayr hand the pile of passports to his bosun who then went off down the quay. Half an hour later he came back, waving across at myself and the Somali youths. We jumped down and hurried across. There were five more passengers: two Djiboutian ladies, each with a small child, and an old Yemeni greybeard.

The well-dressed policeman arrived in a four-wheel-drive car and checked our passports as we climbed on board, al-Gisayr giving a chivalrous hand to the ladies. I kept glancing nervously along the quay but one of the sailors whispered to me: 'Do not worry. They returned to the town to look for you there.'

The engine thumped into life. The crew were chivvied by the captain. Ropes were thrown. Ladders lifted. We drifted sideways away from the quay, then with a clank of the rudder began to turn and make headway. I sat on the quarter deck, bare feet on the warm planks, my gaze on the receding coast of Africa. A solitary pelican lumbered up into the air and all the hundreds of small black flies that were plagueing everybody, suddenly and quite miraculously, abandoned ship for the shore. And the cares and worries of the previous days, the doubts about Cedric and the fear of arrest, all that flew with them. I curled my toes against the warm timber and smiled.

# The Red Sea

# 10

From half a mile out, the seedy decaying reality of Djibouti was replaced by a vista of fresh white buildings rising from sprays of green. Sea approaches always promise the best. I sat on the quarter deck and the cook served the passengers lunch, an aluminium tray piled with rice and huge knuckles of meat, washed down by a glass of sweet black tea. I heard al-Gisayr ask one of his men to check on the 'harem': the two Djiboutian women and their children who had been shown to their own deck space on one side of the engine house below the half deck rail.

I leaned my elbow on the stout gunwhale, shaded by the poop deck above, and looked north to the pale mountains of Tadjoura across the gulf. The sea was no longer the lifeless corpse of the beaches but hissed and sucked at the stern, flashing with bubbles that coiled and spun, easing the ship to roll, so the rudder chain clicked with the strain. Nothing, not even al-Gisayr's quick commands, could keep the smile from the sailors' faces as they moved to lash down luggage and rig up a sunshade over the lower deck. They were pleased to be out on the sea, away from the numbing boredom of the land with its filth and petty bureaucracy and endless waiting. Here there was a warm wind cuffing the waves to life and horizons of blue water widening east for two thousand miles till you reached Bombay. The youngest of them sang to himself.

As the sun wheeled, I moved to the other side and sat with an old man, Yahya, at the head of the quarter deck from where the timbers curved out and down steeply, giving the impression of riding on the end of a gigantic bow, arching to arrow the mast into the depths of winding green.

Yahya was ninety years old and after visiting his wife in Djibouti was returning to his wife in Mokha, a monthly exchange that had continued since 1925, with a few breaks for war; it had once suited his merchant trade but now was purely personal. His robust good health he attributed to a diet of fish and rice, no alcohol or cigarettes, and regular supplies of qat. We shared mine, half-reclined on rolled blankets, flicking the denuded sticks into the waves. In a lifetime of sailing these waters Yahya had been ship-wrecked twice, lost at sea once and seen his brother swallowed by a whale.

This area, he told me, was full of the creatures and he and his brother had once come out fishing in a huri, an open canoe. Far out in the Gulf of Aden they had come into a school of whales, all blowing until the sea appeared full of fountains. Then one had come towards them, its huge mouth gaping. Yahya jumped but his brother and canoe disappeared inside the jaws. Moments later it spat him out, battered and bruised but alive. His brother, thinking quickly, had thrust his dagger into the roof of the leviathan's mouth.

They had clung to the wreckage of the canoe until a passing sambuk stopped to pick them up.

'Did you think you would die?'

He pointed heavenwards. 'Who knows when he will die? It is the will of God, not of man.'

In Arab seafaring tales, the sea becomes a monster of capricious cruelty where winds blow men to their doom, magnetic mountains rear up and tear the nails from ships, and islands turn out to be whales. But the man who can hold his nerve must cross the dreadful oceans if fabulous treasures are to be discovered. That was the very real goal of the Arab sailors who made it as far as India, Java and China, returning laden with silks, spices and tall tales. In Yemeni stories of the two-horned conqueror, Dhu al-Qarnain, he journeys across the sea of darkness to find men with no heads and eyes on their shoulders, people with giant ears who wrap their heads up inside them to sleep, and tribes of single-breasted Amazons. Many such legends are undoubtedly concerned with ancient journeys across the Red Sea and on into the Saharan wilderness and the heroes of such epics are often Himyari kings, a people who succeeded the Sabaeans in governing Yemen. After the sea of darkness they meet the great sand river which can be crossed only on Saturdays but all who do so die.

Nevertheless, in story after story they try again and again, all dying until a thoughtful king put up a border sign: 'There is no way beyond the limit I have attained. All who cross, perish.'

Herodotus wrote such things down and earned himself the title Father of Lies. He wrote about the same single-breasted Amazons that appear in Yemeni tales: women who cut off one breast in order to draw their bows in battle more easily. Archaeological evidence of the Pazyryk culture in the Siberian Altai mountains has recently begun to suggest a culture of mounted warriors with female archers that precisely fits elements of Herodotus's description. Valued for their horses, the Pazyryk nomads had trade connections with India and Persia – places Yemen was in contact with 2,500 years ago. One thinks of James Bruce, vilified and disgraced for suggesting the existence of eaters of raw meat. And that is why, when Yahya told me his brother was swallowed by a whale, I kept an open mind.

An Indian dhow came in the opposite direction, a ship far bigger than ours and capable, Yahya told me, of carrying 350 tonnes cargo – about twice the capacity of al-Gisayr's boat. To the south were some low coral outcrops, one with a large thatched hut on its peak, about twenty feet above sea level.

Strange sensations are provoked when visiting places long since left behind and forgotten. Looking across to the madreporic island and the thatch-roofed hut in the centre, I had the thrill of recognising a place that had survived the vagaries and changes wrought by my memory and by time.

A decade before, newly arrived in San'a and suffering from red wine withdrawal symptoms, my wife Judith and I flew into Djibouti for a three-day binge. On the first night we met up with Robert, an old teacher friend from my days in southern Sudan. 'Let's go for a drink,' he said. 'What about here? No idea what it's like – never visit the bars much.'

And as we walked inside, the geisha girls at the bar turned and flung their arms wide. 'Roberte! Mon cher!'

'They say it to everyone,' he snapped as the girls rushed over to fondle him. 'Roberte – it's like saying Joe to a GI.'

Before the evening disappeared in an alcoholic haze, I noted down something he said about an island out in the Gulf of Tadjoura where the coral was particularly beautiful. Two days later we persuaded an unwilling fisherman to take us there. We had no name for the island – I looked up the word for coral and the man nodded and pointed vaguely out east.

His little boat was painfully slow: we took four hours to achieve what al-Gisayr's sambuk had done in an hour, but eventually a low white line appeared with a hut on it and he pointed and we nodded: 'Yes, that's it!' – out of desperation rather than from any knowledge.

Approaching the island we could see figures moving around in swimming trunks which confirmed that this was the place. Then we were bumping over big knolls of coral and the water was pale shimmering green over the white sand and a pale shimmering shape came zipping under the boat and hauled itself up onto the tailboard – a muscled Steve McQueen who did not smile or speak but merely pointed at the beach, ignoring our greetings.

I studied his tattooes: strange cabbalistic swirls, dots and numbers surrounding four main pictures. On the left forearm was a baby and on the upper arm a naked woman; the story continued in less cheerful vein on the right upper arm where there was a decaying corpse and finally, on the forearm, a grinning skeleton. Judith and I exchanged a glance.

I smiled at the man and made a pleasant comment in halting French about the coral. He stared at me through icy blue eyes, then frowned threateningly. It made the tattoo on his forehead move. When we scraped onto the beach, our fisherman took four large strides down the boat, flung himself onto the sand and sprinted for cover. Steve McQueen man-handled the boat up the sand a short distance and we stepped out. He gesticulated towards the hut.

As we climbed through the coarse grass and broken dead coral, I saw that something was written in French over the entrance to the hut and with sinking heart I realised that the man was indeed Steve McQueen, playing Papillon, and this was Devil's Island. The sign read: 'Légion Étrangère'. We had stumbled, it appeared, onto an island reserved for the recreational pursuits of the French Foreign Legion.

We stopped in the doorway. Before us, seated at several wooden trestle tables and dressed in identical black swimming trunks, were about fifty sun-tanned men who simultaneously swivelled round and stared at Judith. In the left-hand corner of the hut were their shorts and shirts piled up; in the right, a stack of automatic weapons and hand grenades.

'Bonjour,' I said in what I thought was a pretty passable accent.

One of the men leered. 'So what the fuck are you doin' 'ere?'

Before a witty riposte could be sent sparkling back, another even harder-faced character said in a Brummie accent, 'Don't mind him – he's from Bethnal Green.' Then they both turned back to an older man, a mean shaven-headed thug, and asked something in French. They seemed to be asking permission to speak. He nodded curtly and spoke in French. The Brummie grinned. 'Chef wants to know if you'll join us for lunch?'

Chef was not a title given for cooking: he was the one other Frenchman, apart from Steve McQueen and the man in charge.

'I really think you should accept,' said the Brummie. 'Chef gets annoyed when people don't obey his invitations – he buries them up to the neck in sand.'

We accepted.

Space was made at the tables. There were two Englishmen, an American, one Japanese, several Germans and Spanish, the remainder looked Mediterranean. No one spoke but for the Englishmen and the American. 'We're between wars,' he said drily.

Lunch was fish in tomatoes and potatoes served in mess cans. 'Watch out for shrapnel,' warned the American. 'We caught it with a hand grenade.'

The two Englishmen painted a grim picture of life. Neither had learnt much French at school but to speak English was forbidden – unless Chef nodded his agreement. English books were thrown away if found. Punishment beatings were regular and they were not allowed out without the uniform. They had fought in Chad, which they hated, and visited Belize which they liked – except for the Mennonite Christians. 'They deny the modern world, don't they? Stupid bastards.'

Chef was disappointed to learn I had never been in the army and suggested a career change from teaching. I made a joke about 'press gangs' but nobody laughed.

Dessert was large hacks of water melon, pips spat on the table. We told them that we were living in Yemen.

'Are there white women there?'

'There's a lady at the Embassy who's very helpful,' said Judith.

'What about guns?'

'You can buy them everywhere outside the capital.'

The general agreement was that Yemen sounded a pretty decent place.

'Where are you from in England?' asked the Brummie.

Judith answered, 'A place called Beverley near Hull.'

There was a cry of amazement from down the table. I had noticed him earlier, a freckle-faced youth who looked a good deal less murderous than the rest, but until then he had not even looked at us let alone spoken; now he was smiling broadly.

'I'm from Beverley!'

Chef did not make any sign or movement, but in a voice loaded with menace, he murmured, 'Did I give you permission to speak?'

There was a silence. The youth's moment of hope, his look of amazed delight, was instantly crushed. He returned to staring gloomily into his empty bowl and never spoke again.

We drank some thin sugarless coffee then made our excuses.

'Yes, go now,' said the American. 'Before Chef signs you up for five years.'

At the beach, we shouted for the boatman but he had disappeared. Eventually Steve McQueen hunted him down for us, handing the man back, a little reluctantly, in one piece.

I doubt the poor fisherman was accustomed to launching his boat with such single-minded swiftness, but the journey back was not so speedy and we arrived after nightfall, our swimming things still dry.

Seeing the island once again from the height of al-Gisayr's quarter deck made it all seem different. I recognised the hut but could see no sign above the door and some thorn bushes had grown up around it, as though it was abandoned. There were other islands, similar low coral outcrops, and of these I had no recollection, except a single image of a dead turtle beached on its back and Judith saying, 'If it was alive we could have turned it over to save it.'

Now I could see these outcrops were home to itinerant fishermen who lived surrounded by bits of driftwood and piles of broken coral removed from nets. The Red Sea abounds in such desolate atolls where men have traditionally made camp in seasonal hunts for various sea creatures. In the years before and after the First World War a colourful Frenchman, Henri de Monfreid, scraped a living in these waters sometimes going on such hunts when, as he put it, 'there was an unexpected spurt of activity in the sea snail trade.'

He describes the disgusting stench of the rotting creatures and the hardships of the collectors who could easily see all their work wasted if the market prices dropped at the wrong moment. Then they might try their luck with the holothuries – sea cucumbers – a creature six to eight inches long, as thick as a child's wrist and with a habit of stiffening when in the hand before emitting a jet of water. Once in a Malaysian Chinese restaurant I had foolishly asked for 'whatever you recommend' and been given a plate of what the Arabs call zubb al-bahr, the sea penis.

Monfreid himself had used these islands as a base for hiding pearls but soon moved on to the more lucrative business of smuggling hashish and people. Even at the beginning of this century the town of Tadjoura was still a well-known slave market. We could see it to the north from our position, a narrow crusty stain where the blade edge of the mountain cut into the sea. According to Monfreid, the slavers had little trouble catching girls – life as a slave in Arabia could be preferable to that of a wife in Djibouti. The men were less willing.

I asked Yahya if he had known Abdul Hai, Monfreid's local name, and he nodded.

'When I was a youth we would see his boat out here. He was known as a brave man and a smuggler but I never met him. My father said Abdul Hai sold guns and kept them hidden on an island near Ras Bir.'

This is confirmed by Monfreid's own accounts of his life which seems to have hovered somewhere between the doomed romanticism of T.E.Lawrence and the money-spinning capitalism of Voskan's employer, Antonin Besse. He was brought up in France but from an early age was filled with a desire for danger and travel. Perhaps he read the letters Paul Gauguin sent to his father from the South Seas or he heard tales of Rimbaud, who had simply disappeared. But it was a desire largely unfulfilled until he reached thirty. Then the death of his mother and failure of his dairy business finally pushed him to act. He sailed for Djibouti in July 1910 and trusted to good fortune for his survival. It worked. One night a Sudanese pearl diver swam out to his hired boat and offered him an illegal pearl for ten dollars. Monfreid sold it for one thousand. Another stroke of luck with a second pearl brought him three thousand and his own boat.

He began to do a little surveillance work for the Governor of Djibouti but when he had a narrow escape from Mokha while spying on the Turks, the Governor loftily disowned him. The incident brought Monfreid to the conclusion that his world and that represented by the Governor were to be separate. 'We did not even speak a common tongue,' he wrote. 'To me, that other world, its confused objectives, its preoccupations, its stifling proximities, its "honourable calling" that permitted so many interpretations, seemed purposeless. My world, the clean world of the sea, was to the Governor a secret garden, remote, shadowy, poisonous.'

Sitting there on the quarter deck I understood that an escape from the world of 'honourable callings' was still possible, although it was a dangerous undertaking and one full of false promises like those of the Legion. But in Monfreid's world, borders were less concrete and more easily subverted. In the intervening years, crossing the border has become the kind of bureaucratic nightmare he loathed and, in making the physical barriers harder to pass through, I wondered if the mental barriers of crossing the shadow line between the Governor's world and Monfreid's had become more difficult, too. Cedric had crossed but I hadn't. I wanted a foot in both camps, to deny that any line existed, like the qat leaves I was holding which danced between the legal and the illegal on either side of the Red Sea.

It had been my indecision that had disturbed the balance of fate. If I had agreed immediately to the search of the car, Daud would never have had the chance to steal it back. Cedric would never have conceived the idea of killing him. I would not have dashed to the port and made it in time for our departure. My hesitation had become a turning point. When I opened my notebook I found the line running up off the page where the pen had jumped in surprise at Cedric's anger. After that was blank paper.

We sailed on eastwards with al-Gisayr snoring in his cabin and the Somali youths half asleep over their qat while the sun sank lower behind the sternpost. When the lighthouse of Ras Bir appeared on the point where the gulf turns north, the currents changed and the boat began to roll to a different rhythm, a deeper and stronger swell. Al-Gisayr woke and emerged wearing a brown woollen balaclava, a blue football jersey and grubby futa. Then, kneeling on the quarter deck, he prayed and read the Koran until the light had gone. It seemed as though our voyage was governed by his reading, for when he finished, a new bearing was ordered. With a rattle of chains and creak of the rudder, we swung north and began to beat up into the mouth of the Red Sea, the Bab al-Mandab, the Gate of Tears.

Once before, in waters to the east, I had passed on my way to Socotra and the captain had marvelled at the calm seas. Now I understood why. It was impossible to stand without clinging to some support. Al-Gisayr ordered the crew to lay out blankets on the lower deck – the quarter deck was too dangerous, he said, a man could easily be thrown overboard. Yahya and the Somali youths went and lay down but I lingered, talking to the old captain. After a while he forgot that I was not supposed to be there and we lay sprawling on the timbers looking up at the stars.

He began to point out constellations: 'Don't you know them?'

I shook my head.

'Like these boys, they don't know anything except hoping to live in a city with a big car, staring at television all day – all rubbish! Look, this star is for Aden, that one for Zeila, here is Berbera, the headland we call the She-pig's Snout, Socotra.' The whole panoply of stars was a map for him. 'Before the compass we would navigate like this, even as far as India.'

I asked how old he was. 'I don't know but I've been a nakhoda for sixty-five years so I suppose I am about ninety. When I started we had only sails and stars, no motors or compasses.'

As we talked the young sailors gathered round, cross-legged on the half deck, listening to their captain spin a yarn about a shipwreck and siren voices and the jinn in a bottle from Imam Ahmed. With the wind and al-Gisayr's toothless dialect I lost track after he mimicked the siren song, to guffaws of laughter. Then I lay back and watched the stars simply hearing the voices and the rush of the water below. Meteorites left burning trails around Orion, the Hunter, forever striding towards Eridanus, the River, but never reaching.

I was roused by al-Gisayr: 'Go and lie down there – the wind is getting stronger.'

In the hold the eye could no longer hang onto any horizon, the sky wheeled in crazy arcs and I shut my eyes to quiet my stomach, feeling the engine thump through the boards under me. Despite this I was asleep in minutes.

I woke suddenly, surprised to have slept for what I imagined was a few minutes, and a little disoriented. When I stood up, I found the eastern sky was lightening and above the glowing horizon hung massive storm clouds of shark-skin grey. But then I realised the clouds were mountains hovering over the sea mist and they were Yemeni mountains, still forty miles off. Somewhere between, on the unseen sandy coast, had been the port of Musa from where the Himyaris had sailed into the sea of darkness. But now it was the land that was mysterious, the port ruined and lost, its position only vaguely known from references in ancient texts.

The sun rose, a red eye bleeding from the mountain ridge, while al-Gisayr prayed and read his Koran; then the wheel was spun a few clicks to starboard. The galley boy handed out glasses of sweet tea and flaps of flat bread cooked in clarified butter. After an hour the lights of Mokha could be seen but in the strengthening sun they shimmered and faded and finally vanished, as though our destination had been spirited away the moment it was within our grasp. The mountains, too, having appeared to loom so close, now mysteriously withdrew in a rising storm of dust and soon there was no trace of either port or land. Without any points of reference, without even another boat to fix on, we seemed to be motionless, the engine thumping ahead but to no effect. The passengers, having risen from their beds, lay down again; there was no wind at all and the temperature was soaring.

I went to the bow, clambering over the coiled ropes and spars to lean there, gazing forwards until, quite suddenly, as if propelled upwards by some magical force, Mokha appeared.

It could only be about two miles off the starboard bow and we altered course again. On the right was the modern port with its oil storage tanks and a couple of small inshore vessels standing off. To the left was the town, a facade of white buildings, stained and gapped in places but still evocative of the times when the East Indiamen would anchor off the shore, sometimes to buy coffee, sometimes to bombard the town for kidnapping an officer, and once in the search for a colonial foothold in Arabia that led them to Aden.

Rounding the mole and gently moving into the wharf, the town was closer and less impressive: the coffee merchants' houses could be seen for ruins, the casement windows hanging over empty doorways and the stucco, long unpainted, faded and flaking like the icing on a forgotten wedding cake. The beach was a rubble where dogs ran and, of the two forts that had once guarded the sides of the town, only one crumbling relic remained.

Now my attention was wholly taken up with landing: the sambuk was manoeuvred against the wharf beside a filthy rusting freighter, ropes were thrown and tied, a few soldiers sauntered across and watched. Then the engine died and we waited.

For a long time nothing at all happened. Then a man on an ancient Suzuki motorbike with tasselled velvet seat-cover came and took away all the passports. A further hour passed. From the end of the quay a group of men now came, five soldiers with Kalashnikovs strolling behind a young man dressed in a pearl grey tuxedo with cuffs rolled up to reveal a purple silk lining, a mustard yellow futa with fluorescent scarlet pom-poms down the side, monogrammed calf-length sports socks and patent leather mulberry loafers. I almost expected, like John Jourdaine the first Englishman to enter Yemen in 1609, also through Mokha, to be seized by the arms and carried forward to kiss the Pasha's shirt, which in this case was a rather surprising plain white.

Instead, the ladder was fitted, our names called and I climbed over and down, at last, onto Yemeni soil. The Pasha, who was actually a simple immigration clerk, shook my hand warmly and said enthusiastically, 'Welcome. Welcome in Yemen.'

# Arabia

# II

There was an old battered pick-up truck to take passengers into the town after the long-winded process of stamping passports. One young soldier made a brief attempt to worry up a small bribe by picking through my bag and muttering over the film I had. The driver told him to bugger off.

We bounced over some stones and took a curving rutted track along the foreshore, then rounded a breeze-block shack. The ground was completely covered in greyish dust through which poked various whitened bones and some scraggy thorn bushes. Blasts of wind whipped up sudden twisters of scrap paper and grit, rushing down main street where the tarmac was disappearing under swollen tongues of sand. We all got out here and the Somali youths went to find a taxi for Ta'izz, the main city up in the mountains to the east. I left my bags in a grocery and set off exploring.

A first glance at Mokha is not encouraging. The name that lends itself in some form or other to millions of chocolates and cups of coffee is an *appellation contrôlée* of sweets and beverages, a Champagne or Havana – a guarantee of excellence. It is perhaps better that few of those contented consumers ever see the unappetising reality of the place behind the name. Scabbed and patched, bristling with rusted reinforcing rods on which every passing plastic qat-wrapper can catch and flap in the never-ending wind, the modern buildings must represent the nadir in the sorry tale of concrete. Nothing redeems this pitiful mess, even the mangy dogs hide their eyes in their arses, curled up in piles of refuse. The ground is littered with tin cans, bricks, syringes and millions of plastic bags – that twentieth-century tumbleweed, flying past the hungry goats. And you tell yourself that this was once, in its day, what Dallas is to oil.

Behind the ramshackle line of modern buildings I found an open area of dust dunes and a minaret snapped off at fifteen feet. The fragments of elegant lime-washed stucco were wasting away to reveal bricks below, and the spiral stairs inside were nothing more than a vague undulation beneath the sand. A hundred yards to the west one house stood empty, the windows gone and the roof timbers bare, sand dunes banking up on the leeward side. All its neighbours had been reduced to piles of rubble, leaving only the mosque of Sheikh Shadhili still complete, a brilliant white range of domes and an elegantly tapering minaret surrounded by debris and dust. I found the mosque locked and, despite a helpful horde of children who hammered hard, no one came to open up. I went and sat a few yards away and sketched the building into my notebook.

This was the same Sheikh Shadhili that Haj Ali had mentioned: the man who is widely believed to have brought qat and coffee to Yemen – so much so that one of his nicknames is Abu Zahrain, Father of Two Flowers. The founder of the Shadhili order, Abu Hassan Shadhili, died around AD 1258, having travelled from Morocco to Cairo, part of a larger movement of holy men and scholars towards an Egypt renascent under the Ayyubid dynasty founded by Saladin. But the Shadhili who may have carried the precious cargo would have been a successor or follower of the founder, since some accounts have him dying in Harar in the early fifteenth century.

In Gerald Brenan's classic book on Spain, *South from Granada*, there is a mention of a poet, Shishtari, whose verses were used by the followers of Shadhili to reach religious ecstasy. Brenan mentions the man in his memoirs of Andalucia because he was born in Guadix near Granada. Curiously, the area is home to a sub-species of qat, catha europaea, from which a tea was brewed in Shishtari's time. This poet also moved east, towards the great cultural revival of Sunni Islam, bringing perhaps some knowledge of plants useful to the burgeoning sufi movement.

Leaving the brilliant white domes and minaret of Shadhili's mosque, I turned west and walked towards the sea, passing the lively qat market, then into the abandoned courtyard of the old customs house. This had once been an expansive paved area surrounded by arches, colonnades and offices where merchants would settle their bills before loading – a process apt to take far longer than the actual journey ahead.

By 1600 Mokha was already a prosperous port but its peak came between 1720 and 1740 when French, Dutch, English and American ships were regularly visiting. Bales of coffee were sent down by camel caravan from the town of Beit al Faqih, Beetlefuckee to the foreign merchants, then despatched for Europe. East India Company records for 1733 reveal their man in Mokha, Francis Dickinson, struggling to arrange the loading of 3,000 bales, a process that required two and a half months, extensive distribution of 'presents' and a threat to completely destroy the town.

Forty years later the customs house witnessed another set of Europeans being run ragged by the locals. Carsten Niebuhr was leading the first expedition to Yemen to be run on a scientific basis. Having had great success in the north, they arrived at Mokha in good spirits. It was not to last.

As customs men ransacked their baggage, glass jars containing dead animals were discovered. One can imagine the glee, the mock horror, the genuine horror: 'You are dangerous men! What witchcraft . . . what sorcery is this?' Substantial presents all round must have been expected. But with Niebuhr was Pehr Forsskal, a man of passionate disposition and by train-ing a scientist not a diplomat. He flew into a rage to see his prized collec-tion of molluscs manhandled so contemptuously. In the mêlée a bottle was smashed and the scent of alcohol enraged the mob (no one seems to have asked how they recognised the smell). To add to hostilities, a helpful bystander suggested that the shellfish were actually valuable jewels the foreigners had bewitched. Then a jar of snakes was found. It could not get much worse – plainly the evil intent was to poison pious Muslims. The explorers were forced to flee the customs courtyard, their possessions scat-tered in chaotic heaps. One of the party, the linguist Frederik von Haven, collapsed and his condition rapidly deteriorated. His death was recorded by Forsskal without much compassion. 'Professor von Haven died here on 25 May (1763), and by his demise made the expedition incomparably easier for the rest of us. He was of a very difficult disposition.'

Within six weeks the scientist would be dead himself, buried in an unmarked grave in the Yemeni highlands. But before that calamity over-took him, he picked and described a specimen of an unrecorded and rather innocuous bush. Later it was given the botanic name *Catha edulis Forsskal,* but to the locals it was known as qat.

I wandered for some time amongst the ruined houses between the customs post and the sea. Roofless rooms, piled high with sand, where goats were sleeping, and remnants of fine plasterwork hanging over empty spaces, all reduced to a playground for the children with tea-stained teeth and runaway hair. Of the two forts which once guarded the extremities of the seafront, only one remained. Between it and the town was a door attached to a fragment of wall leading from nothing to nowhere. As the wind and dust became unbearable I returned to the grocery shop where I had left my bag and waited for the Ta'izz taxi.

It was a long wait. The shared taxis in Yemen are Peugeot 405 and 504s: in fact, in the colloquial Arabic, Peugeot has transformed into 'biju' and become the word for a long-distance shared taxi. With their three broad seats, the drivers can easily squeeze nine passengers inside. The only problem, apart from discomfort, is waiting for the other eight travellers if you are first to arrive. This car was clearly a Mokha car: it had no internal side panels, no speedo, no handbrake and no lock on the boot. The floor was awash with discarded qat, empty plastic water bottles and cigarette butts, and when we eventually came to leave, it refused to start. The driver gave no sign of displeasure, neither did the passengers; he simply got out, raised the bonnet and stabbed around with his jambiyya for a bit. Then, flicking some non-essential wiring onto the road, he shouted, 'Swiss!' (another cannibalised word, meaning car-keys – this time from the English 'switch'). A passenger fired the ignition. It started.

There is a long straight tarmac road that heads east out of Mokha towards the mountains. Few major routes exist, even today, into the lofty mountain range that runs down the entire length of Yemen and this is simply because these peaks rise so abruptly and precipitously. The only practicable roads have to follow valleys and these are often narrow gorges, prone to devastating flash floods, choked with house-high boulders and, most of all, easily ambushed. Mokha developed because it was the nearest point on the coast to a major route down from the city of Ta'izz, a place that had been the capital at various times and also a way-station for travellers heading up to its rival as capital, San'a.

This first part of the journey was across a desiccated flat plain where the wind howled relentlessly, whipping clouds of dust across the asphalt and keeping visibility to a few hundred yards. Occasional ruined structures suggested it had not always been so barren and during the town's heyday a sixteen-mile-long aqueduct had once passed through here.

'Have you heard?' the driver asked as we started across this unhappy desert. 'They kidnapped a Frenchman yesterday.'

'Who did?'

'The gabail – the tribes in Marib.' He shook his head. 'The world is a strange and wondrous thing!'

I might have said his comment was the strangest of all because the tribes have been kidnapping visitors ever since visitors started coming.

'Is he an oilman?'

'No,' a man at the back of the car had unwrapped his scarf from around his face and spoke in English, 'he is a diplomat.'

We began to chat. He was a tour guide who had been given an unscheduled holiday himself after a long stint of overtime.

'I was kidnapped,' he explained. 'Like this Frenchman.'

A month before he had been taking a party of French tourists to see Marib and the relics of the ancient Sabaean dam, when some armed men stopped them on the road. They were forced to drive north into the notorious Wadi Jawf where they came to a small village.

The tribe were expecting a large group and had prepared a house for their guests. Food, qat and hubble-bubble pipes were laid on, and soon the tourists relaxed and began to enjoy themselves. There were ancient sites unknown to archaeologists near by and the group were taken to see them. They played with the kidnappers' guns, learning how to fire a Kalashnikov. They could walk around freely and explore what to them was village life from the Middle Ages: a life without television, roads, schools, hospitals and shops – many of the things, in fact, which the kidnappers were hoping to extract from the government by kidnapping French tourists.

For Nabil it was not so easy to adjust. He was a Ta'izzi and a town boy, one who had grown used to the standards of hygiene and food that his tourists normally liked. The Europeans could draw on a long tradition of admiration for those who adventure and explore, particularly those who suffer in remote places. They could imagine themselves back at home, treated as heroes. Nabil did not have that cushion. With his neat short hair, spectacles, shirt and trousers, he felt utterly different to the swarthy, ban-doliered tribesmen who wore the same rough tunic day and night. At the daily qat chews he acted as an intermediary, helping the hosts and guests to converse. And slowly he relaxed, the slightly superior attitude he had adopted was worn away. He began to enjoy himself, too. Then he made his discovery.

Nabil's family were from Ta'izz and had been for many generations. But his father had told him they came originally from Radaa, a town north-east of Ta'izz, and before that they had fled the flood following the destruction of the Great Dam at Marib in about AD 570, that same cataclysmic event that Sheikh Muhammad had spoken of in Harar. For the tour guide and his captors there were many names to remember, genealogies to be gone through, but after much discussion and recollection, after many after-noons with qat, he realised that the tribesmen and he were related. He had been kidnapped by his own family.

They had been tribal guests for three weeks when negotiations with the government failed and a pitched battle was fought with troops a few miles away. Following this an agreement was reached and the hostages released. The kidnappers gave each hostage a gift of ancient artefacts, frankincense and myrrh. When it came to final goodbye, a few hostages said they did not want to go: 'Please could they stay?' The authorities nipped this rebel-lion in the bud, whisking the group off to San'a in Landcruisers. Nabil himself planned a family reunion in Marib shortly.

Hostage-taking in Yemen has not always led to such successful cultural exchanges, although there are few cases of a hostage being harmed. In the early years of a European presence on the South Arabian coast, there was increasing perplexity and confusion amongst the Arabs. No one knew quite how to deal with these barbarian infidels and their peculiar business practices which condemned perfectly honest 'presents' as bribery but tolerated crimes like bloodthirsty piracy, habitual drunkenness and bewitching molluscs. All too often the Yemenis could do nothing but respond in the traditional gentlemanly manner: by taking hostages.

Sir Henry Middleton was one of the first to fall foul of the communica-tion breakdown. Arriving in November 1610, he was received with great distinction by the Turkish Governor and given a house for himself and companions. Once lulled into complacency, however, they were attacked and Sir Henry taken prisoner at the cost of eight men dead and fourteen wounded. Meanwhile the Turks tried to board Middleton's ship, the *Darling*, but a cask of gunpowder thrown among them by the English crew thwarted the attempt. The *Darling* then stood offshore and waited.

Sir Henry and his remaining thirty-three men were now sent to San'a where they suffered from the cold and were warned not to darken the shores of Arabia again. Transported back to Mokha, Sir Henry managed to escape and, boarding the *Darling*, threatened the town with his guns until compensation was handed over. When he then embarked on a little piracy, it only confirmed local suspicions: Europeans do not behave properly.

The modern Mokha to Ta'izz road follows much the same route as the one Middleton and his men were taken along. Fortunately, however, the three-day mule ride is now a four-hour car journey. By mid-afternoon I had arrived.

Superior and faster communications have yet to erode the individual character of Yemen's cities. And Ta'izz has character. It is built on a number of low hills at the foot of an imposing mountain, Jebel Saber, which soars to almost 10,000 feet. The mountain is well-populated itself: white-painted houses wind down vast buttresses like broken strings of pearls. This is the source of qat for the city, a trade unique in Yemen for being controlled by the women and reminiscent of the situation in Harar.

In the town, especially the souks, there is a colour and vitality lacking elsewhere. Silky irridescent greens and mustard, swirling patterns of cinnabar and mauve, purple pom-poms with snazzy belts – the young men wear their futas with at least as much panache as any catwalk queen could ever do. The country girls likewise are gorgeous: shiny, pinch-waisted, puff-sleeved, ball gowns over bright baggy harem pants gripped at the ankle by hand-made hoops of embroidery. Their scarves are piled in vast turbans of yellow and white, with orange blossom or marigolds tucked inside to hang low beside one amber-smooth cheek. Their faces are handsome rather than pretty and the old ladies can be as striking as their grand-daughters; and all this beauty selling onion tops or mooli radishes in the street market.

The town ladies are more sophisticated and so rarely seen. They wear the fashionable black that covers everything, but the briefest glance at the contents of shop windows reveals a similar love of sequins, silk and strong colours.

After finding a hotel, I bought some qat; it was late in the day and I was lucky to find anything: in the mountains of Yemen, qat times tend to be a fairly inflexible three o'clock onwards and so the market only operates from mid-morning to four-ish. I chewed alone in my room gazing up at the green terraced slopes of Saber.

At sunset I ventured out again into the streets below the souk. Having just left the deadly decay of Djibouti, I was struck by Ta'izz like a surprise party. Tahrir Street was jammed with hawkers whose shops folded out like magic lanterns from inside wheelbarrows. There was everything here for the real man, you could tool up with a spare Kalashnikov magazine and twenty rounds, buy a flick-knife, a flak jacket or a furry key-ring, there were tough guy perfumes like Rockyman, Emir and Grenade – this one in a silver hand grenade-shaped bottle and when I took a test dab it left a nasty weal across my wrist. Then with the battle won, Action Man could change into a smoke-grey silk shirt, pleated midnight blue trousers, white socks, black shoes and a pair of Big Daddy underpants, Made in China and complete with zipper pockets for the safe-keeping of Lionel Ritchie tapes.

I loved this market. Whenever I stopped to look at something, a small knot of interested bystanders would come to see what I was looking at. Everyone talked all the time. 'Do you know James?' someone asked.

'James who?'

'James the Englishman.'

'Ye-e-s, maybe.'

He turns to another complete stranger. 'There! He knows James.'

'James who?'

'James the Englishman.'

At a tea-shop, I had two much needed glasses of spiced milky tea and the waiter insisted on paying for them. One young man in robes grabbed my arm. 'Say "There is no God but God and Muhammad is His messenger."' We settled on the first part only. No one asked me for anything or sidled alongside with some dodgy proposal. All that was required was to be part of things, not an observer. I realised then how tense I had been, how the lack of sleep, the qat and the heat had screwed me up into a tight little ball. I needed a good rest.

[164]

Ta'izz was an excellent place to recuperate with daily quotas of top-quality leaf. Each day I meant to have a day without it but somehow I would find my feet walking into the souk.

In the mornings I explored Ta'izz's old buildings, many of them relics of its heyday as capital of the Rasulid dynasty. This fascinating family ruled most of Yemen south of San'a from 1228 until they were ousted in 1454. Quite probably it was during their reign that both qat and coffee arrived, though it is unlikely that either tree followed quite such a tortuous route to fame as the Rasulids themselves.

The family's forebears had at one time lived near Marib, but the destruction of the dam sent them north. For a while they ruled part of what is modern Syria, then moved to Constantinople, before drifting east into central Asia. There they lived with the Turkmen but kept their family identity until the twelfth century when one of them, Muhammad bin Harun, moved to Baghdad and distinguished himself as a diplomat. This gave him the title, al-Rasul, the messenger, a name which they retained as they moved west again, eventually into Egypt at the same time as the Kurdish warlord Saladin came to power.

For reasons that are obscure, Saladin decided to invade Yemen. Certainly the control of lucrative trade routes was an attraction but Saladin may have also wanted to find a remote destination for his unsettled and dynamic brother Turanshah. In 1172 the expedition left for Nubia and with it went al-Rasul's son and four grandsons. Perhaps like Turanshah, they too were perceived as a threat.

The Rasulids served their masters well, both during and after the conquest but it seems that by 1228, the Ayyubids had had enough. When the last of them, al-Masud was called to Syria, he abandoned Yemen, taking care to fill seventy ships with a few personal possessions – the only problem being that they were other people's personal possessions, namely:

1000 eunuchs
500 cases of gorgeous stuffs and clothing
300 loads of aloes wood yet fresh and of the finest ambergris
400 slave girls
gems, pearls and precious stones an untold store

70,000 pieces of Chinese brocade wrought with gold and of works of art what cannot be limited as to number.

In his place al-Masud appointed a deputy, Nur al-Din al-Rasul, one of the four grandsons who had come with Turanshah. Al-Masud, however, never made it to his comfortable governorship in Syria and his successor never arrived. On the north-eastern fringes of the Islamic empire a new and terrible force was being unleashed: the Mongol hordes. As they rampaged west, Yemen was quietly forgotten. For two years Nur al-Din played a cautious game, then he announced himself as ruler of Yemen. Several thousand miles of wandering and 650 years after departing, they were back.

With the rest of the Islamic world in turmoil, the Rasulids were left to consolidate their power and enter Yemen on one of its most prosperous and creative periods. Ta'izz was their capital. The second of the rulers, al-Muzaffar, built the beautiful domed mosque that bears his name in the old city. The gate into the market is Rasulid too, as are the twin minarets of Ashrafiyya mosque, an unmistakable landmark standing above the city. These poet-kings built mosques and schools and gardens in abundance; they wrote astronomical treatises and constructed astrolabes, one of which can be seen in the Metropolitan Museum of Art in New York; they lined their pavilions with gold and silk and ate off Chinese porcelain from Annam; they reformed taxes so agriculture flourished and, though they fought amongst themselves, it was a time of peace for the ordinary man, at least until the decline and, finally, the fall in 1454.

It was during Rasulid rule that the mystical movement of the sufis became a major social force as followers of men like Shadhili arrived with the promise of guidance for those seeking closer understanding of God. Missionaries passed through Mokha and Aden on their way to Africa, including one Abu Zarbay who is credited by some Hararis with founding their town, and by others with introducing qat to Yemen in 1430. The name sufi itself comes from the Arabic word meaning wool, perhaps a reference to the simple cloth they wore. This asceticism was one major part of the sufi tariqa, or path, but even more revolutionary was their use of stimulants to help them along to spiritual enlightenment.

Religion of a mystical nature has long been assisted by chemical means. Cannabis seeds have been found in the frozen tombs of central Asia, dating back 2,500 years. Herodotus witnessed its use in fifth century BC in what some scholars believe to have been a rite to purify the spirit, something akin to the North American Indians' sweat lodge. Opium appears to have been used in cults at least as far back as 4200 BC. In the Late Minoan III period of Cretan civilisation it was taken during religious rites to induce ecstasy.

In the 1960s, when hallucinogenic drugs became widely known in the west, there were many claims that a sense of God might have arisen in prehistoric man through drugs. Mary Barnard wrote, 'The experience [the accidental discovery of hallucinogens] might have had, I should think, an almost explosive effect on the largely dormant minds of men causing them to think of things they had never thought of before. This, if you like, is divine revelation.'

In one well-known experiment, subjects were given either psilocybin or nicotinic acid at a Good Friday service. Those who took the hallucinogen reported an increase in mystical experiences – results seized on by the 'sixties drugs guru Timothy Leary as proof of the mystical and religious benefits of drugs.

Certainly, drugs seem to be able to push experiences in the directions people are hoping and expecting to go. And for the sufis, like the ancient Cretans on the island of Aphrodite, that direction was religious ecstasy. Their beliefs were varied but centred on the idea that, by repetitive rituals of prayer and meditation, the individual could approach God. From this developed an idea of a secretive select group, above the laws of man. Some took this to be licence for a life of sensuality and luxury but most advocated simplicity and austerity. One of these was a certain Ahmed ibn Alwan whose father was a scribe at the thirteenth-century Rasulid court.

Ibn Alwan moved to Yufrus on the western side of Jebel Saber where he founded a religious school and became noted for his outspoken attacks on the kings. In legend he is credited with using qat in his meditations and prayers, the drug lifting him and his followers on their path to religious ecstasy.

It was a time when the 'mystic saint' was a figure of great influence and importance, and qat, with its power to work some strange alchemy of the mind, must have been a valuable tool: that mix of dreamlike unreality and sharpness of thought that bestowed instant mystical experiences – a short cut to sainthood. As ascetics too, the holy men were sympathetic towards a substance that tended to deprive users of sleep, appetite and libido.

The first coffee and qat trees to arrive in Yemen were probably planted on Saber or its neighbour, Jebel Habashi, a word from which the old name Abyssinia is derived. Initially they may have arrived in the form of powder, mixed up as teas, rather than as seeds or plants. What is clear is that both substances began to be used as part of religious ritual by sufistic sects, knowledge of them spreading anywhere that the sufi missionaries travelled. But the secular world was not far behind, and, when qat and coffee moved out of the narrow circles of the sufis, they became controversial almost immediately.

It was the Ottomans who discovered coffee being used in Yemen during their first occupation of the country from 1536 onwards. Twenty years later, Istanbul and Cairo had coffee-shops; by the 1630s coffee was being drunk at Balliol College, Oxford as a social beverage; Paris had 250 coffee-houses by 1690; in America Boston had its first in 1689. The coffee-shop had quickly become synonymous with dark-dealings, intrigue and sedition. In the Islamic world learned men denounced the substance as 'haram' – a practice forbidden to Muslims. In Cairo, to be found in a coffee-house was a crime punishable with a flogging; recidivists were sewn in a bag and thrown in the Nile.

Qat was a less successful traveller than coffee: its active chemicals deteriorate quickly and the dried tea is far weaker than the fresh leaf. Consequently, while coffee began to become a vastly profitable world commodity, second in value only to oil nowadays, qat stayed at home. Within the Yemen it was no less controversial, with occasional bans and attempts to limit its use even early on. King Abdulwahhab ibn Tahir had briefly done so in Ta'izz at the end of the fifteenth century, apparently because the town's women complained it was diminishing their husbands' sex drive. Stimulation of religious debate, however, went on and poets duelled in verse over the relative merits of the two substances.

*Qat says:* They take off your husk and crush you. They force you in the fire and pound you. I seek refuge in God from people created by fire!

*Coffee answers:* A prize can be hidden in a trial. The diamond comes clear after fire. And fire does not alter gold. The people throw most of you away and step on you. And the bits they eat, they spit out! And the spittoon is emptied down the toilet!

*Qat scoffs:* You say I come out of the mouth into a spittoon. It is a better place than the one you will come out!

The genre has fallen into disuse in modern times – perhaps extended and animated argument between a bean and a leaf has its limits. The best, however, are masterpieces of wit and verbal dexterity. The modern equivalent perhaps would be Coca-Cola and Fanta battling it out in rhymed couplets, or fifteen stanzas of Land-Rover versus Landcruiser.

It is undeniable that qat and, to a lesser extent, coffee have provided a real impetus to Yemeni literature from the fifteenth century till the present day. Much of this literature came from the sufis in the form of poetry – poetry whose translation can be almost impossible. One traveller to Yemen who grappled with the problem was Ameen Rihani, a Lebanese Christian who spoke Arabic as his native tongue and English fluently. He visited the country in the 1930s and wrote eloquently on the poetic contests of the time and the thorny problems of rendering obscure sufi verse into English.

Even the sufi poet descends from his starry heights to crown its 'emerald leaves' with mystic rhymes. Here are two, which I am able to render into a tolerably English accent:

> The winged horse of my heart, my spirit feeds
> And on it rides up to celestial meads.

But the original line of the poet staggers with figures and allusions. The winged horse, he calls Buraq, the steed of the Prophet Mohammed: his heart is a ladder; and his ecstatic spirit is the Angel Gabriel. Now, imagine the said Angel riding upon Buraq – Ghat[qat] – and galloping up to the highest heaven, and you will get an exact idea of the poet's fancy, as well as an appreciation of the translator's plight.

One can understand the importance that the sufis attached to qat and its properties, and it was for that reason I decided to take a small side trip, over Jebel Saber to the mosque of Yufrus where Ibn Alwan had lived and worked. I wanted to walk up but the sheer overwhelming height of the mountain persuaded me – soft after so many lazy afternoons – to ride up and walk down.

# 12

The shared taxis for Saber left from the market gate. Amongst the wheel-barrows full of oranges, the waiting motorbike taxis, the men in jackets and white zennas carrying paintbrushes was one muddy four-wheel-drive containing sixteen passengers. They had that eager, bristly look of a hyaena pack when they saw me. I was number seventeen, in the worst place at the back, and as I pulled the door shut someone said: 'Oh, look, an Israeli spy come to photograph our land from the mountain.'

'And you, my brother,' I said loudly, 'you must be Michael Jackson, you sing very well.'

This was obviously in the spirit required because they all laughed.

'No, he is an American come to chew our qat and see New York,' said a youth. He had startling green eyes under a black tasselled headscarf tied at a rakish angle.

The driver now got in, pushing passengers along the seat to make room. Money was collected and we set off up the steep streets towards the Saber track, stopping once to resecure the back doors which had burst open, almost throwing me out.

A woman in the middle seat, her bronzed face wrapped around with white scarves and a sprig of white blossom tucked in over her left temple, turned to speak. 'Takhazzin? Do you chew qat?'

'Don't buy her qat!' cried an old man. 'She grows it on a graveyard.'

He was soundly ticked off by the woman while everyone else chortled. She was a qat-seller from one of the many villages on the mountain and having sold her wares the day before had stayed with her sister in town.

Not all the qat trade on Saber was controlled by the women, she told me, only certain villages kept that tradition.

'Test her mathematics,' suggested the green-eyed youth, the numerical ability of the Saberi qat-sellers being the stuff of legend.

I tried a few simple multiplications but she simply gave a contemptuous snort and disdained to even answer.

'Okay – eight seventeens?'

The reply was immediate and confident. 'A hundred and thirty-six.'

'Fifteen nines?'

'A hundred and thirty-five.'

The youth clicked his tongue. 'I seek refuge from the stoned devil!'

'Twenty-three twenty-twos?'

'Five hundred and six.'

In admiration I gave up, checking her answers was taking an embarrassing length of time.

We now left the asphalt road and started up the steep track that winds back and forth across the face of the mountain, climbing ever higher. Jolted and shaken in the back, windows occasionally obscured by schoolboys who had climbed up to stand on the rear bumper, I caught tantalising glimpses of fabulous views over the city to the parched brown mountains beyond.

The roadside was well populated: crude tin-shack shops were busy with schoolchildren, the girls all in black veils and the boys in brown trousers and white shirts. This was a place without flat land and they all looked extremely fit and healthy from a life spent either going up or down.

An old man in the front began to declaim verses, his finger jabbing heavenwards with the rhythm of the words.

'It sounds wonderful,' I said to my neighbour. 'Who wrote it?'

He looked surprised. 'It is his own.'

The top of Saber is actually a broad craggy upland but there is one peak slightly higher than the others and on it is a radio mast. When we passed the bottom of the track leading up to this, I got out and watched them drive off. If I had hoped to walk to the summit, however, my hopes were instantly dashed. Two soldiers came out of a stone shelter and with great friendliness said no. I chatted to them for a while, thinking they would relent but when it became clear they would not, I set off back down the Ta'izz road on the lookout for a footpath that would take me westwards.

The day was magnificent with a brilliant deep blue sky and the air cold on my face. Fan-tailed ravens rode the breeze, then chased a hawk that sprang off a boulder below them.

Not reaching the summit was a disappointment. I had wanted to follow in the steps of the first European to climb Saber, one of the more remarkable travellers to visit the Yemen.

When one examines the comments passed on Yemen by outsiders in the nineteenth and early twentieth century, two things are always repeated: one is how dirty, poor and tyrannised the country is, and the second is that the 'debilitating time-wasting scourge' called qat is the main cause of all the dirt, poverty and tyranny. During the Second World War, Naval Intelligence reported on the 'insanitary habits' of Yemenis, 'especially promiscuous spitting . . . in ill-ventilated rooms at qat parties'. Doreen Ingrams, wife of the British administrator Harold Ingrams, stated in forthright colonial manner: 'I saw no possibility of Yemen developing into a prosperous country so long as qat was allowed to exhaust the people's talents and sap their vitality.'

There is a distinct sense of, 'if only they would see reason and do things our way'. A medical report on qat for the Aden Colony government in 1950 lamented, 'Unfortunately addiction to qat appears to be more widespread than addiction to whisky.'

But there was one notable exception: an Italian doctor named Paul Émile Botta. The son of a politician, Botta had broken off from medical studies to travel in Asia where he had become an opium addict before returning home to complete his degree and became personal physician to Muhammad Ali, the Viceroy of Egypt. This Turkish adventurer had come to power in 1811 when his ragtag army of Albanian brigands had lured the last of the Mamluks into a trap and murdered them. He was avaricious, cruel, bloodthirsty, and given to assassination by beheading. When he encouraged Botta to visit Yemen, the Italian obliged, publishing his account of the journey in 1841.

He found the country very much to his liking and gave what was destined to be almost the only positive report on qat for the next 150 years. 'For myself, I promptly took up the habit and derived much pleasure in the gentle stimulation which it gave and for the dreams every bit as much striking as the reality which followed.'

Botta climbed Jebel Saber, wrote two books about Yemen and went on to discover Nineveh – not at all bad for someone sapped of his talents and vitality. According to his friend Fresnel, the French Consul in Jeddah, he valued qat more highly than opium.

On the high plateau of Saber there is no qat at all, it is too cold and exposed. I had arrived just after the short rainy season had failed and the land was dry. Between outcrops of bare, eroded rock were shallow bowls of agricultural land, the lines of terrace walls curving and whorling around the contours like a vast ancient thumbprint. Here the people grow dwarf barley, dwarf sorghum, ful beans and garlic, and they build their houses of tawny yellow stone on the crags, partly to maximise farm land and partly for defensive reasons. Far away, across a fading bluish void, rose the face of Jebel Habashi and gleaming like a tiny beacon on its lower slopes was the white mosque of Yufrus.

'There is no way down on that side,' one old man told me. 'You must take a taxi to Ta'izz then a taxi to Yufrus.'

But a little further on, two schoolboys showed me a path that headed west, striding along terrace edges, then scrambling down crumbling cliffs to pick up a new stack of terraces and repeat the process. They came along with me, chattering gaily about the baboons that come to be fed at their grandmother's door, about the man who trained a falcon to dance at qat chews, about their impossibly tall Somali teacher and occasionally passing me shoots of herbiage to sniff.

Eventually we came to a final terrace where an old woman was cutting dry sorghum stalks. Beyond the mountain dropped precipitously to a promontory on which was a village. From there a deep narrow valley curled downwards between towering ridges. In the shelter of the valley I could just see the beginnings of qat terraces, the pale green leaves shimmering in the sun. The boys pointed out a house set apart from the village, a simple stone cube amongst some unkempt terraces. 'They are akhdem. They are not allowed to live in the village.'

The akhdem are a people of African origin, remnants of the slave trade and the various pre-Islamic Ethiopian invasions. Although the 1962 Revolution swept away the rigid hierarchical systems of Yemeni society, the akhdem remain among the poorest and are still discriminated against – as the boys had revealed. They had other prejudices too: when I stood up and said I would climb down to the village they protested vehemently. 'No, you cannot. Those people are bad. They are all qat-farmers. They will cheat you. Come with us and have lunch at our house – it is very near.'

But it was still early and a good time to be out walking. I thanked them and set off down, skidding on the dry scree and clambering down gulches full of vicious grey thorn bush and the sharp-tipped tongues of aloe vera. There seemed to be no path joining the upper and lower zones of this stretch of mountain and, only after descending for a couple of hundred feet, did I find a narrow footpath leading down into the village.

The houses here were perched on bare rock above the terraces: simple unmortared constructions in handcut yellow stone with squeaking iron doors and windows. Along the flat rooftops were rows of old tins holding geraniums and marigolds and each window was marked with splashes of whitewash. A man directed me onto a path that twisted down the terraces deep into the valley before flattening out and curving around the valley head on the edge of a terrace wall.

To drop those few yards was to drop into a different world. Gone were the dry, thorny screes and barren wind-scraped terraces of the upper plateau; this was an enclosed place where water could be heard trickling over stones, qat trees rose high above and tiny powder-blue butterflies flitted between sun spots on the bare earth. Two men, at work in their terraces of coffee trees, called across the valley to each other. The sound of an axe on wood echoed around. I passed a small white mosque with a single dome, shaded by tall cypresses, and passed through a hamlet. 'Look,' I heard a woman's voice say from below me. 'There goes the Sudanese teacher.' The houses were always either above or below. One moment you were looking down on the patches of coffee beans drying on the roof, then a few steps and a slide and you were passing the front door with a glance inside to catch the soulful eye of a chestnut cow munching on straw. The people occupied the upper floor, and on this occasion the white stubbled head of an old man peered down at me from the marigolds: 'No! That's not a Sudanese – that's a Christian.'

Doubling back along paths beaten flat by bare feet, I noticed that the little yellow butterflies drank from the little yellow flowers and the powder-blue butterflies had a powder-blue flower. There were almond trees and peaches not yet in blossom, the leaves brownish and curling as though autumn had come to the tropics. Women passed me carrying bundles of faggots on their heads. The older ones answered my greeting, but none spoke first. They wore loose red and black turbans, smock-like dresses with huge embroidered bibs attached and sirwal, the baggy harem pants tight at the ankle. Their bare feet were stained with henna and their eyes rimmed with kohl. Younger girls who would have once worn exactly the same now favoured the flouncy, shimmering colours of the town.

As I passed along one section, an old man called to me from his roof: 'Ya Khabeer! O friend, come and drink qishr.'

I stepped from the path on to his roof and he poured me a glass of pale straw-coloured liquid from a flask. It was bitter, slightly gingery and unsugared. In coffee-growing areas qishr, made from the husk of the berry, is preferred to tea. 'Stay for lunch,' he said and we wrangled good-naturedly over it for a while then his young grandson appeared and tottered along the parapet – much to my concern.

'Don't people ever fall off?'

'Masha'allah,' said the old man, grinning. 'We are born to this life. But sometimes a man will fall when repairing the fields. You can see how high they are.' He pointed down the valley.

There was about a half mile of terraces in sight, stacked above a boulder-choked stream that dived out of view as the valley turned south. Some of the terrace walls were more than twenty feet high and such was the steepness of the hillside, this might secure a field only five feet wide. Into that was packed two rows of coffee bushes or qat.

I thanked the old man for the drink and stepped off his house onto the path. 'Go down and cross the stream,' he told me, 'then follow the terraces to the next village.'

I walked on in the shade of the trees, following the valley as it wriggled through the ridges. Once I came to a fork and hesitated. A woman's voice said, 'Go down!' and I looked around at the blank trees but seeing no one simply shouted a thank you. Later, I stopped by a bank of white flowers where dragonflies were hovering and listened while two men discussed the price of qat. One was a few terraces below me, the other across the valley, and though they could talk perfectly easily the valley bottom had plummeted five hundred feet and to shake hands would have entailed a two-hour walk.

The footpath now began to twist and turn, descending fast; a few times it made long detours back up side valleys. There were fewer trees and it was growing hot out of the shade. Having scrambled down a thousand feet, I crossed a stream and reclimbed the same height up to a ruined tower where a youth named Habib showed me the path.

Once again there were trees and scattering bands of sparrows and sun-birds moving before us. We came down into a hamlet, twenty or so stone houses divided between two rocky outcrops on either side of the arc of terraces. Habib took me to meet his uncle who was picking qat in a field directly below his own front yard. They were picking for themselves, the best stuff having gone off to market earlier.

'Stay for lunch and chew some qat with us,' he said and this time, after politely allowing myself to be persuaded, I agreed.

Uncle Saeed was a tall stooping man with a rather lugubrious face. He wore a rough robe tied with a jambiyya and belt, then over that a vast shaggy black overcoat that appeared to have been torn directly from the back of a monster sheep. Like everyone he strolled up vertical terrace walls with nonchalant ease, stopping to hammer a loose stone back in and shout commands about lunch to the house.

I followed him up the thirty-foot south-west face of his patio only with difficulty and had to be helped over the final lip, much to the amazement of various children: 'Is he a cripple?' enquired one. The house faced across the terraces to the ridge where the rest of the village was poised over a cliff. The front yard was three steps of beaten earth, scattered with chuckling chickens. On the right was a black doorway to a smoking stone shelter where food was being cooked. To the left was a second stone shelter where the cow was kept: in these mountain areas cattle are brought their food by the women who go out chopping forage every evening.

Saeed took me to the upper room which was furnished with one foam mattress, two uncovered loaf-shaped hunks of grubby foam and a pile of blankets. I was seated in a corner and a bright-eyed gang of all ages assembled around me. Lunch was fatut, a large bowl of bread soaked in sour milk and oil, a dish of boiled potatoes, a dish of sohawig, a type of sour relish, and sour milk flavoured with herbs. The men ate together with great lip-smacking pleasure and when the first of them sat back replete, I followed suit. This proved to be a mistake as Saeed became convinced I disliked their food and, despite my protestations, threw some money at a boy with instructions to fetch biscuits: 'Foreigners eat biscuits, don't they?' The biscuits duly arrived and I reluctantly ate the entire packet in front of my audience. Any attempt to stop was forcefully and loudly discouraged.

Saeed's wife came in and ate a little of what the men had left. She was a strong-faced country lady who delved into her headscarves and removed some qat for me. I sat in the corner and began to chew with Abdulkarim, a handsome young man with a wispy black beard. A three-way conversation ensued with Abdulkarim translating his mother-in-law's impenetrable dialect into comprehensible questions whenever I failed to understand her.

'Is London an island?'

'How do you farm in your country?'

'Are you married?'

'How do Christians pray?'

'Do you eat pig?'

Each answer set off discussions amongst the listening crowd and frequent handfuls of qat were plucked from the headscarf to keep me going.

'How much did you pay for your wife?'

I hesitated. In Yemen the man must give the bride's father a considerable sum of money. Not only that, he must cover the cost of the actual wedding and find money for the girl. All this can become a serious financial burden and many men are forced to work abroad for several years simply to save enough to marry. It was with some trepidation then, that I admitted to paying nothing.

There was a shocked silence, followed by whispers.

'You mean your father paid it for you?'

'No, I mean I paid nothing. And her father paid for the wedding.'

Saeed's wife slipped down against the wall and called for a cigarette.

'Does she cook bread well in the tanour?'

'I don't think she has ever cooked bread – her father does sometimes.'

I could see they were thinking: So that's why she was free of charge.

'And how does your wife carry the grasses from the fields for the cows? On her head?'

'She doesn't carry grasses.'

Mrs Saeed had wrapped her face in her scarf but I could hear strange hooting noises coming from within, then the muffled question: 'But she carries things on her head?'

'No – never.'

She screeched in appalled delight. A small boy bolted outside in fright. 'Who would marry such women! Their cows will die!'

'She hasn't got any cows.'

Mrs Saeed hid behind one of her sons. Eventually she rallied and, sitting up, wiped away a tear and accepted another cigarette.

'Our women go to school and university,' I said, eager to restore some pride. 'They become doctors or teachers.'

'What use is that?!' she snorted. 'Who will carry the water and the grasses? Educated girls will not want to do those things. None of the girls go to school here. Men don't want educated wives.'

I asked about her children.

'I've had seventeen but five died.'

'God have mercy upon them. Was it disease or an accident?'

Abdulkarim cut in. 'It was God's will.'

More people arrived, others left. We talked about growing qat: something that all were agreed was a very good and profitable thing, but held back in the village by the lack of a road. Abdulkarim told me how qat had become the main crop.

'If you grow sorghum or beans, like on the top of Saber, you can harvest twice a year and there is a lot of work to be done. Even coffee, which we grow here, it brings good money but only once a year. Qat gives you money all year and more money too – that is why everyone wants to grow it.'

'But not everyone has the right land.'

'That is God's will.'

He described the process of farming the tree, from planting cuttings to harvesting five years later. Everyone in the village was involved, whether in picking the shoots or running it down to market. His brother-in-law went to Ta'izz every day, leaving with a sack of qat on his back at 6 a.m. and not returning until 9 p.m.

Qat grows in Yemen at altitudes of between 3,500-8,000 feet, with some leeway at each extreme, depending on local conditions. Though tolerant of poor soil, it tends to prefer low humidity and annual rainfall of about thirty inches if it is to produce the active alkaloids. When the rainfall is below

[178]

sixteen inches, irrigation becomes necessary; the sound of the water-pump is a feature of drier areas.

It is often said that qat has replaced coffee in Yemen but the true situation is more complicated. While Abdulkarim admitted cutting down coffee to make way for qat, in other mountain places coffee grows in profusion and farmers say qat is not suitable to replace it. The two, then, do not occupy exactly the same ecological niche.

I asked Abdulkarim if they used seeds. He shook his head. 'No, we take sticks from other qat trees and plant them. In two years they are ready.'

'Five!' protested Mrs Saeed. 'It takes five years before you can pick enough to sell.' I detected a certain pleasure that she took in correcting her son-in-law and airing her superior knowledge.

'And how long do they produce?'

'Maybe thirty years normally, but they can go on for a hundred or more.'

On the origins of qat and how it had arrived on Saber, both were less certain.

'They say Sheikh Shadhili brought it for us,' said Abdulkarim, 'but we do not know when. Even we do not know where we come from. Some years ago we cleaned out an old rainwater tank and found figures of people, dogs and animals – Himyari things. One man found some gold coins and sold them in Ta'izz. After Islam came, these things were of no use anymore.'

He stood up. 'Excuse me, I want to pray now.' He went to the far end of the room and laid out a small rug that he took off the shelf.

Habib, who had been quiet up to now, took his place. I guessed he was a little in awe of Abdulkarim.

On his arm was a deep infected wound caused when he had fallen off a terrace. There was no medicine or doctor and I could do nothing except suggest cleaning it.

'I am married,' he told me in a whisper. 'But on the wedding night I had no money to pay the girl the dukhul, so she went back to her family.'

The dukhul is the 'entrance fee', paid on the wedding night to the bride. 'How long ago was that?'

'Three years.' He thought for a while. 'It is good you pay nothing in your country. Here it is too expensive to get married. And . . . ' He glanced at Abdulkarim. 'I want only two children – seventeen is too many.'

It was as if he had uttered a daring thought.

Later in the afternoon, I began to feel the pressure of the people. There were just too many crowding around firing questions and I had suffered one too many lectures on becoming a Muslim. It was then I realised it was much later than I had thought. I was escorted outside and shown the impossibility of descending further that day. I would have to stay with them.

In the late afternoon light, the village was bathed in gold, while far below, the plain was in shadow. There was a glorious sense of space and freedom in a world where the only directions were up or down. But it was an illusion, the village was a prison guarded by Abdulkarim and his new improved Islam. The qat had brought sufficient wealth to ensure complete stasis: girls would never be educated because farmers' wives do not need education. They married at twelve years and were grandmothers before thirty. Up the mountain the land offered no future to all the children and education was the obvious route to a job in the city. Here qat kept the land alive, the terraces in repair and the villages full.

At night we sat around a candle. Spiders came out and crawled over the walls. Then Saeed threw a blanket over to me and grinned. 'Sleep. Watch out – fleas.'

I slept on the floor and woke at dawn, cold to the bone and covered in bites. Saeed and the others were already gone.

It was 5 a.m. and the sun was gilding the very tip of Jebel Habashi. All the village was out in the terraces feverishly picking qat and stuffing the leaves into small plastic bags. I stood on the roof and shivered, watching and waiting as the line of sun dripped down the sides of Habashi, spread across the plain and suddenly burst around the mountain ridge and across the roof. Almost immediately I was warm.

After a glass of qishr, I said goodbye and a small boy in a red beret showed me the footpath. At first we went up and over the ridge behind the village, then he left me to take a well-made stone path down through qat terraces. Everywhere people were picking. A man with a sack over his shoulder came bounding past me, shouting a greeting: 'Sabah al-kheir!'

I could only stagger down, thick-kneed and awkward, always managing to slide on smooth boulders and land on my backside, usually when a large audience was available.

Passing through a village, I noted that the faces were more African. Then I was into a long, scrappy descent through thorny badlands where only goats roamed. There were traces that this had once been terraced but the walls had collapsed and all that remained was an unproductive desert. One could well imagine the same happening further up the mountain, had not the qat tree created a flow of money from town to country.

I walked for a couple of hours into cultivated valleys where the people spoke in a different dialect and the square fields were full of sorghum, papayas and bananas. This was Tihama culture, the Red Sea plain, a place of broad-brimmed straw hats, men in white futas and jackets, women in loose robes, donkeys tripping along dusty bunds between fields, camels groaning and the endless thump of water-pumps.

In the late morning I reached the asphalt road that runs from Ta'izz to Turbah and there was a market going on. Under shelters of straw matting and cloth, people were crowding around baskets piled high with dried fish, tomatoes, garlic, onions and guavas. The men carried little axes and wore jackets with the sleeves torn off. The women were in brilliant blouson-sleeved dresses and turbans, with their faces painted an alarming shade of yellow to ward off the sun.

I had a drink and some lunch, then walked out of town and found a tree to sleep under. Two days of walking downhill had left me stiff-kneed and tired. I made a bed from my headscarf and lay down in the shade. I slept for an hour, then got up and started to chew the qat Saeed had given me. If I was to make it to Yufrus before dark, I needed to move.

From high up on Saber, the white walls of Yufrus had appeared to be close to the plain, just a few ripples in the land separating them. Now I discovered the long dusty truth as I plodded onwards through the clouds of cloying white dust. Eventually I rounded a high promontory and saw the mosque ahead, its domes gleaming against the shadows of the countryside. The sun was sinking fast behind Habashi and I would have to hurry.

The road led below the walls of the mosque and I found a footpath leading up through banks of prickly pear where yellow-vented bulbuls were singing. There was an archway, then a rising tunnel under the building that emerged beside the main door. I wandered inside to the courtyard, even in the dying light it was a blinding white with shimmering pools of water along one side. A wall separated this area from an inner one where old men with white beards were reading the Koran at small rosewood lecterns.

A young man in a long white zenna called me over to the parapet. He was sitting with his legs tucked under himself, watching the line of darkness creep down the mountain towards us.

'You like Yufrus? You know about Alwan?'

He told me that the mosque had been built by King Abdulwahhab ibn Tahir around five hundred years before, but its reputation as a place of healing had begun with Ahmed ibn Alwan, seven hundred years ago. Families would bring relatives, especially those who were mentally ill, and leave them for weeks or months at a time, hoping the atmosphere of calm and sanctity would somehow work on them. And yes, he assured me, it did work.

The line of shadow crossed over but there seemed to be little diminution of light inside the courtyard, such was the vast expanse of brilliant white. Now everything seemed to glow.

'Where are you travelling to?' he asked and I told him that San'a would be the end of my journey.

He swayed gently forwards. 'Is there something for you in San'a?'

'I have friends there,' I said. 'Insh'allah, I will take qat from the Wadi and sit with them – that will be the best ending for my journey.'

He tapped his head and gave me a crooked grin. 'Perfection comes from Allah and not the minds or creations of man.'

Then he descended from the parapet, and as he did so I heard the clank of iron; glancing down I saw that he was manacled. He made no mention of this, but stooped to take hold of the chain that joined his ankles and shuffled along beside me. It was his second visit, he said, and expected to last a few more weeks. I asked about the chains and he replied that they were necessary because sometimes he attacked people, but his family could not bear to see him locked up in a cell.

At the gate of the mosque he called a youth to take me to meet the Imam of the mosque. We said goodbye and he shuffled back inside.

The Imams of Alwan mosque are all descended from the saint himself. I found the latest incumbent in an unfurnished room, sitting by the window and writing furiously in the dim twilight. He was writing the Koran from memory.

'When ibn Alwan came back from being a missionary in Africa,' he told me, 'he started a religious centre here. Being a sufi, he disagreed with the wealth and luxury of those kings.' He pointed out the window up the hill. 'You see, there is an aqueduct that brings our water from a spring high on the mountains. Pure cold water. Ever since ibn Alwan we have drunk that same water.'

I asked about qat and the saint. 'Yes, he used qat in his prayer sessions – to help him reach God – like a ladder.' He leaned forward and touched my notebook. 'Do you want me to write something about qat for you?'

He took the book and scribbled in fast flowing hand. The light was very dim and he hunched right over the book. I could see that he was writing over the same words twice, occasionally crossing out, sometimes using the next page to finish a long line but also bending lines up the page edge. For me it was totally illegible and, when I later took it to others, they gave up after picking out a few words. A search of ibn Alwan's known writings revealed no poem that matched this one, and so what the Imam wrote remains a puzzle – appropriately perhaps, given the enigmatic nature of Alwan's verses.

# 13

Some years before I went to live in Yemen, I taught at a secondary school in southern Sudan. It was a small village on the border with Zaire in the territory of the Azande people, a group made famous in the world of anthropology by the studies of Evans Pritchard during the 1920s. After I had been there about a month, someone told me about an American couple who were studying the tribe at a camp about twenty miles away. One Sunday I cycled through the bush to visit them.

The Azande do not usually live in villages but in small family groups scattered through the forests and in one of these the anthropologists had taken over a chief's compound. There was a circle of mud and thatch dwellings with a couple of grain-store huts on stilts. In the centre of the beaten-earth yard was a large dome tent, all fully mosquito-proof with windows and doors and flysheet extensions, and when I finally arrived after sunset it was lit up with storm lanterns. Ralph was wearing rainbow braces and shorts; Sheila had round-rimmed glasses and a smock. They were both assiduously writing up their notes from the day's researches on a plastic picnic table.

No wonder the locals were suspicious, as my Azande friend whispered, what on earth could they teach such fabulous creatures. It was as if an alien spacecraft had flown over Big Ben and the Houses of Westminster only to touch down on the coast at West Wittering and the little green men, coming forward with pads and pencils, had demanded of the awestruck inhabitants: 'Why do you have three layers on your wedding cakes?'

I was allowed to enter the tent and sit in a folding chair. They told me they were soon to be leaving for home and would be selling off all their gear. Would I like to buy anything? They produced a list, all neatly marked with prices in dollars and nothing crossed off. A lot of work had gone into that list, but I wondered who they expected to sell to: I was the only foreigner within a hundred miles and my arrival was obviously unexpected. As for the local population, they were subsistence farmers who managed to get through whole years without handling more than a few piastres. Then I realised: they knew the locals could not possibly afford anything but the most menial of their possessions. They had stacks of disposable plastic drinking cups, all tidily marked up at five piastres each with supermarket stickers. Nothing was to be given away; that was made clear. After two years living with the Azande the Americans had learned one over-riding, all-consuming, irrational lesson: to hate the Azande. They loathed them with a passion that spilled out in a second list – a list of complaints and whinges that took some hours to recite.

I left in the morning with a Rolling Stones tape and an Azande dictionary and saw them once more, briefly, when they passed through the village on their way out to Juba. They had most of the stuff with them and had left nothing behind.

In the beginning of anthropology, there was Sir James Frazer. He wrote the classic *Golden Bough*, a catalogue of human cultural diversity and adaptation whose central premise was that human development culminated in rational scientific man – coincidentally, a man not unlike Sir James Frazer. If all the strange and bizarre practices of primitive man were of interest, it was a historical type of interest, good for telling us where we had come from. By the 1960s and '70s when I grew up, this was almost perfectly reversed. Primitive peoples were of importance because they had something we had lost and, as such, might tell us where to go. The obvious conclusion was that if you could get as far from western influence as possible, all the better, all the more to learn. Somewhere out there were pristine primitives, full of archaic wisdom. It is the Shangri-La notion: that paradise is out there, very difficult to reach, but definitely out there somewhere.

Even a year spent in a leaking grass hut on a diet of cassava leaves did not cure me of this romantic idea. Ralph and Sheila's stock of noble savage romance had proven less durable. 'When you read Evans Pritchard,' said

[185]

Ralph wearily, 'you get a totally different picture.' The reality fell so far short of the dream, and they had blamed the Azande for it. Not me: even when the local witchdoctor failed to divine the whereabouts of my stolen kettle, even then, my unshakeable belief that wisdom is something found far from home never wavered. Like Abdulsatar in Harar, tuning in to the BBC every day, I kept on believing that truth would come from remote people. 'Better you ask me about a bicycle,' the witchdoctor had said, a little petu-lantly I thought. 'A kettle is a small thing and very hard to find.'

I still wanted that golden bough of scientific rationalism to break from under me, and I still wanted the remote paradise. Jebel Saber had been beautiful and invigorating but it had not satisfied that need to get further away. Riding back to Ta'izz in a shared taxi, I reflected that Abera had been right to call this a pilgrimage because, like a pilgrim, I was determined to make it more difficult than necessary, to head for the stony wilderness where golden boughs lie broken. But it was not until I reached Aden that I picked up the thread that would lead me to such a place.

The night after visiting Yufrus I woke at dawn in a Ta'izz hotel room, then fell back asleep and dreamed the same dream I had had in Harar. There were two splinters in my knuckles and I picked at them until they came out as sticks. And as I pulled the second of them, there was a sickening mus-cular twitch and it turned into a snake that flicked its body free, as if from an egg, and fell to the ground. I woke with a start, still feeling the disgusting presence of its body inside my hand. All through the morning, as I waited for a taxi, then headed off for Aden, I was haunted by that feeling in my hand.

The last time I had been to Aden was shortly after the war in 1994. At the bottom of the mountains, where the land flattens out into shimmering dunes and gravel pans, there was a petrol station that had taken a direct hit from a tank shell. I pulled in hoping to find fuel but the forecourt was lit-tered with glass and mangled pieces of metal from the defunct pumps. Still hopeful, at least of some water, I got out and walked around the side. In the wall was a perfect circle about five feet in diameter and behind it on cushions arranged to enjoy the new view that this unexpected opportunity presented was a group of qat-chewers.

This time, as the taxi sped past, I saw that the hole had been repaired with breeze blocks and the pumps were working once again. But Aden's recovery appeared to go no further than such patching of holes. From the causeway there were precious few new buildings to be seen. In the dazzling white shallows once earmarked for reclamation, the pink flamingoes stepped as daintily as before and up ahead was the same old magnificent jagged claw of Aden's skyline.

For centuries, the volcanic plug with its safe anchorages and defensible positions has attracted mariners but annoyed visitors. The climate was supposed to be the worst in all the British Empire, the natives peculiarly unwholesome. In what must be one of the few towns in the world to be built inside a volcanic crater, sweated the flotsam and jetsam of four continents. Even to be linked to such a breed was to court infamy in British eyes. The 1917 military handbook lists personalities of leading citizens of the north and a certain Salih Shadli is comprehensively denounced: 'A man of about 44 whose eyelids are heavily lined with antimony. Of somewhat insolent bearing, unreliable, shifting and dissolute. A bad man. Keeps in touch with Aden natives.' You could not get much worse than that.

There are men who look much like Salih Shadli still to be seen in the narrow lanes of Crater, beards stained blood-red with henna, eyes black-rimmed and teeth touched with gold, stage villains from the days of music hall and silent film. The Brits never did feel at home in such company and built themselves compounds of villas out on the salt flats of Khormaksar. The habits of foreigners, as Queen Victoria noted, were 'extraordinary and very often disgusting'.

But it is Crater where the life of Aden always was. And it was there I went and took a room in a small upstairs hotel. There was a bed, a ceiling fan and a wall of shutters that opened over the street.

The buildings of Crater were put up by the British, square three-storey blocks built in grey volcanic stone, with plenty of shutters, no glass, and narrow lanes between to hold out the sun. On the ground floor are shops where the cosmopolitan nature of the town is revealed: an Indian dabbing lime on a betel nut wad, rugs from Socotra, apple-flavoured tobacco from Egypt, cups of tea speckled with nutmeg or cloves. In the evening the people come out to shop: the men all in futas for the heat, the ladies swathed in black. Two girls pass, one looks Indonesian the other Somali;

their hems ride up, scarves slip. A herd of goats tug at some qat rubbish, their udders wrapped in bright scarlet brassieres. Two Russians amble out of the chip shop, fingertips red with ketchup.

Despite the dislike felt by many British residents, an empire without Aden was unthinkable. In 1955 Lord Lloyd, Under-Secretary of State for the Colonies, condescended to inform the Adenis that 'for the foreseeable future it would not be reasonable or sensible, or indeed in the interests of the Colony's inhabitants, for them to aspire to any aim beyond that of a considerable degree of internal self-government.'

The Adeni answer was to strike and demonstrate but the British were intransigent. In a country where access to arms and ammunition has never been a problem, the next development was a surprise only to the colonial government. On 2nd April 1958, two bombs exploded.

Governor Sir William Luce was careful to downplay the incidents in his secret telegrams to London: 'At Little Aden . . . an unskilled attempt was made to damage an oil pipeline. One of the 3 sticks of explosive used exploded and dented the pipe. Although in this instance use of the time delay fuse indicates some degree of expertise, the execution in both instances was crude.'

This was almost exactly two years after the French were humiliated by the crude and unsophisticated Viet Minh at Dien Ben Phu but the British were not worried. For them the threat was from the north, across the border in the royalist north, and the answer was to build a buffer zone, a paper minefield of agreements and treaties with the petty chieftains. The grenade attacks intensified. One was lobbed through the bedroom window of a senior British officer and the local *Daily Telegraph* correspondent filed a story of how the officer and wife had escaped with cuts and bruises. A few weeks later the paper announced the officer's divorce: his wife, a *Daily Telegraph* reader, had been in England all along.

Despite rigorous checks, the arms and ammunition got across the causeway. Part of the traffic that came through was the daily qat caravan: dozens of camels laden with carefully-wrapped bundles of the leaves. These were checked and taxed, the colonial government derived a healthy income from the drugs trade. But, despite the searches, nothing was ever found secreted in those bundles, until one day a camel exploded. Subsequently, the British checkpoints on the causeway would run a metal detector over the beasts and any that triggered a beep were handed over to bomb disposal for an inspection of its stomach contents.

The British had problems but none was bigger than their complete misjudgement of what they were facing. The tangled web of treaties and petty sultanates, a classic nineteenth-century divide and rule situation, was simply unravelling in the face of an ideologically motivated and disciplined guerrilla army. Not only that, when withdrawal negotiations were held in Geneva, the British were shocked to find the enemy sitting opposite contained high-ranking men from the local army and police forces, people they thought their own. Twelve years after Lord Lloyd's declaration the British had gone.

The new communist government did not have long to celebrate before the grim economic squeeze began. The Suez Canal was closed and Aden port went into steep decline. What had been the world's fourth busiest port in 1964 was soon nothing but a forgotten corner of Arabia where international terrorist Carlos the Jackal could relax.

There was a joke around in those days, although you had to be careful who you told it to, concerning an American, a Russian and an Adeni on the beach at Crater. The American took off his jeans and threw them into the sea. 'In the States,' he boasted, 'we have plenty of jeans.' The Russian swaggererd forward and, taking out a full bottle of vodka, lobbed it as far as he could. 'In Russia we have plenty of vodka.' The Adeni thought for a while, then stepping forward, he picked up the Russian and threw him in the sea.

What the joke does not tell you is that the poor Russian was probably grateful, for being an ally was proving as vexing as being the enemy. The problem was continual divisions, often on regional lines, that led to civil wars. From the first spat in 1968 they managed one approximately every four years, culminating in January 1986 when an estimated 3,000 died in Aden during 'an ideological correction' sprung by then President Ali Nasser. Unfortunately for him, it backfired and he fled into exile in Syria. The victorious faction gave the world's press a tour of his HQ located in the former British Army mess above Steamer Point where they noted the Louis XVI chairs on which qat parties had been held.

The Adeni way of life, however, remained unaffected. The brewery kept on brewing, women worked unveiled, the night clubs rocked. It was cosmopolitan, it was increasingly decrepit and, when unification came in 1990, it was an anachronism. For four years it survived. You could drive from a firmly Islamic capital where few women go unveiled, and that same night be drinking local Sira beer over a plate of chips while watching belly dancers have money crammed in their sparkly brassieres by men in sharp suits. Next morning you could go to the supermarket, along with everyone else, stock up on booze and drive north, only to be stopped at a checkpoint if you were unlucky and have the whole lot smashed on the road by zealous troops.

Then came the Socialist Party's rebellion which was rapidly quashed by a coalition of its own enemies in the south, the northern armies and the mountain tribes. The secessionist leaders escaped by boat to a life in exile after a last desperate retreat on Aden.

A short time after the dust had settled, I had driven down to the port from San'a – the last forty miles of road still littered with burned out tanks and pick-up trucks, almost every building holed or damaged in some way. At the end of the causeway, the up-market Mövenpick Hotel was a wreck, gutted of everything. In traditional style the tribes had descended on the sinful city and sacked it. Public buildings and unguarded houses were looted: the museums lost priceless collections of ancient artefacts, the Mövenpick had even lost its light switches. San'a was flooded with second-hand goods for sale.

I had stayed with the brother of a friend on that trip, and this time I went back to find him, a bundle of qat under my arm. I wanted to know if Aden had survived, if the old dog was running rings around its new masters, just as it always had done. In 1994, in those heady days of post-war euphoria when everyone was just glad to be alive, he had told us stories of dodging press-gangs, of Katyusha rockets slicing through his neighbour's front wall, of a tank that had rumbled down the street lobbing shells over the houses and behind it a boy pushing a wheelbarrow, shouting 'Tomatoes! Potatoes!' He had seen the champagne celebration of the tribesmen, smashing Moët et Chandon on the kerb stones and yelling 'God is great!', and he had seen the renegade al-Jiffri speeding towards the port for his last-minute getaway. But it was too soon to know what the future would be; everyone was just waiting to see.

I found my friend's euphoria long since soured, leaving only a despair that life would ever improve. What little progress had been made was being thrown away, corruption was choking the life from government and public institutions. The only ordinary people with money were qat-sellers, supplies had never been interrupted all through the war, and they were ignorant country folk without a clue as to what to do with their unwarranted wealth. Life was a struggle without many compensations – none of those with which Aden had traditionally distracted itself.

We sat watching the television and he flicked over the satellite channels: football from Bahrain, soaps from Egypt and Lebanon, MTV via India, CNN news, live Koran recitation from Saudi. The world was visible from Yemen now, beaming down into dishes on every roof, but for all the promise it was scarcely any closer than before.

I left him after dark and went in search of other old friends, Ramzi and his band, the musicians I had met in Djibouti.

The natural bowl that forms Crater is broken on one side for about six hundred yards between two rocky headlands. It was in 1839 on this stony beach that Captain Haines of the Bombay Army first landed and claimed Aden for Britain. On that spot now stands a Pizza Hut, but it was from an Arab restaurant next door that the music was coming.

I wandered through a deserted gateway and past some darkened buildings full of empty tables, each screened from the others by cream-coloured curtains. There was a high wall and beyond that a large patio where the music was reverberating – amplified Arab rock, a swirling complex sound under soaring falsetto voices. A man in a fez carrying a hookah pipe appeared in a gateway and beckoned to me. I followed him but when I reached the entrance I stopped in the shadows to watch.

The band had a small stage under an awning to my left. I recognised Ramzi on keyboards and Waleed the bass player. In front of them was a small open area on which about twenty young men were dancing in flouncy little groups while waiters in tarboushes weaved through them to the tables at the rear.

This is it, I thought, this is Aden. This is proof that it never died. The outrageous ability to gobble up your invader and spit him out lives on. Then two young men took the floor in pink shirts and harem pants with waistcoats clasped at the navel with single pink buttons. And they danced. Shoulder shimmies, snaky hands, cow-horn arms, and when they were done, then down came a single fluttering forefinger to that single pink button on the belly and pressing gently, as if a ruby might drop out, held the centre steady while all else flailed.

'Are you Englishman?' A voice in my ear. I saw a face in profile, wide-eyed and moustachioed. 'Then look at this.'

He held up a hand in front of my face and hidden in the palm was a medallion inscribed with two crossed rifles under a red star.

'Do you know what that is?'

I nodded.

'Do you know we want the British to come back? The Adeni people want this, I tell you.'

A double-breasted peach waistcoat with front tails teased to halfway down the thigh came wriggling forward from the throng.

'I'm not sure that they will,' I said.

He took my hand and pressed it against the medallion. 'Tell them to come – you must do it!'

'But this is a . . . ' My voice dropped. 'This is a communist star – not British.'

He screwed his eyes shut in irritation. The peachy tails had ridden high up over the blue satin shirt and were now being tickled back down to the thumping beat. A silver brooch winked from a white polo-necked shirt, a fluorescent futa belted with diamante hearts flared as the dancer spun.

'The communists were not corrupt. Stupid sometimes – but not corrupt. Good fellows, like the British. My father told me. He fought them. He threw a hand grenade once – do you know the Café Zaku?'

'The British will not come back. They want to be European now. They don't even remember where Aden is.'

'It's not true. They have no friends in Europe. Here people love them. You must tell them – swear it.'

Out on the floor, arms were reaching for an imaginary lover, shoulders quivering, spinning and down to knees and limbo back, hands clutching up and caressing and dying further and further back until pink pants was flat on the floor with the sinuous arms fading like flames on a forgotten fire. The drummer was bent over his kit, doubled up with laughter.

'I can't promise.'

'Swear it. We want the British back.'

'All right. I swear to bring British government back to Aden.'

He snatched the medallion away. 'There!' he cried in triumph, 'you are an imperialist – you British never change!' And with a roar of triumph, he leapt away into the shadows.

Later I had dinner with the band.

'We can't understand it,' they said. 'We haven't seen these people since the war and now they turn up on the same night as you!'

The second set finished at 11 p.m. sharp and there were no belly dancers or beer, but I knew that Aden was very far from being finished.

My days began to take on a pattern: I would explore in the mornings then take a lunch of fatut, a sort of minced banana sandwich with honey that they kneaded up in great earthenware pots, then a steak of roasted tuna with delicious flat bread hot from the tanour. Then I would retire to my room. I had given up thoughts of missing even a day without qat – an afternoon unassisted by the leaf was too horrible to contemplate. By noon I would be restless and fidgety, ready to snap at any wisecracks. I found my memory for recently heard names failing. If called on to make sudden feats of recollection, I floundered. My own telephone number in Britain suddenly dropped out and it was three days before I retrieved it; I had never even thought it necessary to make a note of it.

It frightened me a little but there was another side to it. The past was so clear it was in front of me. I dreamed the names of my classmates at school and saw every one of them as though I had sat down and memorised the register. During the night, a girl I had known at thirteen and never thought of since marched into my room as a woman of thirty-five and demanded to know why I had never told her I loved her. I ran out into the street, a Nottingham street, torn up by regrets for things that might have been but never were. When I woke up I was under the fan and it took me a full agonising minute to recall where I was. Dreams were too real, they came striding up and slapped me across the face; I could smell the inside of my school desk, that woody mixture of dust and bubblegum. One night I woke to find a black cloud pressing down on my chest, choking the life from me. Then I forced my hand outwards, inch by inch, and broke through. I was on the floor on my hands and knees, not flat on my back as I had thought and I was shouting at the top of my voice.

Outside the door was where the hotel life went on: twenty-four-hour television and qat. There were men who took the leaf every waking moment of their lives but these were the rarities, seen as different and a little bit crazy. If addiction to qat is possible, then these men were addicted – mudmin in Arabic. But should you take one such man off to a qat-free country there would be no withdrawal symptoms beyond an occasional bad dream. Yemenis who go to study abroad, like Khaled in London, manage perfectly well without qat for months at a time. When they return, they take up the habit once again – probably with a sigh of regret – but life without qat in Yemen can mean life without friends.

Studies have failed to find any typical signs of an addict in need, and yet laboratory tests on cocaine-addicted monkeys showed that the qat chemical cathinone could be substituted without altering their behaviour. One assumes the monkeys were not sprawled lazily on cushions with a waterpipe and a few close friends. 'Qat is nice,' says the Yemeni proverb. 'There is nothing worse than it.'

I had lost weight. Qat dampens any appetite for food after the session. Then you sleep late, miss breakfast and end up eating a large lunch. My teeth hurt. I was constipated. But at one o'clock, without fail, I would find myself passing through the gate and into the qat souk.

One day I got talking to one of the muqawwat, the qat-sellers, and asked, 'Where is the best qat from, the very best in Aden?'

He smiled and shook his head. 'Not now, not this time of year, but in the summer, then is the time for the qat from Yafa – then you will know good qat.'

'And where is this place, Yafa?' As I asked the question I remembered that I had heard the name before: Abdulsatar in Harar had originally come from there.

He waved vaguely. 'Oh, it is too far. Up there. North.'

'Near Dhala?' This was a major qat region on the San'a road and the place I had in mind for my journey north.

'Not that one.'

'Near Abyan?'

'You must not go to Yafa. It is too far and its people are not good.'

And he would say no more.

I began to ask everyone I met about Yafa but most were equally vague. 'They are Jews,' said one man. 'They make trouble,' said another. I discovered that it was a day's journey from Aden and that the main town was Labus. In bookshops I looked through indexes and found no reference but a map revealed that it was a large province of 8,000-foot mountains and deep valleys. The old colonial memoirs were equally unforthcoming, but I did glean two things: first that the Upper Yafa tribes had never been subjugated by the British or Turks, and second that the Governor of Aden, writing in 1953, described the area as 'uncivilized and turbulent in the extreme'. I resolved to go there immediately.

# 14

It took over an hour to find the taxi stand for Labus. No one seemed too sure where it was but I eventually tracked it down to a tin shelter behind the market in Sheikh Othman. There was a special rank for the off-road vehicles, a bunch of ageing heavyweights long past retirement date with their balding tyres, crooked doors and windscreens strapped up with tape. I walked among them calling, 'Labus! Labus!', and two men in zennas and jackets came bustling over: 'Aiwaaaa! Come, come.'

I was bundled into the back seat of a twenty-year-old Landcruiser and found myself in the middle, two men on my right, another on my left, a big man for a Yemeni I thought and then he turned his head and I saw a large Father Christmas beard and twinkling blue eyes.

'What are you doink?' he asked in a Russian accent. 'No one goes to Yafa. In one year I never saw any other foreigner go to Yafa.'

He held out his hand, and I noticed that for a big man it was surprisingly delicate with carefully manicured nails.

'My name is Sergei.'

I introduced myself and asked, 'Are you going to Labus?'

'Not exactly Labus, I am a surgeon at the hospital – it is not far from Labus.'

The driver climbed in, tying a tasselled headcloth of black and gold around his grizzled head and shouting, 'In the name of God!' several times. Some of the passengers echoed his words and we set off.

'Don't we pay first?' I asked Sergei. The shared taxis in Yemen always demand money in advance.

He grinned. 'Now you are in Yafa. Huna Yafa. This is Yafa, not Yemen.'

The other passengers took up the cry, 'Huna Yafa.' They were a danger-ous looking crew: unshaven rascals who kept their Kalashnikovs on their laps and a constant excited chatter about everything they saw. 'Look at that driving! What a donkey! You son of a yellow-eyed whore! Your mother's crack! Fifty rials for a kilo of oranges, in Yafa we pay forty only. By God, driver! Why are you going so slow? Where will we take lunch? And we must buy qat – the foreigners will want to see London.'

Our route was back along the San'a road, past the Anad military camp at the Ta'izz turning, the place where the fiercest battles of the 1994 war were fought. Then the mountains began to rear up from the plain, choppy waves of black rock, the strata running vertically, as if poured from the noonday sun. The road criss-crossed the valley, splashing through the stream several times. In the rainy season such watercourses can become swollen torrents in seconds: I had once seen a Toyota pick-up snatched by the water as it entered and tossed like a stick against a boulder fifty yards downstream.

At the town of Habilain we turned east still on asphalt and headed up a side wadi surrounded by jagged peaks. At one low hill the man behind me tapped my shoulder.

'This is where the British reached – they had a camp on top of that hill, but they never dared go further.'

In this province of Radfan the first rebellion had started and spread like wildfire. Like all the invaders who had come before, the British were to learn the impossibility of ever subduing such a country and such a people. They desperately attempted to shore up their defences with a barrage of treaties, accords and mutual compacts, but many of the sheikhs they dealt with had no more authority than the colonialists. The problem was that the Yemeni system was fluid: a man might be sheikh and command his people, but it was all a game of personality and individual charisma that each generation had to win anew. And some of the men who presented them-selves to the Governor in Aden as rulers of some remote territory, and were signed up with stipends and salutes, had no more right to claim to be ruler than a dozen others who promptly set about toppling the upstart.

At midday we reached a small town of shacks and roadside workshops, a real frontier place with everyone armed – except myself and the doctor.

There were two restaurants here and after some discussion, one was chosen.

A Yemeni roadside restaurant at lunchtime must be one of the most memorable culinary experiences available. You have to remember that every man in that place is set, absolutely fixed, on the idea of qat. He has got through the morning somehow and now he is at fever-pitch, the expectation is killing him: the qat is out there, outside, qat-sellers are selling on the steps outside, others are buying. 'It'll all be gone, look at the crowd, no qat, there'll be no qat!'

Up the steps and under a lean-to roof, shouldering our way inside a yellow-walled cave with iron tables crudely welded to the iron benches, and a heaving mob of brigands, great fistfuls of bread waving over blackened scalding bowls of fizzing green slime, howling for soup, bring more soup! Men squatting around common bowls on the tables, no one talks when shouting is better and everyone is shouting at everyone they know. 'Hey Ali! You devil! Come and eat!' Sweat runs down the walls. Waiters run. Marag! Marag! Meat soup. That life blood that pulses in every good lunch and sohawig so sour it sears your tongue and hunks of greasy meat for teeth to tear into. But most of all there must be salta, green and frothy, sizzling in a stone pot, the primordial soup on which we will float to paradise. The essential ingredient is halba, fenugreek, then marag and maybe meat balls, potatoes, chillis and eggs. There is no set recipe: forget Delia Smith cook books and dainty manners, this is medieval banqueting.

Then you realise that there are manners, that this pack of ravening beasts, who are apparently intent on tearing apart various chickens, goats and cows, are actually behaving with all the elegant courtesies of the Knights of the Round Table. The sink in the corner is cracked and stained and full of discarded onion tops but they wash their hands rigorously. And then they try to give away their food or at least entice strangers to share it with them. The right hand offering gesture. Come on and share. Everyone wants to share. If you catch their eye they'll try and share. If you're sharing a table, then you'll share the food. They heap bread, great flaky flaps, heap it across to you, and hanks of meat plop down before you, ten-foot lobs of generosity. They share the water cup, a plastic beaker, greased and stained by a hundred mouths. And their hands, right hands, go to the common bowl but always with the instinctive turn-taking. And they won't have the meat. You would think they only ordered it to tear off the best bits and give them away. Then they make a break for the door and fight over who is going to pay before making sure everyone has a glass of sweet, red tea in which a sprig of mint gently rotates.

I bought qat with the others from the muqawwat at the door: good green shoots with long succulent tips. I had not seen qat like it on the entire journey but I did my best to contain any obvious glee. The other men were better at it. 'What's this stuff? Off the bottom of the tree where the dogs piss? You bugger, Muhammad, selling poison to the Englishman. Don't you know he built Aden? Shame on you!' They grabbed his headscarf off and threw it around like a gang of school truants.

But they ordered bags to be filled, just as I did, then watched hawk-like while he loaded up three hundred rials worth. In the mountains, this method of qat-selling, with the sprigs and leaves not tied into bunches is becoming more and more common. And when he stopped and folded the bag shut with an exaggerated flourish which said 'That's your lot', they grabbed their money back. 'What! You jinni, I suppose you'll be asking for dollars for it. Zid addi! Increase this!'

And the muqawwat, as he did every time, leaned across and taking back the bag threw in a few extra shoots as if he had just snatched the last morsel of bread from his only son's mouth and given it to a thief.

Back in the car, we all settled with pleasure. 'Praise be to God,' said Nasser, one of the men behind me. 'This qat is honey and almonds. By God! We can relax.' Cold water was bought, cigarettes offered around, then we moved off.

Sergei did not take qat, but he talked about his life. He had been brought up on Novaya Zemlya, an island in the Soviet Arctic, son of a doctor who had fought for communism. As an idealistic young man he had worked overseas, not for the money but the satisfaction. Then, while he was away in Niger, his bit of the USSR had become Russia and the government agency that employed him had become a privatised company. When he returned home it was to a country he could neither afford nor like. His savings were meaningless, a pathetic pile of useless money that would not buy a secondhand sofa. Then they offered him Yemen.

It was a good job: a thousand dollars a month in a major regional hospital at Lahej and, though he spoke only Russian and a little English, he had arrived with high hopes. At San'a they put him in a taxi to a large town where they put him in a second taxi to a small town. Here he was met by another man who despatched him in a third taxi through some incredible mountains and hair-raising tracks to a large village where a car was waiting to take him to a small village where, at last, he found the hospital. He worked there for a fortnight before a kindly soul took pity and told him it was not Lahej.

At first he was furious and wanted to leave immediately. He was a good surgeon and it was a poor hospital. But they had kept his passport and when he did get it from them – which took ten months to achieve – he discovered that no visa had ever been stamped into it. He could not leave because he had never arrived. Nor did his salary come. How could a man who did not exist receive a salary? In a year he had never had more than a fraction of it. He was trapped in a capitalist gulag. His eyes twinkled, he shrugged.

'This is Yafa. You will see.'

The tarmac road was gently disintegrating as we moved further up the wadi: the concrete pans where the stream ran were pitted and crumbling, in some places entirely washed out. On both sides the mountains were too severe for any life except the grey scrub thorn that clung to the boulders. Then the valley narrowed to no more than fifty feet; there were walled terraces tucked under the overhangs and, in the centre, the road ended in a wall of white boulders.

'Yafa!' shouted Nasser excitedly. 'From here you are in Yafa.'

Engaging four-wheel drive, we now proceeded to climb the wall of boulders and when we got to the top we were in quite a different world altogether.

Ahead was a long V-shaped valley down which a boulder-strewn flood course wriggled between vast mountain buttresses. In the lee of each of these massive ribs, presumably where the floods did not rip quite so mercilessly, terraces had been built up, stacked on top of one another, some only large enough to stand a donkey in. And on flat land that had been hacked out from the slope stood the tall square houses. They were built completely without cement and tapered to white parapets with sharp wolf fangs of stone on every corner. Each floor was also marked by a white band on the exterior, some smaller dwellings with only two lines, others with eight or nine, like measures of a man's wealth. The wooden shutters were brightly painted in blue, the sills chequered in red and white. Amongst these houses were simpler places, just as tall but unpainted with smaller, meaner windows and these were the pre-1967 houses, so Nasser told me.

'Believe me, in those days people would fight with their neighbours. The houses on opposite sides of the valley might be at war for years. Sometimes it was impossible to get out the front door without the risk of being shot. Look at the watch-towers – even now they use them.'

These were elegant towers of stone, nicked all over with gun loops and trimmed at the top with crenellations or zig-zags of rough-cut stone. Most stood over the lower fields where qat grew; higher up, in terraces that needed climbing gear to be reached, were the dry stalks of the last sorghum harvest.

For some time we bounded and bounced up the valley, the driver receiving occasional offerings of qat, the youth at the back who had no money constantly attempting to ward off presents of stems.

'Why are you coming to Yafa?' he asked, but whatever I said met with incomprehension: 'But why come to Yafa? People leave Yafa.'

At the head of the valley, the road began to wind upwards to Naqil Ihyar, the pass into Wadi Ihyar. Slow vehicles ahead had formed a convoy of smoke-belching Russian trucks – it looked like the retreat from Afghanistan; indeed, the same thought must have passed through Nasser's mind because he told me that many Yafa'is had gone to fight as mujahideen and discovered Afghanistan to be much to their liking.

The province has long been an exporter of soldiers: the Nizam of Hyderabad's army was once staffed by Yafa'is, as were many of the Sultans' forces within Yemen and the British-run Federation Army.

The long climb up the 3,000-foot pass took over two hours with frequent stops but the road was actually quite good, having been recently bulldozed. At the top a lorry had broken an axle and we came to a halt. I walked up to a cairn with Ahmed the driver.

To the west was the long bluish valley from where we had come: the mountain buttresses now touched with late rays of sunlight and looking like some giant skeletal remains. To the north and south were steep, stony crags, rising to great height.

'That is the land of my people,' said the driver, pointing north. 'And this rock marks the boundary with the land of the people in this valley. In the old days I could not have gone further, but now it is peaceful and the road passes this way.' He pointed down into Wadi Ihyar, a deep narrow cleft in the mountains that descended to a village below and then divided in two. From the bows of the mountain that separated these two side wadis sprang a single crag, perhaps 400 feet high but appearing quite lost in the general grandeur. On top of this crag was a castle.

'That was the house of the Sultan of Yafa al-Ulya – Upper Yafa. He is dead now.'

Beyond this any view was cut off by high ridges, some of them dotted with houses. It is this combination of deep narrow valleys and high ridges that have made Yafa so impenetrable throughout its history, both to ground attack and communications. The road we were travelling on had been blasted through in the mid-seventies, the first motor link for a vast swathe of territory.

The broken lorry was finally moved to one side and we went on, the mountain-tops fringed with golden light while the valley was in darkness. In the village, the Sultan's old house still dominated, but the walls were unpainted, the windows unshuttered and cracks appearing between the stones.

'Now the road is a special one,' said Sergei and he was right. We began to bounce over boulders, lurching and thumping up what was no more than a rockfall, the tyres hissing as they slipped on smooth dusty stone. Loose scree hammered at the chassis and Ahmed got out to inspect – a smashed brake pipe or fuel line could be disastrous. Nasser took my address. 'I may visit England one day.' Then he climbed down and with a wave, stepped over the lip of the precipice into the darkness.

When we reached the plateau it was night and all I could see was lights dotted everywhere, like constellations. There was nothing that could be a town. The track deteriorated though we were no longer climbing, the lurches more violent even at walking pace. A yellowstone wall on either side hid what the headlights might have revealed. We entered a compound.

'The hospital,' said Sergei.

'This is it? Is there a hotel?'

He chuckled, out of habit holding his hands as if they were gloved and sterile and ready to hold a knife. 'Hotel? What are you saying? There is no hotel in all Yafa. You will stay with me, here at the hospital.'

Ahmed was already unlashing my bag from the roofrack. 'Stay with Dr Sergei. He is a good man and everybody knows him. You will be safe with Dr Sergei.'

It was then that I heard it for the first time: the urgent stuttering of a distant machine gun and, arcing across the night sky like a bloodstained whip, the lazy red lines of tracer bullets. Sergei sighed. 'More work for me! Ah, Kevin. Welcome to Yafa – you are our first tourist.'

Sergei had an apartment in a two-storey concrete block next to the hospital building. There was a kitchen, piled high with dirty pots, a living room and two bedrooms. The windows were barred and shuttered, the doors all had curtains, there was no heating and it was bitterly cold. We slumped down in the leatherette armchairs, keeping our jackets on. The only attempt at brightening the place was a picture of George Bush with his face scratched out, the caption was in Hindi.

'Before me, an Indian doctor lived here. He was in Yafa for seventeen years but two years ago his salary stopped. After seven months he left. Here it is very stress for a surgeon: no electricity, no instruments, staff problem. The people are very tammam, very good, but corruption is problem. Even an important man may get only seven thousand rials a month: that is not enough to survive. For me they come. "Dr Sergei, can you come to this house and perform operation?" But I am say, "No! These are gunshot wounds." Of course, all are gunshot and maybe criminal. If I go they may decide to pay me or simply to silence me.'

'Are there a lot of gunshot injuries?'

He began to laugh. 'Not only gunshot: bazooka, mortar, shrapnel, rock shrapnel – you know a bomb explodes here, everywhere is rock, so we get people with rock shrapnel inside. Once a shop in the souk exploded and we had ten people for amputation. One man was almost dead, we amputated both legs and seven days later he went home. These people are very tough, really, and very tammam.'

He went out into his room and came back with a stack of blankets. 'These will be enough – it will get very cold later.' I was already shivering, my feet were numb. The spare room had a huge wooden bed, a stack of Indian magazines and the sound of a baby coughing pitifully from next door.

# 15

At first light I was awake but unwilling to leave the warm blankets. I could see my breath in the cold. Then I heard Sergei moving about and forced myself up to the window. The view through the dusty glass was limited, but I could see a stony mountain plateau dotted with houses, the older ones huddled together in villages on the bare rock. Light was bursting across and drawing thin beadings of gold up and down the walls. A couple of these buildings were larger, each of them stone-built and tapering like the others but with dozens of blue shuttered windows and a water tank on the roof housed inside a brightly painted Chinese pagoda. There was no sign of people, however, and I later discovered they belonged to Yafa'is who had gone to Saudi Arabia as poor boys and were now millionaire merchants in Jeddah. The houses were rarely used but performed the useful function of informing those back in the old country how successful the owners had become.

All the houses were built on patches of bare volcanic stone and between these were low terraced fields filled with a coffee-coloured loam. The land fell away to the west into a hidden valley beyond which another ridge rose, also dotted with houses. The view north was blocked by a low mountain about three miles away.

Sergei had boiled up a pot of water for me to wash in and then there were date sandwiches and hard-boiled eggs for breakfast. 'I will go to the hospital now,' he said, 'to make my rounds. You can come with me and I will introduce you to some people who will help you.' I had already told him how I wanted to walk north towards my final goal, San'a.

A glass of thick black coffee and five sugars cranked us up to face the cold outside, but once out in the sun I found it was warm, the bitter wind of the night having died away to a breeze.

The hospital was a single-storey concrete building with barred windows sited on a flattish crust of rock. At the entrance Sergei was surrounded by people waving X-ray plates.

'Doktor! Doktor! Please look here!'

He smiled and shrugged, taking each one in turn and holding it up to the light, communicating in a faltering mixture of Arabic and English with mutters of Russian to himself. 'How many years this one? Bint or walad? She is seven. You must bring her to the hospital – immediately – bi sura!' Tutting and shaking his head. 'Only seven, terrible, terrible. If we waste one day it will be double amputation.'

No one was ignored but all the time he was shuffling towards the entrance, managing to arrive when the last petitioner had his answer. We now took even longer in our arrival. Sergei had been away for a few days and not only that, he had a visitor with him. There were many hands to be shaken and questions answered. I was introduced to the hospital director and sat in his office waiting for Sergei to call me.

The door was open all the time and a stream of people wandered in and out, some to look at me or sit and chat, others to see the director. A youth in a gaudy yellow futa escorted his aged mother to the desk. She was bent double with the years and her face was painted a startling yellow with the local anti-sun preparation. Over her orange long-sleeved undershirt she wore a brilliant yellow and green traditional dress tied at the waist with a red chiffon scarf whose ends touched the ground, and on her hands were tight black gloves trimmed with fur. A second woman wore the same but she had a tiara of blue tinsel. Everyone in fact had some unique touch about their clothes: amongst the men I could not spot two headscarves the same. An old man, in a stripy blazer that would have graced a Henley regatta and a futa that would not, came up to me and raised a finger: 'Tatatata-tata?'

I nodded. His hands turned palms up. 'Tatatata-tat.'

I smiled and he shook his head: his hands became hard flat spearheads that slashed the air. 'TATATATAT!' One eyebrow arched. 'Tata?' He made a cow's horns with forefinger and little finger, waggling them at me as he shuffled away.

The guard brought me a cup of tea. 'We must take qat today, shall we? I visited your country in 1990. Birming Jam. Oh, it was very nice. People were very helpful in the street if you were lost, and they even brought letters to the sheikh's house. I stayed with him and every day I saw it happen with my own eyes. There was a small door in the door of his house and letters came through it every morning. Then the sheikh would open and read them. It was a wonderful thing.'

The old man in the stripy blazer came back. His right hand made a steep dive, attacking his knee. 'Tatatatata!!'

'He has a problem and cannot speak,' explained the guard. 'But he is telling you about when the British bombed his house. It was in the 1930s.'

'Does he hate the British, then?'

'By God, of course not. They dropped warnings before the planes came. Very honourable men. He loves the British – we all loved them as they fought as honourable men. But they never conquered our land. Nobody has done that.'

I smiled at the old man who was watching us questioningly as we spoke then I brought my hand down from high, making gun noises. He sighed deeply and grabbing my hand, pumped it up and down warmly with a huge grin. 'Tatatatat!' So it was that an aerial bombardment became a point of human contact some sixty years later. He ambled out the door with that knees-splayed flat-footed mountain man walk that somehow makes progress on level ground look more arduous than up a 5,000-foot cliff.

The guard went out, too, confiscating a Kalashnikov from a youth of about thirteen. There was no problem, the lad was quite happy to lodge the weapon with all the others in the corner behind the director's desk. In Yemeni tribal law some places have a sacrosanct status, places within which it would be an enormous dishonour to violate the peace. Traditionally, markets and mosques have such a status, but in Yafa it had been extended, and never once broken, to the hospital.

For patients and their families, getting an audience with the director was not a matter of queueing or appointments. Newcomers simply pushed into the knot of people around the desk, shaking hands and kissing cheeks, then thrusting forward bits of paper or placing them over the one the director was in the process of reading. There was nothing especially rude about this, quite the reverse; rudeness would be coming in and hovering silently. But the country folk, the dusty-footed farmers with jackets out at the elbow and their tiny bent-backed wives whose faces rose like yellow moons from under their scarves, these people were more diffident. I could see their eyes flicker across the group, searching for a relative or friend. Such a person could then be relied on to ease them through to the front and intercede on their behalf. Without family and friends you were lost, forced to tip an orderly to help.

Sergei returned, but not in his gown. 'We have no electricity, so I cannot make operation. Come – I will show you.'

We toured the wards which were clean and tidy but obviously lacking in anything except basic equipment, and that was old and delapidated. 'One time I went to Aden and my Russian friend there gave me a sub-clavial catheter,' said Sergei. 'He had one to spare, by chance. When I arrived here, a girl was lying on the stretcher. She was ten years old and had been shot by accident in the abdomen in a village nine miles away. You remember that last road yesterday? Well, believe me, that is the best road here. How she survived I don't know. When I saw her she had no pulse and no pupil dilation. I pulled the catheter from my pocket and put it in immediately – to give her blood. Then we stitched up the liver, the small intestine and the stomach. We got the bullet out and she lived. Without that catheter, she had no chance.'

We stopped at a bed and he examined a blood stained bandage around a young man's knee. 'Bullet wound.' He indicated the top of his knee and bottom. 'What goes up must come down, yes? Someone fired into the air and the bullet came back down through the kneecap. It is not too serious. He will walk.'

Yemen is one of the most heavily armed societies on earth and yet there is a sense of safety and security you do not feel when in many European cities. I had often tried to explain that to people before, but following Sergei around I saw that there was a human cost and one frequently paid by the innocent. I emerged from the hospital feeling as though I had been through a war zone.

We walked through the souk, an open space where pick-up trucks were piled high with oranges and old women were selling onions. Sergei had a Yemeni friend he wanted me to meet and we found him in a small office, working on some business accounts. Yahya was a small round man with the face of cherub and a gleaming bald pate. He had trained in Russia and Sergei's relief at the chance to slip away from the strain of speaking English was palpable. We went next door into a tea-shop and they chatted in Russian about Sergei's trip while we drank tea from cups and saucers and ate chips with ketchup. The owner, Yahya explained, had worked in Sheffield many years before and picked up English habits. The tea however was Arab: black, sweet and heavily spiced. When we came to leave, my money was refused: another customer had already paid and left.

'We will chew qat this afternoon,' said Yahya. 'I know a good place.'

Sergei returned to the hospital and we went over to the qat-sellers who were selling the goods from the back of trucks. Each had a simple hand-held balance with two pans which they loaded: one with five large batteries, the other with qat.

'Kam tishti?' they demanded. 'Rotul?'

It was the first time I had seen qat sold by weight, and not only that but by the pound – the rotul being an ancient measure equivalent to a pound whose ancestry goes back to the Greeks and Phoenicians. Elsewhere in Yemen it has largely been ousted by the kilogramme, but not in Yafa.

We took a pound each but it was disappointing stuff: large tough green leaves hiding tiny shoots. Some qat-eaters like this type, it can be stronger than others, almost as if the active ingredient is more concentrated in the tiny leaves. But for me it was too fiddly and too difficult to judge the quantity of usable material. Yahya was adamant that he would pay. 'You are our guest – will you shame me with your money in front of these people?' I put the notes away reluctantly, consoling myself with the thought that everyone had seen his generosity and I had done my bit in buying qat for large numbers of people in Harar.

As we returned across the market, we were stopped by a small middle-aged man. I was immediately struck by his eyes: they were black and heavily kohl-rimmed with an engaging hypnotic quality to his gaze. His hair, oiled and equally black, curled out from under a tightly-wound white headcloth.

'Hello,' he said in English. 'Are you Britishman?'

I nodded. Yahya, I noticed, was already a few feet away, as if in a hurry.

'I worked for the British in Aden,' the man said. 'My name is Idris. Will you take qat with me this afternoon?'

I looked at Yahya. The fact that the man had worked in Aden interested me. Yahya made a gesture as though to say, 'It's your decision.' There was also the guard at the hospital to consider and at least two other members of staff who had mentioned qat sessions. But reasoning that Yemenis are generally relaxed about such things, I agreed to go to Idris's.

He nodded. 'Good. Come at three o'clock, Yahya knows the house.'

When we resumed our walk to the hospital, however, Yahya seemed a little put out by my decision. 'I had spoken to another friend – but don't worry, I will see you at Sergei's apartment at 2.45, okay?'

He left me to go back to his office and I dropped my qat at the apartment, wondering if I had committed a blunder and knowing that I would probably never be sure.

I was keen to see something of the countryside around the village and also survey the land to the north for possible routes. There were no vehicle tracks – that I had been told already – but Yahya had mentioned that before the road had been built, people had walked north-west to Dhala, a three-day march. 'No one does that now,' he had added. 'You should take the taxi back to Habilain, then another to Dhala or to San'a.'

I had not tried to explain why I did not care for that idea: that going back along the same route would be like a failure, that I wanted to go beyond the reach of the motor car to the wildest places. I set off through the village towards the low mountains to the north. From there, I reasoned, I would get a good look at the land.

It was mid-morning and the sun was well up, but the shadows remained chilly. I wandered through the alleyways between houses, then crossed a low area of terraces where the qat trees were covered with rags to protect them from frost. Lizards skittered away into the stone walls. The land was dry and only a few people were around to do the work: cutting the dry stalks of sorghum or ploughing. Men waved at me, but the women hid their faces. In the far distance I could hear the irregular rattle of small arms fire and an occasional explosion, but no one paid any attention.

It took a couple of hours to reach the summit of the peak. Then a vast panorama opened up before me. The land fell sharply away to a deep valley through breathtaking sweeps of terraces, some stacked over one hundred tall. The bottom could not be seen, however, because there was a kind of double valley: the land scooped down and projected as a wide ledge on which villages were perched. Beyond these was a bluish haze and a second precipitous drop. A few miles and many hours walk beyond, the far side of the valley rose up, a black featureless wall on which I could see no sign of human life. Beyond that lay further and further ranges of similar ridges, all running east-west. I knew that this first deep gorge had to be Wadi Bana, one of the great valleys of South-West Arabia which skirts Yafa along the northern and western sides.

There seemed only one possible pass through this impressive natural barrier. Far to the west, close to where the massif of the Yafa mountains blocked any further view, was a place where the rock wall was streaked with red. There I thought I could see a slight difference in the rock, an oblique line separating two minutely different gradations of grey. It was possible that this marked a side wadi entering the main course of Bana. Whatever the route, I could see that the walk was a serious undertaking.

I scrambled back down from the summit and found a path along some terraces where a farmer and his wife were spreading fertiliser.

'Are you the Russian doctor?' he called.

'No, I'm British but I am staying with the doctor.'

'And where are you going, O Britani?'

I told him why I had been on the mountain and he clicked his tongue.

'That way is not good,' he said. 'There is a long walk to some hot springs at Hammam. From there it is also bad. You will die if you take this route. Do you have a gun?'

'I do not need a gun as I am guest in your country and have no dispute with anyone.'

'That is true,' he said. 'But the Great Satan lays many traps. There are wild animals: tigers, hyaenas, snakes and scorpions. Also bandits who will prefer to kill you lest you live to recognise them. And water is very scarce in that region. It is likely you will succumb to thirst and hunger as you do not know where to find anything. Then the animals will eat your body and no one will be able to bury you according to your customs as should be done. Only the bedu live there because they know the manner of survival. If you find those men, it may be you can live. But you will not find them as nobody knows where they will be.'

'Yes, but apart from the wild animals, the bandits, the thirst and the hunger, is it a safe route?'

He began to laugh with me. 'By God! One hundred per cent safe – excepting in those things.'

'And where is the place to take the path?'

'You must ask others about that. I have never travelled that way, nor do I wish to. Take my advice and go by car from here to Habilain.'

I said I probably would but his admission that he had never actually travelled the route himself had cheered me. All he had told me might be nothing more than hearsay and exaggeration, not to be credited with any great reliability. This was the big test, I told myself: would it be the wilderness ahead or the ignominious retreat along the road? As I walked back to the hospital I began to develop a bloody-minded attitude about going north, an attitude that would be sorely tested in the following days. I saw Ralph, the American anthropologist, in his rainbow braces going home in disillusion when he had not even bothered to walk over the border into Zaire and see the bizarre and wonderful sights it offered, allowing his great romantic myth of remote people to wither and die for want of effort. And there was something more, too: that precipice with vast expanse of smoky ridges beyond . . . It was as though in reaching the end of Yafa I had reached the end of everything. I had the same feeling that I had had as a child of six standing on the very edge of the Dorset cliffs. I wanted to throw myself off.

My thoughts were interrupted by the realisation that the sporadic gunfire had now become constant; the volleys of Kalashnikovs were being answered by the deep hacking cough of a heavy machine gun. By the time I reached the hospital apartments, I was convinced some sort of tribal war had begun.

Sergei was in the kitchen. 'Ach, Kevin. Good. I have cooked Russian soup for you. Let us eat.'

'Wonderful! Thank you Sergei, but what about the guns? What's happening?'

He paused over the stove, a spoonful of soup poised for testing, listening carefully. 'Guns? Oh, that. It is normal here. Every day is like this. They shoot for any reason and no reason. I don't mind unless they use my roof to shoot from when I am having a siesta. Then I go and tell them to stop.' He poured out two bowls of vegetable soup and added some boiled chicken.

[211]

'Usually it is weddings when they like to fire, and they always manage to shoot somebody. One wedding gave me four operations.'

We went through into the living room and ate. 'By the way,' he said when I told him about my morning's walk, 'it is not safe to do that. If you ask a woman the direction, her husband may see you from the house and shoot. You must ask me and I will arrange for someone to go with you when you walk.'

'But I hardly saw anyone, and very few women.'

'Many houses are empty, as the people like to go away to find work. Here, especially in this village, most houses are empty. Plus there are many problems. Before the communists were strong here, now it is the turn of the fundamentalists. There are many changes. Those who were down are up, and those who were up are now down. It is the way, like everywhere.'

He yawned. 'Now I will take my siesta and the shooting, inshallah, will stop.'

He went to his room and I waited for Yahya. As the time approached three, the gunfire died away: most men were settling down with their qat.

Yahya arrived carrying a large vacuum flask of qishr, a futa for me to wear and a pack of cigarettes for me. 'We'll buy water on the way,' he said.


Idris's house was a typical seven-storey tapering tower which, from below, looked immensely tall. He greeted us warmly, dressed in a white zenna, tied with a broad leather belt full of bullets.

'Come and look at something,' he said, leading us across the lime-washed courtyard and under a peach tree. There was a large grey stone with some wavery white quartz running through it. 'Do you see?' He traced the lines and I realised that they spelt out 'Allah' in Arabic.

'Where did it come from?'

He took me to a spot where we could see over his yard wall and pointed to the mountain where I had walked that morning. 'There – near the Himyari ruins on top of that mountain, where you went this morning.' He gave a secret smile and led me back to Yahya.

Our session was to be in a side room, separate from the main house. These annexe qat rooms, or diwan, saved guests from any potential embarrassment, namely seeing a woman of the family without her veil.

Contentment. Reclining on cushions, smoking a hookah with cheek full of qat.

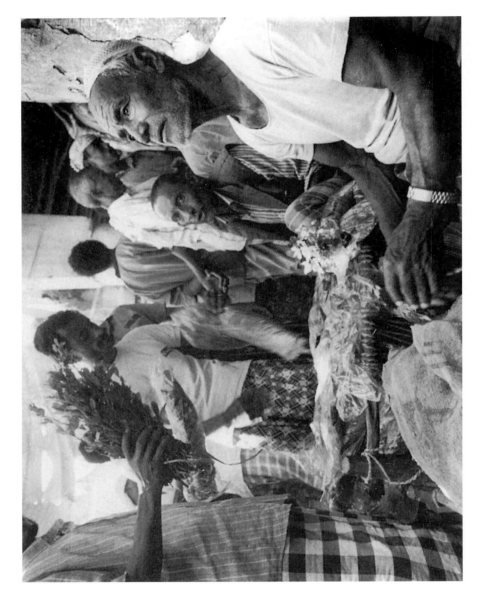

Qat market in al-Khowkha on the Red Sea coast. The sellers sit on rope-strung beds with the bundles protected from the sun by damp sacking and plastic.

Shopkeeper chewing qat outside his lock-up in Sukhnah. Popular wisdom in Yemen is that better bargains are to be had earlier in the afternoon before introspection and melancholy sets in.

Qat-runners taking bundles to outlying villages on Jebel Bura.
In the background, below the village, are qat terraces.

In the old city of San'a, heading off to a session laden with bundles of Dhula'i qat, each carefully cocooned in pink plastic and with a bottle of mineral water on the handlebars.

The city of San'a, looking over Talha mosque.

A salta restaurant in San'a. Only served at lunchtime, the frothing, green delight is a San'a speciality requiring an alchemist rather than a chef.

The once magnificent merchants' houses of Hodeidah are crumbling and neglected, held together it seems only by a web of electrical wires.

They undoubtedly saw us, however, peeping through the upper windows where there were tiny corner shutters for just such a purpose.

The diwan was cave-like with a roof of stone slabs laid on beams and pale green walls. Two windows gave some light and showed the walls to be almost a metre thick. There was a cupboard recess with wooden doors, a hookah pipe and cushions on three sides. We hung our jackets on large iron hooks above our heads and sat down in one corner. Yahya clicked his tongue in annoyance, 'We forgot to buy water – well, just drink the qishr, there is plenty.'

But Idris came in with bottles of mineral water. 'Here,' he said. 'It is special water, quite safe, I prepare it myself.'

'You have a well in the house?'

He just smiled. Yahya put his to one side. 'I only drink qishr with qat – really.' It was all very polite and the significance of it only struck me later.

A third guest came in and we stood to shake hands. Men often kiss cheeks on greeting old friends but Idris and Yahya restricted themselves to a smack of the lips, a sort of symbolic kiss. I did likewise.

The visitor was a young man with an unhealthy yellow complexion and deep-set eyes that burned with feverish intensity. He settled himself next to me but scarcely spoke for the next three hours.

'He is sick,' Idris said in English. 'In his mind.'

We began to pick our qat. It was far better than I had expected, but the ambience of a room can often help and this one was perfect: dimly-lit, warm and convivial. Qat rooms are always about nine to twelve feet wide, sufficient to allow space for access down the centre and for pipes, water pots and piles of qat sticks. The drug acts on the body's temperature control, sometimes causing sweats but generally cooling down: my feet are unusually susceptible and have often had to be wrapped in a blanket, even in ninety degrees of heat. Although most reactions are less extreme, rooms are kept closed, especially in cold mountain areas, but ventilation is still necessary with hookah pipes and cigarettes going. In Yafa the smaller secondary shutters allow air flow without causing draughts.

Idris's pipe bubbled gently, Yahya sipped his qishr. We chatted about the British and their rule. Idris had gone to Aden as a young man in the 'fifties but had soon been politicised against the colonial government.

'What job did you do?' I asked.

He gave his sorcerer's smile. 'By day I worked in a laundry and by night I shot British soldiers.'

He had joined the underground movement, the National Liberation Front, and as a young firebrand was quickly involved in violent protests.

'One night we went out to Little Aden, walking silently along the shore. Then we planted explosives under the oil pipeline. Some others had gone up to the settlement nearby and began to shoot. This was our signal. We triggered the charge and escaped by mixing with all the people running from the settlement. The bomb caused an enormous fire.'

I wondered if it was the same explosion that Aden Governor William Luce had discounted as 'crude', but Idris was not sure about the date.

'The British became very tough then. They had a regiment, we called them, al-zenawat, "the bastards"'. They wore a long tail of hair from their caps.' I assumed he was talking about the Argyll and Sutherland Highlanders whose tours of duty in Aden led to many controversies.

'They made any young men line up – the line stretched from Mualla to Crater, all standing with their hands on their heads. I was beside one man who was chewing tobacco and he reached in his shirt pocket to get some more. A soldier turned round and shot him dead.' His eyes glittered. 'But not all the British were bad – actually, we liked the ordinary soldiers. Many would wear futas and take qat with us.'

I asked about the aerial bombing of villages in Yafa.

'You see Yafa was a problem for them. It produced many fighters and from Yafa they could go to Dhala, Beidha, Lahej and Lawdar very easily. But the British could not get into Yafa. It is protected by deep valleys and mountains. So they sent planes: when I was a boy my village was bombed.' He paused to draw on the hookah pipe and frowned because it was almost finished. 'They dropped a paper saying we should leave, so we went to some caves above the village. Then the planes came and destroyed the houses. I remember one old man became very angry and rushed out with his rifle. By chance he shot down a plane – it crashed over in Wadi Ihyar. We lived in the caves for a month in case they came back.'

Like the man at the hospital, the years had softened any rancour but the undeniable fact was that following the bombing he had gone to Aden and become a freedom fighter.

The policy of aerial bombing started in 1937 as a punitive measure for highway robbery but by the late 'fifties was a means to control 'dissidents'. According to the British these were outsiders, trouble-makers, sent across the leaky frontier from North Yemen, particularly via Yafa. The possibility that the enemy was within could not be contemplated.

The memos sent back and forth on the topic between various governors and Colonial Office officials are striking for their bland arrogance. 'When such punishment becomes necessary,' wrote Sir Bernard Reilly in 1959, 'it is inflicted in as just and humane a way possible.' Another official explains to London that a woman who was collecting water from a well had been killed by 'mischance' when 24,000 pounds of bombs fell on her and her village.

No one in Idris's village had been killed but resentment had spilled over against the man seen as the British stooge: the Sultan of Upper Yafa. The silent third guest, Saleh, was moved to speak when the Sultan was mentioned.

'He left by helicoptor in 1967,' he told me in a low voice. 'And it was he who had called the British to bomb his enemies in Yafa – so people hated him.'

Idris stood up. 'I will bring a fresh pipe – do you want anything?'

I shook my head. Yahya followed Idris outside.

'Did you see any bombing?' I asked Saleh who was leaning back gazing at the roof. His forehead was covered in tiny beads of sweat.

'I am of the family – the Sultan's family. It is because of this that I know what happened. The British took him by helicoptor to Aden.'

'But you did not go?'

'His children went but not us. We stayed and things were very difficult after 1967. For many years I told no one who I was – none of those officials. If they knew I would have been killed.'

This had some credence as relatives of the Sultan had been assassinated.

'People here do not like government – any government,' he said. 'In Labus there is a cassette shop and most of the music is songs, poems about politics, protesting about government. I can remember when the pro-British sultan was here, a poet sent him a verse.' He frowned trying to recall.

> Your grandmother must now leave the port,
> Her time is passed, she is aged and mad,

And you who are sick with grief and woe,
Then London is your cure, so go now, go.

He wiped a hand across his forehead. 'In Aden they were about to send the Sultan to London but before it could happen someone killed him.'

Yahya returned and Saleh lapsed into silence once again. Idris brought in the smoking earthenware cone that holds the tobacco and fitted it onto the pipe. We sat quietly, listening to the sound of him drawing on it. I was relaxed, the qat was good. There is a point in any session when the world stands back. The outside is forgotten, scarcely seems to exist. At that moment there is a feeling of cameraderie and shared experience that is rarely disrupted by any doubts: they come later, the petty suspicions and paranoias that creep out of the shadows as the qat recedes from the mind. But even then, content as I was, I felt something niggling away at me, some vague uneasiness and it became stronger when Yahya, taking the chance of Idris and Saleh talking, leant closer and whispered: 'He is sick, this man Saleh. I mean in his psychology and Idris is trying to cure him. But for me, a man who trained in Russia, I cannot accept such things. I am a scientist.'

I had no clear idea of what he was talking about but I began to understand that each of the three had their sympathies in radically different places to the others.

As the sun set, Idris rose and lit an oil lamp. I asked him for the bathroom.

'Do you want light or heavy?'

'Er . . . light.'

He showed me through a door at the far end into a small bathroom. There was a tub of water and two foot blocks. The urine went out of a small hole at the base of the wall in front. The 'heavy' bathroom would be in the main house. The system of separating solid and liquid wastes is used all over Yemen: the solid stuff drying rapidly in the thin air before it is burnt and the ashes spread as fertiliser.

When I went back to the others, Yahya was getting ready to leave.

'It is time we should go, Kevin.'

But Idris would not hear of it. 'Yahya has work but for you there is no reason to leave. Stay and we will discuss more things. Is not the qat a good thing – bringing us to talk together like old friends? And when will we ever

[216]

have the chance again? Stay. The way to the doctor's house is easy to find when it is time – I will show you.'

And I felt he wanted to speak to me about something that he could not, or would not, mention in front of Yahya and, curious, I wanted to know what that might be. So I chose to stay and Yahya said goodbye.

Some time passed before Idris got up and opened the cupboard. He took out an attaché case, a cassette player and a set of headphones. Then he unravelled the wires carefully and placed the headphones on Saleh. He had stood up, ready for what was to happen, removing his belt so he was dressed only in shirt and futa. Idris took his hands and placed them, hand over hand on the belly, in the position of Muslim prayer. Then he took the man's shaven head in his hands and bringing it close to his mouth blew sharply three times in each ear. Saleh closed his eyes. Idris selected a tape and inserted it in the dusty machine.

The connection between headphones and cassette was faulty, some noise spilled out and I could hear quite clearly that this was a recording of Koranic verses being chanted by a group of men. Saleh started to sway slightly.

Idris sat down and began to smoke his pipe. In the gloom, with his black eyebrows and wild black hair, there was something almost demonic about him. After some minutes he flicked the catches on the case and took out a photograph.

'I want you to see that there are things . . . You do not understand everything, nor does any man. This man has been sick for four years: he went to every doctor, took many tests and tablets. None has done any good. And why?'

He passed the photograph across. It took some time to work out what was meant to be there: red swirling colours surrounded two dark holes and straddled between them was a shape, a white creature without a nose but with burning red eyes and elongated fingers. The feet were dog's paws.

'That is a photograph of a jinni, a devil, taken with these new instruments that can go inside a person's body.'

Two things struck me about this photograph: the first was that the head of the demon was remarkably like the sort of shape people habitually give aliens, whether they be film directors or those who claim to have been abducted by UFOs: that lack of nose and hair combined with pointy head and ears seems to be universal. The second thought was more disquieting: it concerned a distant memory of a childhood game of hide-and-seek and an airing cupboard door that got jammed and the small figure of an old man in a tight black suit sitting inside. I can remember the red malevolent eyes and the whitened hand that came scuttling like an insect across the neat pile of flannelette sheets towards me as I crashed out into the hall with a scream. No one ever believed my story of the bogey man in the cupboard, but I was careful never to go near it again.

Idris took the photograph back and passed me two sheets of paper covered in strange writing. Some words were recognisably Spanish but there were Arabic and Greek letters floating through a crazed jumble of stars and symbols.

'These are written by a man with a jinni inside – like Saleh.'

He took back the papers and replaced them carefully in his case. It was as if he was a salesman on a home visit, showing me charts of startling returns on investment; he had the same Messianiac gleam, a desire to convince.

'What can men know of these things? What does a man like Yahya know? He does not believe it is possible. But you, Kevin, you have a mind that is open.'

And I nodded enthusiastically, but I was wondering if I wanted to stay after all, whether I was caught up in some strange power play between Idris and Yahya. And I was wondering what was going to happen.

The answer, at least for the following hour, was very little. Saleh listened to his tapes. Idris prayed, then he and I talked and smoked the hookah pipe. Outside dogs were fighting, a moth came in and began to batter itself against the lamp.

Then Saleh groaned. Idris was across to him in an instant, lifting the headphones off his ears to speak. 'Where? Where is it?' Saleh pointed to his left calf. The headphones were replaced and a stick fetched from a place above the door. It was about the size of the blade from a rowing scull. Gently at first, Idris began to beat Saleh's calf, as if he were swatting a very inoffensive fly. But Saleh called for more power and the blows got harder, and harder. I sat there, next to them, still idly picking my qat from the bag, with my right knee up and elbow resting on it, apparently a man at total ease in the latter stages of a qat dream. I probably had that expression the

Royal Family have when something spontaneous happens in public: a sort of encouraging but glassy smile.

Idris stopped briefly to tie a bootlace around the top of Saleh's shin, tight enough to pinch what little flesh the man had. After five more minutes the beating stopped. Saleh fell to his knees and put his head against the wall. Idris sat down, slightly out of breath.

'I am not beating him,' he said, 'but the jinni. He cannot feel anything. The jinni is inside and we beat it. We force it to hear the word of God and the jinni hates it. He runs inside the man. He is burning up with it. Sometimes he runs to his face and you will see another face, not Saleh's. When he was brought to me, I whispered the words of the Koran in his ear. Immediately he fell down with terrible shaking. When he recovered, he could remember nothing. I knew then that there was a jinni inside him.'

Saleh let out a deep sigh and Idris smiled and raised a finger, a doctor recognising a symptom. He led the patient gently to the end of the room nearer the lantern. Saleh was having difficulty with his breathing, short gasps punctuated with awful halts. He pointed to his back and Idris told him to take off his shirt. His skin was completely smooth, hairless and unblemished, like a child's. Idris began to beat him up and down the spine with rapid chops of the hands, fingers slightly apart. After some minutes he stopped and turned Saleh back to the wall. He was now on my other side, between me and the lamp.

'There are four types of jinni,' said Idris, 'and this is a very bad one, very very bad. Once a patient of mine urinated a huge worm and it wriggled out under the door. That was the jinni.'

I did not believe that for one second, I was totally rational, totally calm and determined to see what I saw, nothing more. I discovered that my left hand was gripping the edge of my futa so tightly my fingers ached. I made myself let go and relax. Saleh began to slap his back and Idris leapt up, grabbing the stick to pummel him. There were no marks, not even a darkening of Saleh's yellow skin. This beating went on and on. Sweat poured from Idris and he was breathing hard. After half an hour he shouted to me, 'Come on! Get up! Hit him!'

I took the stick and started to strike the lower back.

'No, no, no,' said Idris. 'Hard!'

[219]

I redoubled my efforts, drawing the stick well back and bringing it down with all my strength.

'Harder!' cried Idris. I could not imagine how anyone's ribs could take such blows, let alone show no reaction. It was exactly as if I was striking a sandbag. There was no sound from Saleh, no mark on the skin, nothing. With twenty such blows I was panting; after forty I was tiring. I counted another twenty and held the stick out for Idris. I was exhausted, unaccustomed to the thin air, or to beating people.

Idris dropped the stick and helped Saleh lie down. He took a bottle of water and splashed a little on the man's back. Using his heel, he worked it into the skin, moving up and down his back. Then a bottle of oil was fetched and this dripped along Saleh's spine. Idris stood on the man and massaged it in with both feet. This done, he lifted Saleh up to his feet and put his shirt back on.

But the man could not stand and had to be sat on two cushions. His face was black and clenched in pain. An hour or two earlier, I reflected, I might have said he was suffering from a mild case of dyspepsia, a slight fever; he had certainly been perfectly rational. Idris changed the tape and the chanting became more urgent, more intense, an endless repetition of the same verse that caught like a scratched record on one particular line: 'Wa ulqiya al-saharatu sajideen' over and over again. This was from the chapter 'The Heights', in which Moses defeats the spells of Pharaohs' sorcerers and, recognising his superior power, they throw themselves down and pledge themselves to the God of Moses.

Idris was leaning towards his patient, sparkling eyes never leaving the man's face. Saleh's forehead was deeply furrowed and now those furrows began to move. In the low light and shadows it was as if they were emerging from a point between his eyes and slowly wriggling up onto his scalp like drugged worms. His back arched, forcing his head lower and lower until it was below his knees. Strange grunts and yelps came from him. There was another noise too: at first I thought it was feedback through the faulty plug connecting the headphones to the cassette player. But Idris cocked his ear, 'Listen – it is him – the devil.' And I realised that it was not feedback at all, but the howl of a human being on the very edge of insanity. It was coming from the machine itself. Then Saleh slumped forward onto the mattress and Idris grabbed him. 'Quick! Take his shoulders!'

[220]

I caught hold and to my surprise his skin was cold. We pulled him into a kneeling position and Idris poured some water down his throat. Once he opened his eyes and they were fixed on me. It was a look both implacably hostile and remote, far beyond communication. Idris got an armrest cushion and gently brought Saleh's forehead down to lie there. He was in a foetal position and quiet.

'Go and spit out your qat,' said Idris, 'while he is like this.'

When I came back from the bathroom, somebody had brought a small pan full of bread soaked in milk and sugar. This was lahuh, the staple diet of Yafa. We ate our supper next to the curled-up silent figure.

'There are people here who criticise my work,' said Idris. 'But I do this for nothing, for no money. If money is involved, it will not work. Sometimes I treat people only with oils or local medicines that I get from the plants and animals. Not every patient will respond to this. But for some, like this poor man, it is the only way.'

'Have you done this for many nights?'

'Yes, and we may not finish tonight. I will try for forty-eight nights. If there is no success, then only God knows what is best.'

We washed our hands and drank a glass of tea. Saleh had started to pound his fist into the sole of his foot with great, walnut-cracking blows. Idris went over and lifted his head. 'Where is he?'

There was a grunted answer. Idris bound up his knee with the lace then began more beating with the stick, frequently stopping to ask, 'Is there a pain in your head?' When he got no reply, he stopped the beating, untied the lace and removed the headphones. He took Saleh's head in his hands and lifted him into a standing position. His hands were massive, one completely covering the forehead, the other behind the ears into which he now blew three times. 'Bismillahi al-rahmani al-rahim . . . ' His voice was strong, an overpowering deep drone, delivered next to Saleh's ear. He went through the Fatiha, the first chapter of the Koran, and through the chapter 'The Heights'. But each time he paused at that same line, repeating it a hundred times, his voice driving like nail: 'Wa ulqiya al-saharatu sajideen. And the enchanters prostrated themselves,' until I could no longer think of anything, only hear that nasal voice and see those huge powerful hands gripping Saleh's head like a vice as the man sank, his knees breaking. Then the hands would force him up straight.

I was directly in front of Saleh. I could not see much of his face but I could see his shirt, held only with one button at his throat. My arms were trembling. There was a sound from Saleh, the sigh of water poured on scalding stones. And as he sighed, his shirt moved.

I was sitting on an armrest, sitting forward, unblinking. The shirt began to part and Saleh's stomach pushed out. It pushed out and out, beyond what could be done with muscles alone. His shirt hung down at his sides and his stomach kept expanding until it was that of a woman at the end of a pregnancy, a yellowy-white shiny dome of skin, pulled taut. Idris was watching it and his gaze flicked across to me. He gave a gentle nod. The words did not stop. Saleh gave a deep grunting cough, like a lion at night. His stomach went down again. The voice went on and the stomach expanded once more. I thought of Awzulkarnein and the man in Harar who had vomited his dangerous knowledge into the hole from which the qat tree grew. But Saleh did not vomit. The wall of his stomach gave little writhing movements, twitches, it became pointed and stretched again until I thought the skin would simply burst, an obscene fruit bloated and rotten no longer able to contain what lurked inside. Idris's voice was faster now and Saleh's neck strained to twist his head away but the powerful hands were inescapable and the voice had to be heard: wa ulqiya al-saharatu sajideen, wa ulqiya al-saharatu sajideen, wa ulqiya al-saharatu sajideen.

Then Saleh coughed again, that same deep cough and his stomach shrivelled away and Idris glanced across at me. I had unconsciously moved back and was pressing myself against the wall. The tension had gone from Idris's arms and his face told me that we had failed. He intoned the words: 'Qalu amana bi rabb al-amin. Rabb Musa wa Haroun. Saying we believe in the Lord of the Universe, the Lord of Moses and Aaron.' The last syllable drawn out then cut off. The hands released Saleh's head. For just an instant there was something peaceful about him, the lines had gone from his forehead. Then the eyes flipped open again with that same haunted stare. Idris turned to me and shook his head. 'Rest now,' he told Saleh. 'Rest until dawn, then you must drink the preparation I gave you. But for now, rest.'

Idris tidied up his things, locking the case in the cupboard. I put on my jacket and we went out into the starlit night. There was no moon. He led me along the edges of terraces, telling me where to put my feet. It was bitterly cold with a strong wind blowing. We both wrapped our scarves tight around our heads. Some dogs howled but we did not see them.

Outside the hospital apartment block we stopped.

'It is tiring work for you,' I said.

'For me, yes, but Allah,' his finger jabbed heavenwards, 'Allah is never tired.'

His arm came over my shoulder affectionately and his face turned to me. There was something almost menacing in those black eyes.

'Kevin. There are many things that you cannot understand, I only want you to see that. In Yemen, you travel, and you meet many people. A man may greet you as a friend. Some may invite you into their house and they will say, "Come, drink tea." And you may take that glass of tea and drink from it. But that person may be a sorcerer and in the glass may be a curse. Be careful, my friend.' He gave my shoulder a friendly squeeze, then stood back. 'I will see you again before you leave.'

He turned and walked away into the night. Only his white headcloth was visible, floating along the terrace wall, then disappearing.

I stood there looking at the stars. I could hear his words 'in the glass may be a curse' and I was thinking of all the glasses of tea I had been given on my journey so far.

I went inside and climbed the steps towards Sergei's door but halfway up, I stopped dead. Yahya. I felt the cold tingling of the night wind as it rose in the stairwell. Yahya had drunk his own thermos flask of qishr. He had drunk qishr and refused all else. And he had tried to get me to do the same. But Idris had come with his 'special water', his water that he prepared himself, the water that Yahya had specifically avoided touching, just as he had avoided smoking Idris's pipe, just as he had avoided accepting his qat – the qat, the pipe, and the water which I had blithely taken.

From somewhere far off there was a crackle of gunfire. I stood in front of Sergei's door and said to myself: 'It only works if you believe it.'

The door was open and Sergei was sitting in the living room, listening to Radio Moscow on a portable radio.

'Kevin! Come, I have something to share with you.'

He held up a glass of dark liquid. 'This was a present from a patient and today it is my daughter's birthday, so we will drink to her health.'

I took the glass and sniffed it. 'Cinzano?'

'Unfortunately, it is not vodka.'

'No, no, it's fine.' I told him what had happened and he roared with laughter.

'Superstition. What nonsense! Come we will drink.'

I raised my glass to my lips and tasted the sweet liquid.

'Nastrovya!'

He grinned. 'You are not a Yafa'i yet, Kevin, not yet. Cheers!'

I did not tell him that, against my better judgement, I had inspected the bottom of the glass and found written there, not without some relief, the comforting words, 'Made in China'.

# 16

Over the next few days I took qat with various people and accepted invitations from dozens of others. The war which had begun on my arrival continued unabated, and unnoticed by anyone else. I went with a friend of Sergei's by car to look at the old border where it came southwards on the eastern edge of the Yafa plateau. On the way we passed the old Socialist Party headquarters, newly taken over by the Islah Party, the Islamic fundamentalists.

The boundary between British and Ottoman empires had been fixed by the Anglo-Turkish border commission in 1913, and, ironically as it is now defunct, of all colonial boundaries it did have some topographical validity along this stretch. We stood on a hillside, looking across a vast deep valley whose bottom was out of sight to a rock wall several thousand feet high. This natural barrier marked the border for some distance, chosen because it was such a tremendous military obstacle for either side. Even here, however, there were plenty of crossing points and for the following seventy-six years, Yemenis from both sides steadfastly ignored the line. The Imams of the north, first Yahya, then his son Ahmed, would march across and snatch a bit of land; they would dispute a wording or interpret things differently, happily treating the fiction of the demarcation with the contempt it deserved. The British moustaches quivered with indignation. They drew the Violet Line, the Standstill Line and the Note Line but no one took much notice. There would be a skirmish and a face-off in some remote sector. Then memoranda and minutes would buzz around the Colonial Office, telegrams would be fired off, inviting all concerned.

Sultans and sheikhs would duly turn up, there would be fanfares, eleven-gun salutes and guards of honour. The meeting would go terribly success-fully, signatures would be gathered. The whole thing was cleared up. Then the Yemenis went back and had another skirmish.

Occasionally, a brave Englishman, a Wyman Bury, would dress up as a native and go over the line. For the less enterprising foreigner, the line on the map was as solid as a brick wall. During the communist era in the south, a visitor from the North wanting to step over would have had to travel to San'a, fly to London, take a flight to Aden, and travel back up to the border – a journey of some several thousand miles to go one step.

Now the border guardposts are gone, ripped away as if the authorities wanted to obliterate all memory of them. Likewise it is easy to presume the need for disguise is gone too: all the Burtons, the Wyman Burys and the last of their kind, Thesiger, they are not supposed to exist any more. But that would be a false assumption: there is more to disguise than false beards and indigo stains – words and silences can cloak the truth just as effectively.

In Yafa the rise of puritanical Islam had brought yet another dangerous cross-current to the choppy waters of tribalism, communism and capital-ism. Like Yahya and Idris, people circled each other warily, showing only a little of themselves at a time. People avoided positions and dogmatic state-ments; they felt their way forwards. They whispered clues to me when no one else was listening. And, like them, I did not push my questions too far, did not force anyone to draw a line in the sand and put us on opposite sides. There were forces and tensions here that I could only guess at. On Jebel Saber I had received religious lectures and come under pressure to declare my beliefs, but not here.


It was during a qat session with someone I met in the market that I heard about Jebel Khiyaal.

'It is our highest mountain,' he said, 'north-west from here. Let's visit one day, we can visit Abdullah – you will like to talk with him. He studied in Britain and now he is writing a history of Yafa. Maybe there people will tell you about the paths that go north, too.'

So I met them outside the hospital one morning, Ali and Muhammad, both dressed in camouflage jackets and armed with pistols. They had an ancient Landcruiser, the sort that Yemenis call habba, a car distinguished by its rounded styling – although this is very different roundedness to the 'eighties models of Landcruiser. Those are called Layla Alawi after the particularly shapely Egyptian actress. The 'nineties monsters with CD players and suchlike have yet to achieve a popular title, but I have heard them called 'The one whose bottom you touch', meaning the owner is so rich you have to kiss his arse.

Habbas are the donkeys of modern rural Yemen, buff-coloured and sturdy, capable of bouncing and thumping along endless tracks with great loads of people, qat and animals – I've even seen one with a camel strapped to the cab roof. Ali and Muhammad's habba was as country as Dolly Parton: the headlights had huge eyelashes painted around them, the cab was wreathed in hand-painted flowers and the interior luxuriously appointed with tasselled and sequinned velvet. When we got moving, I realised the character did not end there, years of duetting with large boulders had smitten the poor thing with sudden desires, notably the desire to hurl itself to the left without warning. So we took the track down from the market, occasionally leaping left and crashing. Ali and Muhammad thought it all hugely amusing and leaned out the windows, whooping with glee and firing into the air.

The track was either bare yellow rock or seas of white dust where boulders lurked. In this harsh and inhospitable environment men had scraped enough soil to make fields, ox-bows of pale brown earth, stepping down and down into unseen depths. Larger fields had their own stone-walled well where donkeys laden with jerry cans wrapped in sackcloth waited while water was pulled.

'You should come in summer,' said Ali. 'Then it is like a garden – now it is a desert.'

They pointed out a ruined house with a Star of David above the door. 'There were many Jews living here until 1948 – all mixed up with us. There was no segregation here. What fools they were to go to Israel when Yemen was their home!'

We passed a group of women. They had come up from a set of fields with leather bags full of brushwood on their backs, big loads that bent all of them double, but they still ran to hide from us, just a glimpse of a yellow face snatching a brief glimpse of the foreigner. It was like seeing a party of cowed slaves run from a cruel overseer.

'In past times,' said Ali, 'we had men and women very happy together. There were dances held when all the boys would form a line and the girls opposite and they would sing and dance towards each other then step away. It was very nice.

'Before the '94 war we were Socialist, but since then the fundamentalists are very powerful. For those people everything is haram: music, dancing, aeroplanes, qat, alcohol, even trousers! Once I went to chew qat at a house of a friend. It was far from the village and we took a car. When we reached there, we found a brother.' He stroked his chin to show a beard – all the fundamentalists wear beards. 'He was telling us everything was haram and America was using television for anti-Islamic propaganda. I asked him if cars were haram because America invented them and he said "Yes, definitely." When we came to leave, we gave everyone a lift except him. I shouted out the car window: "You will have to walk, my brother. To ride would be haram."' We all laughed.

'But he took qat?'

'Oh, yes. Not all of them say qat is haram. The Koran does not forbid qat, of course. Even for alcohol it says a man drinking in his own home should not be molested. If a man breaks in, his crime is greater. These people forget such things. Islam is not an intolerant religion.'

I asked how things compared with life under the communists.

'People say that there was no progress under the communists – as if progress is the only thing worth having. Now they see how much they have lost. Corruption is terrible, no one can live on their salary, so they are forced to be corrupt. Under communism there was no corruption here, so everyone feels the change.'

Already the process of forgetting the bad times had begun: the communist tyrannies, like those of the British, were receding from memory, leaving only a golden froth of pleasant recollections. But if Ali sounded nostalgic, when I put that to him, he recoiled.

'No! We would never accept communism again. We want change but not to go backwards.' He laughed. 'Don't you know they banned qat – except on Fridays? There is a story about it. First you must know that it happened in the 'seventies and our currency was the dinar and the fils. But the fils was almost worth nothing, even the smallest coin was ten fils and it could buy nothing. In Aden there was a rich merchant taking qat on a Monday with a girlfriend and they had an argument. She ran out and went to the police and told them the merchant was chewing qat – which was a crime. The police came and raided and took him to the police station.

'Now, what would happen these days. The rich man would pay, wouldn't he? But then the officers were straight. We had nizam – proper organisation.' It was a word I was to hear invoked time and time again in nostalgic tones. 'The rich man said, "Come on. Let me buy you something. Don't you know I'm a very wealthy man?" And the officer said, "Okay, you're rich, so please, give me one fils." Of course, for all his money he could not pay only one fils, there was no such coin. They sentenced him to two months in prison – one for the qat, another for the bribery.'

Ali and Muhammad roared with laughter and we crashed. This time puncturing a tyre. It was then I discovered all the tyres were down to the canvas, and we had no jack or spanners. There were no recriminations about this unfortunate lack of proper organisation: we went and sat in the shade of a lone acacia until such time as someone might come along, or the tyre magically reinflate itself.

'During '94 many people here went to fight against Ali Abdullah,' said Muhammad, referring to the President of unified Yemen and previously President of North Yemen. 'So we believe Yafa is unpopular now with central government.'

'Are there troops here who are not Yafa'is?'

He laughed. 'Istaghfir Allah! No, they cannot. All police and army here are Yafa people.'

We took out the qat that we had bought from the market – or rather, they had bought. I had tried very hard to pay, but they became almost aggressive about it. 'The guest is bound by the law of the host. Do not put shame on us!' Ali had said.

It was poor quality stuff, the prolonged dry cold wind was hitting the trees badly. Fortunately, Yafa farmers do not rely on the leaf as exclusively as in other areas. The sheer distance to the markets of Aden make it only profitable when the qat is good and plentiful in the summer months. This seasonality, combined with limited land and restrictive measures under communist government, keep the plantations relatively small and the crops diverse.

'During the time when Abdulfattah led the communists they tried to dig up qat trees,' said Muhammad. 'Not in Yafa – they never had enough power – but in Dhala. So the farmers used to sing,' he began in a high wailing tone:

O Abdulfattah! O Aristocrat!
You will die but not the qat!

He grinned. 'And he did die. He was shot by his own people. No one can take the qat tree away, you see. These farmers will kill you first. Just go down and try.' He pointed into the terrace. I jumped to my feet. 'Okay!'

'NO!' He grabbed me. They were both laughing. 'I am serious. They will do it.'

After an hour a friend of theirs came along and he had a spanner but no jack. We solved that by driving up onto a boulder, packing other stones under the axle and kicking the boulder out. Our spare tyre was so worn I could see the inner tube through the weave of the canvas. Further stoppages seemed likely. Fortunately there was a tyre repair joint further down the track: 'puncturi' the Yemenis call them. This one set up with earnings from Saudi: a breeze-block hut, a compressor and three boys, all completely caked in oil. Our tyre was repaired and the spare removed.

The landscape became more dramatic: a series of mountain crags standing apart from the main massif, outer bastions separated from each other by deep convoluted ravines that burrowed down towards Wadi Bana in shadows as dark as aubergines. Each of these mountain bastions was accessible only by a low saddle of land, connecting it to the main massif. It was towards one such saddle that we moved.

'We call it Shanghai,' said Ali, 'because they sell Chinese things there.' There were a few tin shacks, but the cornucopia of eastern merchandise turned out to be a meagre stock of flowery bedsheets.

From Shanghai a sudden and glorious view opened up to the south: vast folded mountains fading from blue to violet. To the north the prospect was less enjoyable: Jebel Khiyaal rose above us for about 1,500 feet and the track up to the village built at the top was all too clear.

'This road is no good,' said Ali, one of the few times I ever heard a
Yemeni driver admit such a thing. He slipped the car into four-wheel drive,
another rare occurrence, and took his shoes off. This was so he could grip
the pedals with his toes, the bouncing and leaping had become so bad that
his feet were shooting off at critical moments. Although not the steepest
or the most twisted of tracks, the Jebel Khiyaal ascent must be the most
bone-shattering. The wheels smacked down into holes, grabbed at the
stone, hauled us up, thumped up onto others, the sole consolation was that
the precipice was on our right and we tended to leap left. Coming down,
of course, would be different.

The villages were spread out amongst the craggy peaks of the summit
plateau, built around a few small patches of level ground where women
were gathered around wells. When they saw us they turned away, some ran
to hide.

Abdullah lived in a single-roomed stone hut on the far side where the
land seemed to come to an end. Beyond the last stone terrace edge there
was nothing but empty space. Clouds gathered below.

'It's the end of the world,' I said.

'That's why Abdullah is here,' Muhammad answered.

We walked along the edge to a second, larger house where they knew
Abdullah would be chewing. There were fingers of rock jabbing at the sky
and a few short terraces, like the scratches of a giant hand as it fell into the
void. Beside the house was a separate diwan, right on the edge of the
precipice. Muhammad and Ali pushed me forward. 'Go to the door and
shout, "Ya, Naradi!"'

So I appeared at the doorway, looking into a large, stone-roofed room,
well furnished with cushions and two men at the far end. I shouted.

The tall one leapt to his feet.

'Captain Haines! Captain Haines has come! Al-hamdu lillah!' Then Ali
and Muhammad were in the room and everyone was dissolving into laughter and kissing cheeks, while Naradi – apparently this was the taller man's
nickname – shouted about the welcome return of the founder of British
rule in Aden and grabbed things off the wall to give me. 'Hayya lek! Life be
with you! Memory of our mountain for you, take it, take it, Captain
Haines.' Which was how I came to be bearing several large geological
samples.

[231]

I was sat down between him and Abdullah, the smaller man in a home-made sheepskin waistcoat. But for an hour it was all Naradi. He was like a man possessed, raging with a madcap zest for life that had been bottled up at this outer limit of human settlement. He told me about ancient ruins on mountain-tops only accessible with ropes and unknown to all but him. He told me of artefacts he had found and reburied. 'If these fundamentalists see them they will destroy them.' He joked at everything and leapt up and ran outside four or five times to shout at the house: 'Captain Haines is here!' That brought a crowd of old men with black beards to sit and nod at me. And by dint of his energy and enthusiasm we forgot about our tiring journey and settled to our qat.

It was then I began to talk to Abdullah and learned that both men were indeed bottled up in self-imposed exile at this remote spot. Naradi had been a civil servant in Yafa but his steadfast socialist politics and complete inability to stop talking about them had brought him into trouble after the 1994 war. Refusing to kowtow, he had thrown it all up for 'the simple life'. Abdullah had a similar story. He had studied in Britain and become a rising star in a ministry in San'a. But when war broke out it was the last straw for him. The corruption and lack of progress had sapped his energy; he left for Aden and swore that if he survived the war he would go and live in the remote mountains where he had been born. So he had arrived in Jebel Khiyaal, built his own house and begun to research a book on Yafa history. He reminded me of Muhyadin in Harar, a prodigious intelligence sprung, as if by magic, from some backwater who goes on to conquer the capital, only to return home in disillusion and find new work there.

'Yafa has always exported its people,' he told me. 'You can find Yafa'is all over the world. My research shows that this happened long ago, too. The first Sabaeans and Himyaris came from here. Do you know the Chaldaeans from your Bible? They were Yafa'is.'

Somehow all the history of Arabia had become centred on Yafa and why not, I thought. This huge range of mountains produced people faster than it could feed them, so starting wave after wave of emigration.

'We are Yafa'i and no one can come here and take our land,' said one old man from across the pile of discarded qat. 'The British could not do it, nor the Ottomans, nor the Rasulids or anyone. In Yafa a man first wants a dagger, second a gun, then a wife and a house. But most important is the gun, without it you are as nothing – you will be blown like a dead leaf before the wind if you are without a gun.'

Abdullah told how guns had arrived in Yemen. 'There was a great Tahirid king who could control the jinnis. His name was Amir ibn Abdulwahhab.' I remembered the name: it was the same ruler who had ordered the mosque at Yufrus to be built.

'One night the King sent the jinn out to fetch him a beautiful girl,' Abdullah went on, the whole room listening intently. 'The jinn went to Cairo and found a Circassian princess – a Mamluk. He brought her back and the King ravished her. In the morning she woke up in Cairo and told her mother what had happened. The mother was angry but said she would believe the daughter if she could bring something from that place. Next night the jinn took her again and she took some of the King's qat.

'In Cairo this leaf was unknown, but finally a scholar identified it and said that it was a powerful drug from the land of Yemen. The Mamluks tried it and wanted more. So it was that the Mamluks decided to invade Yemen. And they did come and defeated Abdulwahhab. That was the first time guns arrived in Yemen.'

The story was fascinating as it bore some historical accuracy. The King certainly existed, ruling from 1472 until 1517. Not only that, but he was deposed by a Mamluk invasion in 1517 which succeeded largely because of its firearms.

The old men were nodding at Abdullah's story. 'It's true,' they said. 'It was qat they wanted from us.'

I asked Abdullah and Naradi about the possibility of walking north-wards until I reached the San'a road and could pick up a lift. Like everyone else, they were aghast. 'Walk! No. Take the car to Habilain. These paths are not used nowadays and difficult to find.'

But Abdullah admitted he had done the walk as a boy. 'You can start from Mauflehi and go down to Wadi Bana, but it is a difficult way and very hard for you. You have no companion, no gun, and no guide.'

They began to discuss it amongst themselves and there was a great shaking of heads and long faces. 'No, better to take the car – that is what we ourselves do.'

I nodded glumly. Under the weight of constant advice to go back the way I had come, I was losing heart.

At sunset I went outside to see the view. Across a billowing ocean of pinkish clouds the sun was fading as it sank, until all that remained was a faint reddening, as though the clouds themselves had begun to phosphoresce with some strange inner energy. There were no ridges, no peaks to be seen, just that featureless glow extending from below my feet to infinity. With the opening up of roads to cars from the south, the northern reaches had been abandoned and once again had become untravelled and mysterious. As I gazed out over that endless veil of cloud, I made my mind up to go there and to hell with all the good advice.

We said goodbye after a supper of flat bread and hard-boiled eggs served from a gourd. In the dark the road down to Shanghai was somehow less scary as we could not see the precipice and Ali drove with great care, as though he were letting a heavy load down on a rope a foot at a time.

We arrived back after midnight but Sergei was still awake and in no mood for sleeping. We sat around a candle, looking at the empty Cinzano bottle while he talked about his childhood in the Russian Arctic. 'In summer, when the birds would come, it was a paradise. But winter was not good. Now I am in Yafa and I am an old man.' He frowned. 'Pah! Most of my colleagues from medical school are dead from that.' He nodded towards the bottle. 'Those of us still alive are finished too.'

'How old are you?' The big white beard made it difficult to judge.

'I am forty-one.'

We both started to laugh.

# 17

I had met Saeed once before at the hospital where he was a doctor but we had merely exchanged polite greetings. Then he came round to Sergei's flat the morning after my trip to Jebel Khiyaal. They spoke in Russian about the debacle of Sergei's tenure and how he was to extricate himself. There was a hope that it might be possible to transfer to a private clinic where he could earn the same salary he had been promised at the government hospital.

They agreed to go that day to visit the private clinic in Mauflehi. 'Why not come along?' offered Saeed. 'You could stay overnight in my village and return tomorrow with me.'

As we talked it over, I realised that his village was a perfectly placed starting point for heading down into Wadi Bana. He told me that he had walked to Dhala as a youth with his wordly possessions piled up on a camel, hoping to find a place in secondary school. He drew a crude sketch map of the area for me. This sounded promising, but when Saeed realised I was serious about going he began to backtrack and the difficulties mounted. I became deliberately vague and said I would take my bag anyway, perhaps with a view to walking over to Jebel Khiyaal. This assuaged his anxieties for the moment.

In the end Sergei was called away to perform an operation and I was put in the car of a dentist, Yusuf, and left to wait in the market while he and Saeed went to buy tins of sardines. It was hot and my eyes were closed when I heard a voice in my ear calling me. I sat up. Idris was standing by the car window grinning. 'Kevin, I told you I would come and see you before you left.' He appeared to know all about where I was going and who with. 'Do not forget what I told you.'

I asked after his patient and he simply pointed skywards. 'There is no strength and salvation save in God.' Then we shook hands and he left. As he walked away I saw he was wearing a black leather biker's jacket and trousers. I never saw him again.

When the shopping was done, we left on the same route as the previous day. The dentist drove. Modern professions were well represented in the Mauflehi area, each village having a speciality: Saeed was the twenty-sixth doctor from a hamlet with a population of two hundred. A neighbouring settlement followed the army, another sent people to America.

Saeed's village was clustered on a small crag at the head of a terraced valley. There were no streets and no access for cars: we simply parked at the bottom near the tin-shack shop and climbed up the rock to the houses. There were no steps but dusty, smooth toeholds revealed where millions of feet had trodden before. Cleverly built into any available ledges were stone byres for cows and chicken coops. Women dodged away when I caught them looking at me, but they continued to call the news to their friends. All had extraordinarily deep voices, like a colony of Eartha Kitts.

I was shown into a separate diwan at the foot of the impressive traditional house. From there was a view across the fields to the neighbouring crag, also with a village on top. 'Here we have doctors,' said Saeed, 'but there they are engineers. Even our language is different. Here we say "sahira", but there they say "sahara".'

It seemed curious that a doctor should choose the word 'sorcerer' as an example.

The diwan was stone-roofed and about forty feet long. There were two pointed recesses at either end of the room, both about a foot wide and as tall as a man. Each of these held a hookah pipe, and on a spike in the wall near by hung the coils of velvet-covered hose. Three sides of the room were cushioned, with piles of spare armrests by the door. At one end were some handwritten citations from British Army officers given to Saeed's father, Abdulhadi, forty years before. 'He has proved a good worker and can be recommended . . .'

Saeed had disappeared to see his family but a young bearded man in a checked, belted jacket came in.

'Are you a Muslim?'

'No – a Christian.'

He frowned and played with his belt. 'Where will you take qat today?'

I said that it was Saeed's decision.

'In this village the men all go to the diwan.' He pointed down to a single room at the foot of the crag, the equivalent of their village hall. 'But there are those who will ask you your religion and if you say Christian, they will leave. They will not take qat with a Christian.'

He left and Saeed returned. The young man's comments were dismissed as nonsense but after our lunch of lahuh, we began to chew in the room. A couple of other villagers joined us, both friendly and talkative. Slowly, I forgot about the hostile fundamentalists and relaxed. They wanted to know what I thought of Manchester United, of boxer Naseem Hamed and the future of Yemen. Their own views on the latter were pessimistic: 'Our poet Baradduni is blind and his face scarred,' said one. 'When they asked him the future of Yemen, he told people the answer could be seen in his face.'

Saeed's father, Abdulhadi, came and sat with us, for the sake of his health not to chew qat, he said, but to talk of his interest in Yafa'i history.

'The most important event was the destruction of the Marib dam,' he said. 'After that the Yemeni people were scattered far and wide. Some came here to Mauflehi and Yafa was inhabited, others went to the Gulf or to the Maghreb and Spain.' He quoted the Koranic verse from memory just as Sheikh Muhammad had done at the qat session in Harar. 'For the natives of Sheba there was indeed a sign in their dwelling-place: a garden on their right and a garden on their left. We said to them: "Eat of what your Lord has given you and render thanks to Him. Pleasant is your land and forgiving is your Lord."

'But they gave no heed. So we let loose upon them the waters of the dam and replaced their gardens by two others bearing bitter fruit, tamarisks, and a few nettle shrubs.'

He paused. 'Our history begins then, but the history of Yafa is not written.' He began to recite a series of genealogies, the oral history. 'That is all people remember but I will try to write it. I have done two hundred pages already.'

Saeed was astonished. 'You never told me!'

The old man chuckled and got to his feet. 'Yes, for seven years I have worked on it and never told you.' He went to the door. 'I write when you are asleep, my boy.' With a wave he left the room, still chuckling.

There was amazement amongst the others as to how the old man had kept such a secret, then they began to talk of his courage through the years of communism and how he was always a man of hidden strength. 'In the 'seventies,' said one, 'the communists were very powerful. Young men in trousers ran the new government and they poured scorn on those who went to the mosque. They drank whisky in the streets and insulted our elders. It was then that Abdulhadi stood in the mosque here and denounced these new ways. He told the men to pray and to be good Muslims.'

When I first heard that trousers were considered taboo by some extremists, I had laughed. Now I began to see how such a situation had come about. Before the 'seventies, such novelties were unknown and when they did appear it was to clothe men who behaved barbarically. Trousers had come to be a symbol of loathsome deviancy.

'My father was imprisoned for one month,' said Saeed. 'When he was released, he immediately preached the same sermon. He was rearrested and imprisoned again, this time for longer. It happened again and again. They never dared shoot him because he was so well respected, but they never stopped imprisoning him. His health became very bad in those days.'

After sunset, Sergei and three companions appeared, but only to say goodbye. He had arranged his new job, all he had to do was become a real person with papers to prove it and he would transfer. I felt quite upset to leave him, a man totally out of place and lonely.

'Will you walk down to the north?' he asked. I nodded.

'Did you tell Saeed?'

'In the morning.'

He tried one last time to dissaude me but I shook my head. 'It's okay, Sergei, if there is no path I will come back up.'

When he and his friends had gone, Saeed fetched some blankets for me. The night was icy cold. His younger brother insisted on sleeping by the door.

At dawn I woke, stiff with cold, and stepping over the brother went out and climbed on the diwan roof. Abdulhadi was there drinking qishr. It was a magnificent morning: the sky a vault of deep aquamarine split across its eastern horizon with ribbons of saffron yellow light. The village was in shadow, a few figures moved in the lanes, arms clutched around themselves and head-scarves completely enveloping all but their eyes. The light trickled down the far hill, touched the rooftops of the houses in the other village and began to swell across the land between. People there were up and about, some were out on their donkeys, others fetching water. In Saeed's village, they waited.

I told Abdulhadi my plans and he nodded sagely. There were no objections from him or well-meaning advice to take the taxis. 'You will need strength for this undertaking.' He called to the house and a woman appeared with a tray. On it was a round of flat bread soaked in honey.

'This is wild honey from the mountain.' He tore off one half and rolled it up. 'Eat that part and put this in your pocket. May God be with you.'

Saeed appeared, rubbing his eyes, and was instructed to show me the start of the path.

We scrambled down through the village and headed south along the side of the terraces. Ahead was a craggy mountain and, once the valley struck its flank, the ravine dived down to the north-west. The path was easy stretches, followed by steep climbs downwards. Quickly Saeed's village was out of sight and we were in the cold grip of the sunless valley. The fields were bare except for occasional patches of irrigated land where shami grew, a kind of dwarf sorghum hardened to mountain conditions. On the stony hillsides was nothing but the russet and grey limbs of huge succulents.

A man came running up the hill with a large sack of qat on his back. A foot-slogging cossid, bearing qat for Mauflehi market. 'You should buy some,' advised Saeed. 'You will not find much qat down there.'

A little further down he stopped me. 'You do have a gun, don't you?'

'The truth is, Saeed, I have never even fired a gun – not a proper one with bullets.'

This staggering confession took some time to sink in. 'You mean a Kalashnikov? You never fired a Kalash?'

Eventually I convinced him that I meant any kind of gun and with a shake of his head he removed a pistol from his belt, a Russian automatic. 'Here, take this.'

'No, no – I don't want it.'

'But at least fire it, so you know how.'

He waved across the valley. 'Try for those three stones on the boulder.' This was about a hundred yards off, the width of the valley. I squeezed a shot off but the recoil whipped my hands up to the right. The echo of the shot thundered around us but no one shouted or complained. I tried another and managed to hit a boulder quite close to the target. Saeed bagged one of the three pebbles.

'Maybe it is better you don't carry a gun,' he said. 'You will assuredly hit something but not the thing you want.' We shook hands. 'Go with God and remember you must ask in Wadi Bana for help. The way to Hammam is not good.'

I promised to do so and set off downwards. When I glanced back a minute later, the valley had twisted a little and he was lost to view.

I raced down for half an hour. It was exhilarating to be alone again and on the move. On either side rose vast rock walls and far ahead were numerous high serrated ridges; I trusted to luck that I would find a way through them. At a small village on a spur I came into sunlight at last and stood in the delicious warmth while asking a man on a rooftop for the path. He was less interested in giving information than discussing whether I could use God's name as a non-believer. 'You said, "Praise be to God", when I asked how is your health. That is only for Muslims.'

Another man joined in from where he was sunning himself on another roof. 'Verily, are we all not sons of Adam, children, in fact, of the Book?'

This stung the first man. 'Do you pray to your Lord, O Nazarene? Is it not true that you eat what is unlawful and make a joke of prayers?'

But I was not to answer, for the second, warming to his task replied, 'Are not Abraham, Noah and Jesus son of Mary the prophets mentioned in our holy Koran? And did not Jesus son of Mary put compassion in the hearts of his followers?'

They continued to wrangle in such a vein and forgot about me until I moved off and one, belatedly remembering why I had spoken to them in the first place, called out, 'To your right!'

This was timely advice as the village was built on a mound of broken rocks with dozens of paths entering and leaving from all sides. A few steps down and a terrace width brought me to a point hard by the mountainside from where I could see that the plunging ravine divided: the left looked more promising and the right narrower but obviously I was meant to take the less inviting option.

Between these two was a knife-edge ridge heading north until it was abruptly stopped by the wave upon wave of east-west ranges. From up on the main peaks the route had seemed so simple but here it was becoming obvious just how difficult it might be. Not only was Wadi Bana invisible, there was mile after mile of nasty jagged mountains between myself and where it lay. Quite literally, I had overlooked these ridges from above. Now they were starting to look unsurmountable.

The path into the narrow ravine, however, soon became a lovely stone-stepped trail of smooth red rock. There were no roads and as this was the only channel of communications it was well-kept. There were a few qat and coffee trees but most fields were stubbled with dead stalks which the women were collecting, singing happily as they worked. A group of men were down in the bottom hammering at a large boulder and I paused to listen as one youth sang a well-known Yemeni melody:

> Passing by me the tall slender figure,
> Going to draw water down in Wadi Bana,
> Her eyes glancing softly,
> And well-aimed was that arrow,
> It shot my heart.
> O my father! O my!
> O you who are going down Wadi Bana,
> You took my heart and left.

After all the warnings I had been given it came as a surprise when a woman called to me from her kitchen garden above the track.

'Sabah al-kheir.'

'Sabah al-afiya.'

'Where are you from?'

I told her I was British but this made no sense to her, nor did the name, London.

'Is it far?'

'By car it would take a month.'

'By God! Is it true? Why are you here, then? Where are you going?'

[241]

She confirmed that this was indeed the path to Bana and wished me well with a smile. I felt then that I had crossed some unmarked boundary; it was impossible to imagine exchanging such innocent pleasantries 2,000 feet above on the plateau.

I had gone down a further 500 feet when I dropped my plastic water bottle and it split on a rock. As I was yet to feel thirsty and there were houses around, this did not seem such a disaster, but it was getting hotter. I crossed the bottom of the ravine where bananas and papaya trees were growing and an old man called to me.

'Are you British?'

He was delighted to see me, a chance to reminisce about his youth in the Sultan of Lahej's army. There was no path from here, he told me, but I would find the way: 'Just follow the donkey shit.'

This proved to be no easy matter: although the wadi had become less steep, it was choked with large grey boulders and clumps of vicious thorn brush that pulled my headscarf off and jabbed straight through clothing. I would scramble and slide down a thirty-foot boulder only to have to retrace my steps when an impenetrable thicket appeared. I struggled onwards for two hours, stumbling and cursing as I slipped and fell again and again. Heat came off the stones in waves. My accident with the water bottle was beginning to look serious: there were no more houses and when I eventually came across a pool in the lee of a huge rock, it was a brilliant yellow porridge that boiled with frogs.

The valley now began to wriggle through cliffs. This was a bizarre stone garden for zen-like contemplation: the soaring strata rippling into snakes and scorpion's tails; vertical faces pocked with sculpted hollows in which a few round stones had been grinding themselves for centuries, and the white boulders of the stream bed stark against the plunging dark walls of the cliffs. There were steep side valleys where the clinging trees were tugged by breezes that never reached the stillness below.

I sat in the shade of an overhang and thought about water. I was cursing myself for not drinking more than a glass of qishr at Saeed's and for not asking the old man for a drink. But there was nothing to be done except push on and hope to find houses in Bana.

Fortunately, the valley broadened slightly, though there were still occasional gateways where the seasonal floods had piled up trees, earth and stones. Passing through one of these narrow defiles I came to a place where a field of rich alluvial soil had banked up on the inner curve. I felt sure this must belong to people from Wadi Bana rather than those above, but there was no one to be seen.

The end to this descent came abruptly. I rounded a crumbling buttress and there was the wadi in front of me like a dream of an oasis: a shingle bank, then running water, beds of waving reeds where small birds were chirruping, shady trees and a heron, ponderously fleeing the intrusion. Beyond this rose a gravelly hillside with a few box-like dwellings, all apparently empty, then further still a range of rounded hills and an escarpment several thousand feet high; behind me the mountains swept up more dramatically. I ran down to the water, desperate to drink, but stopped when I saw the long yellow beards of algae hanging on every stone. Downstream the valley disappeared between uninhabited cliffs but upstream there was a house on a ledge above some small fields of corn. I could see a boy there, watching his black and white goats from the shade of some papaya trees. It seemed sensible to wait a little longer, just to ask if they drank from wells or the open water itself.

I waded the stream twice to avoid a stretch of cliff then climbed up towards the house. It was a simple stone box with small holes for windows and a narrow set of steps leading up to a yard behind. From around the corner, five female faces observed my approach in silence. When I reached the bottom of the steps I looked up and greeted them. The four younger faces promptly disappeared but the older woman, their mother, answered.

'Wa aleikum as-salaam.'

Two of the four faces reappeared.

'Is this Bana?' I croaked.

Five heads now visible all nodded.

'Do you have water?'

There was a flurry of activity and a glass of unsweetened qishr passed down. I drank it thankfully.

I asked about the path to Hammam.

'That is very far,' said the woman. Her accent was so strong I could scarcely understand her. One of the daughters took my glass and refilled it, a pretty girl with bronze skin and a flowery dress. She was, perhaps, only ten but her hands and feet were already worn and lined with the incessant

[243]

work of fetching and carrying. Their possessions were the minimum: a few cookpots, three glasses, a couple of plastic jerry cans. They grew sorghum twice a year and collected honey in the season. They had a dozen goats, a donkey and a dog. 'My husband is dead,' the woman told me. 'Last year, he was killed in a car crash at Habilain. Have you been there?'

I nodded. 'I passed through it on the way from Aden to Labus.'

'So you've been to Aden too?'

I drank two more glasses then thanked them. The woman pointed upstream to where the river turned sharply and disappeared. 'There is the path to Hammam. It goes behind these hills to the mountains.'

She waved eastwards. Beyond the hills the escarpment ran out in an impressive line of shark's teeth peaks, pale and distant in the midday haze.

'Is Hammam before those mountains,' I asked, 'or after?'

She thought about it. 'It is far.'

I handed back the glass to the girl: all the while she and her three sisters had stared in a mixture of curiosity and horror. As I turned to leave, the eldest whispered something to her mother. The woman's eyes narrowed suspiciously. 'You are not from Yafa, are you?'

I smiled. 'No, not Yafa. From very far – Britain, do you know it?'

The girl whispered again. 'We do not know that place,' said the mother. 'Is it further than Habilain?'

'Further than San'a, further even than Cairo.'

'Ma'shallah!'

I set off along the bank. Small thumb-sized fish skittered away in the shallows. I crossed using some stepping stones and took a faint path up over the hill. On the far side I picked up a broader track, one wide enough for a vehicle, though I could see no sign of tyre tracks.

No sooner was I on this straight, shadeless track than I began to wish I had drunk the algal soup in the wadi. I walked uphill for half a mile, came to the top of a ridge, walked down another half mile into a wadi, then up again. On and on, the jagged range ahead shimmering gently and never appearing to get any closer. I was torturing myself: 'Only four glasses of qishr and an eight-hour walk down 5,000 feet, are you insane? Go back. Go back at once!'

When I reached the top of the third rise, my brain did a sudden back somersault in protest. I sat down heavily. On a hilltop ahead I could see a man sitting with a Kalashnikov and he turned and aimed but no sound came. I shouted something and my voice was so small it seemed I could barely hear it myself.

'Yes, go on shoot – see if I care, you bastard. Just don't offer me any water, will you?'

I stood up. The man was a baboon. Baboons do not carry Kalashnikovs. Baboons carry fleas and this one was scratching furiously.

The next section went slowly. Moments before the baboon went out of sight, I realised it was a man with a Kalashnikov after all. The heat shimmers were playing havoc with my eyes which had been covered with a greatly enlarged microscopic slice of pond-life: strange tadpoles drifted across the sky, black diatoms peppered the edges. I kept up a ridiculous act, berating myself for being a weakling while forcing myself to march in time with 'Shoot me! Shoot me! You bastard, go on shoot me!'

At the crest of the next rise, I looked down in despair at yet another dip and rise, precisely the same as the last. Behind me the assassin-baboon had gone back to being an unusually shaped rock. Apart from the benefit of not being killed, this was rather disappointing as it meant I really was alone, utterly alone. The hills were bleak gravel undulations leading on to the mountains, and these were now revealed to be black rock as the sun got behind them.

The next wadi had some substantial trees in its bed, large enough to shelter from the sun. I sat with my back against a smooth grey boulder and watched some black ants scurrying up the trunk of an acacia. Now my water problems had been superseded by another more pressing matter: the track forked.

There was no way of knowing which was the correct choice but I examined the traces of donkeys and what seemed to be signs of tyres. My conclusion was that a vehicle had come down from the right, down the bed of this wadi, probably from some distant mountain region. This right-hand trail joined the one I had walked along and then turned across the valley bottom and climbed the hillside. I could see the path zig-zagging up the far slope. The lower outlet of the wadi seemed to be an impenetrable thicket of thorn bushes blocking a narrow gorge. The zig-zag trail up the hill, I concluded, was the correct choice. In this I was totally wrong but the mistake saved me from great hardship, perhaps even saved my life.

I felt much better after the rest and I had climbed about halfway up the far side of the wadi when I happened to glance back. There was a movement amongst the trees: a man had come up from the thicket I had thought impenetrable. I had not even noticed a path. He was making for the track down which I had come but I shouted and ran after him. I must have made an alarming appearance: a white man, scorched red and covered in dust. With great dignity he sat in the shade of a tree, leaned his chin on his stick and waited.

Running had not been a good idea. I could not speak for some minutes during which time we nodded at each other and I made vague rasping noises. He was very old and had a pleasant lined face with twinkling grey eyes and a short white beard. Despite wearing an old zenna with jambiyya, woollen V-necked sweater, torn jacket, shawl around his shoulders and a thick headcloth, he looked perfectly cool and composed. Sweat was dripping from the end of my nose.

'Don't you have a car?' he asked. 'Foreigners have cars. I have seen them in Habilain going to Aden.'

I shook my head.

'You have money?'

I nodded but he took hold of his bundle wrapped in a shawl and rummaging around pulled out thirty rials in grubby notes.

'It's all I've got,' he said. 'But take it.'

I shook my head, grunting and pulling my spare change from my pocket – about four hundred rials. His eyes widened. 'God is generous!' He cried, folding his own notes carefully back into his bundle and waving away the offer of my own.

Eventually the power of speech returned and I asked him for Hammam. This drew one of those wonderfully expressive gestures that Yemenis perform with such elan: a wild flick of the right hand that somehow clicked the thumb and forefinger together – a sort of visual exclamation mark.

'That is a long journey,' he said. 'You will walk until tomorrow and all the next day before arriving. Even without halting to take your rest you will not find water until tomorrow at noon.' He motioned with his chin at the wadi where he had walked from. 'Do not walk to Hammam. You must go down there. You will come to Bana again and a village where you can stay tonight. Tomorrow a car may come.'

'I want to walk,' I said stubbornly.

'I think you are tired now,' he observed. 'It is better that you rest in the village. Do you have water with you?'

'No.'

'Then you cannot go to Hammam – you will suffer. God only knows but you may die. There is no one living on this road. Where will you sleep? It is a bad place with leopards and hyaenas.'

I gave him some qat from my bag and we chewed a few shoots together. The heat had certainly affected my mind because I had not given up thoughts of continuing. My rationale was that Yemenis tend to exaggerate distance and dangers, especially for an unarmed single traveller. But then, as he continued to stress the importance of returning to Bana, I realised that he too was unarmed and single, and this was a different place to the mountain. When he said goodbye and departed, I decided to follow his advice and set off down the side wadi towards Bana.

This was an easy stretch. With the knowledge of a village ahead, there was nothing to fear. It is the unknown that requires courage and once that burden was lifted from me, I walked with a lighter step.

Only a couple of miles along the wadi, I turned a corner and found myself back beside Bana – this time even more beautiful. There was an earth bank with some trees, then the shimmering stream meandering across a field of long grass that hissed in the breeze. All around were tremendous peaks rising 5,000 feet in one relentless sweep from wadi to summit. Two boys drove a camel laden with firewood across the stream, an old woman lay asleep in the shade next to her flock of goats.

There were three stone huts, a rusting Landcruiser buried in a thorn bush, and a man sitting in the shade chewing qat.

He made a place for me beside him.

'Ahlan wa sahlan. Welcome. Here, drink some qishr.'

I was handed an aluminium bowl with a half inch of brown liquid in it. Never has any drink tasted so divine.

His name was Muhammad and he had worked in Saudi Arabia until the Gulf War when, like six hundred thousand of his compatriots, he had been summarily thrown out because Yemen refused to condemn Iraq. With his money he had started a shop, the hut with a metal door, but business was slow. I went and had a look around his stock: soap packets, aspirins, safety pins, and bullets. In the corner was a box of mineral water bottles, so I bought one and drank it immediately. We returned to the shade and I relaxed. The qat took hold. I knew, for certain, I would not move again, perhaps for days.

Two armed men came strolling over the river. Old men with hawk-like faces and keen eyes, they came and sat to talk. They were from a valley called Shir'ah and the taller of the two, Abdulqawi, lived at the village of Hammam. He confirmed everything the old man had said. 'Maybe a car will come,' he said. 'Then we will ride. If not, we will walk together.' But he was sick with malaria: his eyes were yellow and he had a fever. I gave him some prophylactic tablets and he promptly fell asleep. The second man was called the Hadhrami by the others and I asked when he had moved from the Hadhramaut.

'I was born here,' he said, 'but my grandfather's grandfather came from there.'

The sun dropped lower and lower until great shafts of gold were laid between the mountain shoulders and the sparkling water. There was a hushed calm to everything, as though the world had roused itself only to watch night come oozing from under the purple cliffs. A cow of chestnut and cream sauntered to the water and drank, a glittering string of diamonds pouring off its chin when it raised its head. At sunset Abdulqawi and his friend stood up. 'We will sleep at a house down the valley – come with us.'

But Muhammad answered. 'No, he will stay with me.'

They nodded and left. Muhammad closed the shop door and locked it, then we set off up the hill behind the settlement. This 500-foot stretch caused me some problems, my legs having stiffened up considerably. At the pass I saw that we had come over to a place where the stream curled around a semicircle of emerald green fields about six hundred yards long and three hundred wide. The gravel banks were lined with brushwood fences designed to catch sediment brought down by floodwater. All around were steep crags and hills, the wadi itself entered and left via gorges. On the far side were about ten houses tucked above the stream on the hillside. They were simple dwellings decorated with no more than crude zig-zags of limewash around the windows; two boasted iron doors and window shutters.

There was still some twilight when we waded across and walked up to the houses. Everyone turned out to see me, children dancing up and down with excitement. Muhammad showed me into his one-roomed place. His wife and mother were at the far end nursing babies. A pole had been fitted across beneath the stone roof to lie clothes and blankets across. There were more than a dozen children, all suffering from chesty coughs and streaming noses.

'Is it customary to shake the women's hands?' I asked and Muhammad looked surprised.

'Yes, of course.'

I got up and greeted them properly. Both were extremely handsome, dressed in red flowery dresses and harem pants with plaits of black hair tumbling to their waists from under loose turbans of scarlet and black. A bowl of qishr was set before me and I began to receive visitors. The entire male population came by: an old man without teeth who stood, hands on knees, and peered closely into my face for a full minute, while the women giggled at him. Then two youths, solemn-faced, and careful of their dignity but too shy to speak. Then three young men with rough hands and feet muddy from working in the fields. Each shook my hand and took his place according to age, the oldest closest. Then an elderly man with a white beard came in with his young wife; she joined the other women in whispers while the old man strode confidently over. His feet were bare, like all the others, toes like huge gnarled roots gripping the dirt floor.

'Anta Britani?'

I nodded. 'Aiwa, Britani.'

'How much,' he asked in Arabic, 'how much is a packet of cigarettes in England now?'

'Thalatha guinea.'

He staggered back with a wail. 'Thalatha guinea! Fuck me! That's daylight fuckin' robbery!'

There was a screech of astonishment from his wife and then a flurry of excited chatter. I really think the assembled village were as surprised as I was to hear the man speak English, though they might have been more surprised had they understood his meaning or grasped that it was delivered in a Birmingham accent that could have tightened wheel nuts on a Longbridge Land-Rover.

[249]

'Where are you from in Britain,' he continued. 'Blackheath, Sheffield or Halesowen?'

I pondered over this mysterious choice for some time before plumping for Sheffield. Apparently, these were the three spots where he had worked in 1967, and the only three that survived in memory.

'I go Aden, take boat to France. Then Victoria Railway Station I show this address to Bobby. I say nothing, not speaking any English. Bobby takes me to the train and I go to Halesowen. Outside station is Bobby. I show him address. He takes me to Taximan. I go to my friend in Halesowen and he takes me to Gaffer. Gaffer find me factory job. We learning English very bloody damn quick. Gaffer says, "Work here!" Then go to dancing hall and meet Baby. Lots of Baby. Dance and talking and learning pretty bloody damn quick. "You Arab boy – too bloody quick!" Ha!'

The young wife was trying to stop the noises coming from her mouth by stuffing it with the end of her headscarf. Muhammad was grinning from ear to ear. 'We knew he went there, to Britain,' he said. 'But we did not know he could speak English.'

'Where did you work?' I asked him, in English.

'Eighteen pound, nineteen pound, twenty pound, good money. John Player five bob.'

'But where did you work?'

'Gaffer says, "Work here!" We learning pretty bloody quick. "You Arab boy too bloody quick!"'

I asked a few more questions but I had guessed already. In the thirty years since returning to Yemen, he had almost completely forgotten how to understand what others said, but somehow retained the ability to speak. He was like a telephone with a broken earpiece. If I wanted to ask, I had to do it in Arabic, but that would have spoilt the effect for the audience.

To his wife, I said, using the Arabic phrase, 'Your husband speaks our language like a nightingale.' She removed the scarf and beamed with pride.

Talking to the men, I learned that the village had been founded eighty years before by two Yafa families. Isolated from the world outside, it was as if they had been forgotten by the violent forces of colonial wars, communism and fundamentalism. Only Muhammad, with his Saudi experience, and the old Brummie spoke Arabic in a reasonably intelligible form for me: the women in particular had such a broad dialect I could scarcely understand anything they said.

'Have you spoken English since you left Britain?' I asked the old man in Arabic.

'Thirty years I stayed here – in this village – and never spoke one word. Then the children came running, "Yahya! There is a white man." And I thought, maybe it is a Britisher, so I came and spoke – the first chance for thirty years.'

Supper of lahuh was brought which the men ate from sparingly then passed the bowl to the women and children.

Later I persuaded them to let me sleep on the roof, and I lay there on my back gazing up as shooting stars sketched lazy lines across Eridanus. The houses were all silent, only the donkeys shifted restlessly in their stalls and frogs called from the river. I was in a hidden valley, a lost world, where people rose with the sun and watched to the stream for survival: twice a year it would flood and they captured the silt, then looked to the stars and planted their crops. Exhausted as I was, I fell asleep in minutes, stirring only once before daybreak when a cool breeze sprang up and pulled the blanket back.

Next day I spent with Muhammad. He showed me how they planted the sorghum on which their lives depended and how they captured the precious soil brought down in the stream. He picked leaves and we sampled their tangy flavour: 'This one is girgir, for the stomach. And this one will prevent back pain. This tree is for henna – for our hair, also the women's feet and hands.' The fields with little bunds between them were full of onions, ladies' fingers, tomatoes and vegetables. Beside them were papayas, lemons and bananas. I had thought the hillsides barren, but there were herbs and medicinal plants hiding behind rocks. 'This one we make tea for headaches. Here is the abab which we pound and put onto bruises and sprains.'

There was pride about his home and the land, but there was a longing to get away, too. He missed the excitement of travel and new places that his brief foray across to Saudi had given him. Perhaps he saw himself like Yahya, thirty years later and still living on memories of that one great trip. His conversation was of escapes, of treasures and chance encounters that turn life around. They were the longings of a man bound to his home hearth and routine.

He told me of his grandfather who had lived on the mountain.

'One night he dreamed that there was a cave below the village and that the cave was full of treasure. Next day he and his friends went in search of this cave. And they found it. Truly, there is no salvation or power save in God! There was a door inside this cave and they used stones to break it down. In this next room they found a door exactly the same and they broke it down. Then they found a room exactly the same but without a door. They began to tap on the walls and eventually they discovered a place where it sounded hollow. So they broke through into yet another room and in this one there were some large jars. They rushed forward but the jars were all empty save for some ears of corn.

'Once again they searched for a door and found one. This next room had jars, too, and in each jar was one piece of silver jewellery – but not good silver, just poor quality. So they searched and found a fifth room and in this were more jars, this time with a single gold coin. The seventh room was empty but it was very dark and without oxygen. No candle or lamp would stay alight in that room and if a man remained long he became faint. Remember this is before torchlights were invented.

'My grandfather and his friends used mirrors to bring light. By reflecting sunlight they managed to light the seventh room and the eighth and ninth. But when they reached the tenth it was getting more difficult and at last they broke into a twelfth room. Here the mirror brought no light and there was a tremendous heat. No one could stay in that room for more than a few seconds. They gave up that treasure search then, but the caves are still there – I have been inside myself.'

'And is it true about the last room?'

'It is true. The room swallows the light of any torch and there must be fire somewhere because the sweat runs from you like water. I did not like to stay there. In fact, nobody likes to go there any more.'

In the afternoon we went to the shop and a youth brought qat to us, manna from heaven in such hot afternoons. We lounged in the shade of the stone hut in companionable silence watching the river. There were few customers: an old woman bought some soap, I took a mineral water – Muhammad prefered to drink qishr.

[252]

My mind drifted with the qat, recalling a journey to Delhi some years before and a day spent exploring the Red Fort. The air had had the same chilled stillness; sounds seemed to grow bigger as they moved further away, like bubbles rising and expanding in champagne. I had stood in the Diwan-i-Khas, the Great Mughal's hall of private audience, and searched for the inscription by Amir Khusraw: 'If there be a paradise on the earth, it is this, it is this, it is this.'

A river ran through that paradise, the Nahr al-Bihisht, a stream cut in white marble across which you have to step to see the view over the sweltering plains. A man approached me with that engaging manner that makes India so irresistible. 'Excuse me, sir. My lady says this is Vanishing Cream.' He passed me a small tube of ointment. 'But we cannot read the description!'

'What lady?'

He looked around, the smile becoming a frown. There really was no lady to be seen. He took the tube back from me.

'Wait. I will locate her.'

And he stepped over the stream and never returned.

The very idea of paradise, it has been suggested, came to the west from the Greeks. They wrote of the fabulous Hanging Gardens, a place that probably never existed but like all good writers they refused to allow the facts to spoil the story. It was a place both lost and longed for, a dream to drive the waking hours.

This was the paradise glimpsed in Persian miniatures, where everyone is posed in profile in gardens of exquisitely refined elegance. Garden in Persian, and Arabic, can also mean paradise.

'The true servants of God shall be well provided for,' says the Koran, 'feasting on fruit, and honoured in the gardens of delight. Reclining face to face upon soft couches, they shall be served with a goblet filled at a gushing fountain, white, and delicious to those who drink it. It will neither dull their senses nor befuddle them. They shall sit with bashful, dark-eyed virgins, as chaste as the sheltered eggs of ostriches.'

And that vision of paradise remains closely related to men's earthly desires in a country like Yemen, where pleasure is a room with cushions, cool water, the pipe and the qat – the leaf that neither dulls nor befuddles. All these things combine, in effect, to produce something congruent with a belief in the paradise promised. After death we get more of the same, only much much better – plus houris. Happiness in this life becomes possible only when we believe it exists in the next.

Sitting on a blanket with the soaring peaks above and sparkling waters before me, I put it to Muhammad that his home was a paradise: he had all those plants, all these mountains, clean air and water, a bag of qat at his knee and a cigarette in his mouth. But Muhammad was not too pleased with my suggestion. In fact, he was shocked: 'Paradise? Paradise! No, no. This is not paradise, this is a prison.'

And I was given a whole list of reasons why, all of which were irrefutable: hospitals, schools, prospects, houses, entertainment. He was right, of course. The daily lives of Yemenis, the qat sessions, might put them in touch with what their religion promises, but it is certainly no substitute – unless you are a godless westerner who needs his paradise on earth. The qat session remains as a comforting symbol for better things to come but nothing more. And yet, I still hoped.

# 18

The following morning my legs were back to normal and I decided to walk to Hammam. However, when we reached the shop there was a Landcruiser sitting under the acacias. There was no sign of the driver but Muhammad knew the man.

'Abdulrabb – he has come for firewood from Yesri. You can ride with him, then walk from there.'

A woman came carrying grasses and loaded them onto the car while shouting orders at Muhammad in a deep thrilling voice. Her appearance was no less unusual: a balled frizz of hair teased from under her scarves at the front, then a red stripe across her forehead and a yellow one over her eyes. She looked like a German flag on legs.

Very soon men began to appear from the grass over the stream, tough gun-toting tribesmen, except for Abdulrabb himself who fluttered up to the bank in a yellow and black silk shirt with trousers, then demanded a camel be brought to carry him across. He had all the big-city ways expected of a man familiar with Habilain and Lahej: an easy assumption of power over non-car-owners, a foppish adornment of socks and shoes and the ability to smoke American cigarettes. Like Muhammad he had learnt to make money in Saudi Arabia and was applying this knowledge. The two stood apart from the others, representatives of a new kind of man, not entirely trusted by the others. The previous night an old man in Muhammad's village had complained bitterly that his nephew required payment – blessings be upon the Prophet! – payment for some cooking oil. When he Muhammad's uncle had wiped the shit from his arse as a child, had he demanded payment then?

It took most of the morning to see the pick-up filled with firewood, then a sheep and six passengers were placed on top. Abdulqawi went in the cab, looking distinctly unwell.

We rolled up the side wadi, dodging the vicious thorns, and rejoined the trail I had walked on two days before. It was then that I realised that the two prongs of the fork curled around a hill and joined each other again. Had I gone right I would have missed the old man. The awful result of such bad luck was soon shown to me: for mile upon mile we hammered and heaved through a landscape of utter stony desolation. Once we passed the abandoned simple huts of some bedu, but otherwise the valley gave no sign of life. At times the trail had collapsed into a morass of boulders and on one precipice the sheep chose to leap for freedom and ended up dangling over a cliff by the rope round its neck. We hauled it back up.

I looked at this landscape and thanked that nameless old man for his advice. By the time Abdulrabb had come this way, a full thirty-six hours after I had passed the fork in the road, I would have been in some difficulty.

After four hours we began to climb up to a high pass. The views back towards Yafa were stunning. At the top we came to the first house, a stone cube inhabited by one old man and his daughter. They gave us qishr from plastic mugs and he told me that his other daughter was married to a Yemeni in Britain – a big city called Halesowen, did I know it?

A long bone-crunching journey down from the pass brought us to Wadi Shir'ah and Yesri: a group of Yafa-style houses built on small crags in the valley. Abdulqawi was now so ill that it was decided to take him to Hammam, saving us an hour's walk in the full heat of day.

Initially, this wadi was barren, a place full of thorns and empty fields but halfway along it was suddenly transformed. The track was a riverbed shaded by tall trees: orange groves sighed in the breeze and blue butterflies drank from muddy pools. It was as though the soaring peaks had squeezed and squeezed until all the green, all the goodness, had been forced into this narrow space. The valley was never more than a shouting distance wide, perfectly straight for five miles with a high pass at either end. In the dead centre, there was a kink around a single crag and on this, high above all others, was built Abdulqawi's house.

'Come and wait there,' he said. 'If a car is coming we will know.'

His sons had come to meet him and carry his guns: a Czech machine gun and a Kalashnikov. Showing no sign of his illness he led us up a winding footpath, past some abandoned houses, to his own. The last few yards were a straight climb requiring hands and feet, then I emerged on a tiny ledge beside a byre holding one chestnut cow and on the other side a doorway to a room. Above my head, on a smaller ledge, was a stone-built chicken house.

Abdulqawi's other sons were waiting inside and came forward on their knees to touch the hem of his robe and kiss the hand that had touched the hem in respect. He then lay down to sleep and left them to entertain me with demonstrations of how they could shoot anything that moved in the valley from the windows of their room. The eldest son, Ali, later took me to see the hot springs, a series of scorching pools ranged down the hillside and surrounded near the top by tiny terraces of huts.

'In summer,' he explained, 'people will come and stay for a month or two if they have a medical problem.'

We worked our way into the upper pool and lay in the clear green waters for an hour, chewing qat and talking. Two other men arrived, one of whom had fought for the rebels during the 1994 war, as had many men from the region.

'I was at Anad,' he told me, referring to the large military base on the Aden road. 'Then in Aden.' But he would not be drawn on what had happened, only to say that his friends had been killed and he was fed up with war. 'There are no grudges in Yemen,' he explained. 'Yesterday I fought you, today we are friends. That is the Yemeni way. The war is finished.'

When we arrived back at the house, Ali's wife was feeding a kid goat from a bottle. 'Its mother was taken by a leopard,' she said.

I slept that night on their roof under the stars.

At first light they gave me qishr and delicious flat bread, then I set off up the valley. It was bitterly cold and I kept stopping to massage cramp away from my calves. The route, however, was easy and flat and I reached the bottom of the pass before the sunlight had penetrated to the valley floor. So deep and narrow was this place that the upper peaks were bleached with the glare of mid-morning before the first houses captured some warming rays.

Even from the distance of Abdulqawi's diwan this pass had looked daunting. The track zig-zagged through dozens of hair-pin bends to a notch in the mountain range, then disappeared. As I walked up, I began to pass through coffee and qat fields, then a small village. The architecture was no longer Yafa'i – these were originally people from over the pass which had only been blasted through forty years before by the British in an attempt to subdue the valley.

I was a half mile and a thousand feet short of the pass when I heard the car coming. It was playing Beethoven's *Ode to Joy* on the horn, interspersed with various honks, grunts and sirens. These, I discovered as it came closer, were linked to a selection of Christmas fairy lights around the windscreen and two purple strobes on the inside cab roof. The driver waved as he passed and then did a clever manoeuvre involving jamming his rear end into the rock wall. 'Brakes no good!' he admitted cheerily. 'Do you want a lift?'

He got out with a jerry can and lifting the bonnet, poured water into the radiator. 'I can take you to Habil Rayda, on the San'a to Aden asphalt.'

Suddenly that sounded like a very wonderful idea. I could be in the town of Ibb that night, in a hotel, drinking tea instead of sugarless qishr and not being eaten by fleas.

There was one other man in the back, a young man in trousers. When we were moving, he asked me what I thought of Yemen and the exiled leaders of the '94 rebellion. I said I had heard that Ali Salem al-Beid was a merchant in Oman and al-Jiffri was in Cairo. He shook his head.

'No. Believe me, they are not sleeping. *We* are not sleeping. The south must be independent to shake off this corruption and chaos. Yemen needs another war and Yemen *will* have another war.'

At the pass he fell silent, as though we had moved from his territory and he was no longer so sure of himself.

The pass was a notch of sheer-sided rock just wide enough to allow a car through. Glancing back, I got a last view of the world I was leaving behind, a vast landscape of blue mountains rising from the dusty shadows of valleys and the very last wave in this turbulent sea, rising above all others, was the shape of Jebel Khiyaal and Yafa.

Ibb lies on the sloping shoulder of a fertile mountain, a green well-blessed land and the one in which many Yemenis would prefer to live. For that reason, perhaps, it had grown five-fold since I had last visited: a remorse-less tide of concrete and breeze-block spreading through the terraces of sorghum. The market is a dream of Yemeni bounty: more onion tops than a man can eat in a lifetime, oranges piled to head height, yams, potatoes, tomatoes, and, of course, very good qat. The best is sold in bundles no thicker than your wrist and at least four are needed, Sha'aibi, they call it, after the area fifteen miles south where it originates.

I spent three days lounging about, consuming large quantities of this superior leaf. After what had been poor stuff in Yafa and Shir'ah, my mind seemed to seize on it with reckless abandon. I would remember words spoken weeks before in Harar exactly as they had been said, but a sudden demand on my vocabulary would leave me dumb, floundering after the most basic of expressions.

On the third afternoon I managed to telephone San'a and contact a friend, Tim, who I hoped to meet up with. I told him my plans to walk down Wadi Zabid from Ibb and then move along the coast and finally head up to San'a via the mountain of Bura.

'Lovely,' he agreed. 'Let's meet in Zabid. There's one of my favourite hotels in all Yemen under the trees in the square. Not everyone likes it, mind you.'

Years before, I had experienced one of Tim's favourite restaurants in all Yemen and narrowly survived. Alarm bells rang.

'It's the motorbikes,' he explained, 'I was with the head of Tricontinental Consultants and they did keep him awake.'

'In the street outside?'

'No, the beds are in the street and they weave between them at night you see. It's all very good fun.'

I thought of the sixty-mile walk I had ahead and how much fun I would see it as.

'Aren't there any others?'

'Well, if you don't mind going back to the coast, we could try Khowkha. There's a man who rents out rope beds on the beach. The only drawback is the cars.'

'Cars?'

'They do weave between the beds at night.' He began to laugh.

I groaned. 'Smugglers going up the beach probably.'

I chose the beach and we agreed to rendezvous at Khowkha in five days' time.

The descent of Wadi Zabid began well. A shared taxi took me to the start of my walk, the town of Udayn. There are those who claim Udayn as the origin of coffee and qat. The name is said to mean 'two shoots' in Arabic. No evidence exists for this and even the name is ambiguous – it could mean 'Little Aden'. A shopkeeper told me that both these were wrong and the origin was two mountains, both called Jebel Ud, on either side of the town. From Udayn I walked, and after a couple of miles picked up the course of the stream, a knee-deep sparkling channel running through tunnels of bamboo where unseen birds sang.

It was all very pleasant but my underlying mood was fragile. The wild freedom and starlit skies of Yafa were in my mind and Ibb, with its crowds and filth, had irritated me. I waded along in the river telling myself how wonderful this was. After five hours the water had softened my bare feet and I kicked a rock.

It was one of those minor injuries that hurt a lot. I put my shoes on but they rubbed the wound. I tried tying a rag around it. I kicked another stone with the other foot. I went behind a tree and had a bout of something messy. After seven hours' walking I was not tired but I was definitely fed up. At a point where the stream dived into a narrow gorge a youth came strolling out of the greenery with a long-handled axe over his shoulder and told me that the river curled northwards, a two-day walk to the first villages. Or, instead, I could trek across the hill to the road and catch a car.

This I did, planning a quick hop around the loop, but once I reached the roadside village my depression worsened. It was an awful place: a few scrappy huts and a shop with a stone verandah where I sat to take qat with a few others. Conversation was limited. They asked the prices of things in England: 'How much are cigarettes? Cars? Donkeys?' Then a long pause while they thought of something else. When that failed they took to shouting 'What-is-yourrr-name?' in English very loudly and often, a game which entertained everyone for almost an hour. Finally we sank into stupefied silence broken only by the pitiful yelps of a diseased dog which the youths were stoning.

I felt my head was exploding with frustration. I went for a stroll and returned to find my qat had been taken. Then I stood in the road and, like a loony, berated them in the name of God for their disgraceful behaviour. I was filthy with dust from the hill, I had a bloodstained rag on one bare foot, the whitish-green foam of dehydration and qat around my lips, my ears had caught the sun and were peeling in pale sheets of skin. When a pick-up truck came along, the villagers rushed out to stop it and forced the driver to take me away.

Inside were six men with Kalashnikovs who caught the end of my tirade and immediately began to shower me with qat, cigarettes and apologies. The sun set and we hammered along the deteriorating track. I had no desire to ask where they were going, only to go as far as possible. They dropped me in complete darkness at a shack and turned back. I slept on some old sacks and dreamed in short intense bursts, waking between each segment of the same dream. I was watching a 'sixties film that started nicely with Ford Anglias pottering up a high street. 'Everyone drove blue Anglias,' said the narrator, and I was in one outside a house from which a man came running, jumped in and drove us at speed. 'The murderer escaped and headed for Cirencester,' said the voice but we did not, we hid up a back lane where a man and woman were sitting in a car. The murderer got out and killed them with a vacuum cleaner hose. Then I was driving and the narrator was saying, 'Police have identified the suspect as Kevin Rushby, last seen travelling east on the coast road.' And I was shouting, 'But I'm only watching this film – how can it be me!?'

At dawn I rose and waited by the road for a car.

I heard it coming long before I saw it: not the ticking of a Ford Anglia but the familiar roar of a habba driven foot to the floor. Then it came down towards me, fish-tailing to a halt. There were two men in the cab, a large load of qat immediately behind covered by a tarpaulin, plus four other passengers. I got the worst seat beside the tailgate on the spare tyre. The first whack of the road drove the air valve into my backside. I managed to climb over the men and grab hold of the qat so I was standing as we thundered forwards, leaning into corners like some runaway stage-coach driver desperately hanging onto his reins. This was driving like I had never experienced it before: crazed acceleration downhill towards precipice corners, bone-splitting crunches over holes, the back veering wildly as it grabbed at the road, then a leap over a hump and my knees forced into right angles. Strapped to the cab roof in front of me was a megaphone and Koranic verses blasted out over the uninhabited hillsides of scrub thorn, a wild 'God is Great!' as we charged towards the apocalypse and martyrdom.

I considered getting off. I considered my chances of surviving if we rolled: should I leap clear, or crouch and hope the cab protected me? In the end I could not face the embarrassment of explaining why I wanted to abandon my journey.

Parties of guinea fowl scattered into the bush; on the hillsides huge purple boulders stared down like Easter Island idols. Then, on a slight bend, he lost control. The rear rose up and planed over the grit. The front wheels hit a rut and were smacked sideways. We spun 180 degrees and came to rest a few yards from the edge.

'You bugger!' bellowed a passenger. The complaint did little good. With a roar of engine, we skewed back on course and went on.

We reached the Tihama plain where the wadi ran out into a heat haze and an undulating plain of sandy hollows, and then we were forced to halt. A man stepped out from under a tree and waved a school exercise book in the air. The taxman.

The government statistical handbook of Yemen makes no mention of qat. Apparently those thousands of acres do not exist, produce nothing and are of no economic importance. A curious situation when qat is clearly the largest crop in cash value and employs, either directly or indirectly, hundreds of thousands of people. The fact that qat fuels road-building, house construction and upkeep of terraces goes unremarked. The fact that qat is the main leisure activity for the ordinary man and cabinet minister alike, all these things are unmentioned. Yet the taxman was there, flesh and blood, ready to be led aside for a confidential meeting with the driver and a small present of his best qat. No money changed hands. We waved and drove off. He did not open his exercise book.

At the small town of Hays, I got down and paid the driver. His journey had not ended yet: Hays is a small place and too insignificant a market for him.

Exhausted by the ride, I threw myself onto an iron bench outside a restaurant. It was not yet nine o'clock but I could feel the heat of the day, coiling itself up like a snake ready to pounce. Flies performed lazy tangoes on the table, a long-dead Simca saloon car lay in a sea of pink plastic bags. The taxi drivers fought over customers: one old man was bundled into a front seat and the car set off only to stop after twenty yards. The old man jumped out, squawking that he did not want to go anywhere. The breakfast menu offered a choice of 'small meat' or liver, but somehow I got rook. Old bandy-legged men wandered around in white futas, white jackets and brimless woven hats shaped like flower pots.

I went for a walk through the market which is a network of squalid lanes, shaded by torn grass mats. There were two dead sheep hung up by the ankles gathering flies, and some pottery jars.

This is Hays's claim to fame: after centuries of sleepless mornings and tireless inactivity, its inhabitants have perfected a perfectly useless pot that will fall to dust should anyone be rash enough to use it. An endless languor hangs over the town as it awaits the long-awaited upturn in the pointless pot market. The last reported activity was during the 1950s when the population took a Chinese roadworker hostage, causing Imam Ahmed to warn them: 'One piece of china will cost fifteen of Hays.' Better known as a lover of Heinz Russian salad, perfume and public beheadings, Ahmed also knew a thing or two about tableware.

As soon as possible I set out for Khowkha, an hour's ride across the barren scrubby plain. The town's name means 'peach', supposedly because camel caravans bound from Beit al-Faqih to Mokha would couch here and eat the fruit from one large tree on the beach. If true, the tree is long since gone and replaced with palms which cover large stretches of the coast. There are two types: dates and dom, the latter an apple-sized bronze fruit of stony hardness from which the people scrape a speckled flour. Both trees have male and female versions which are carefully planted to achieve pollination. The male date also gives its leaves for building ushas, simple shelters of woven palm that the fishermen build as temporary camps.

I stayed on the beach and soon found a fellow qat fiend with whom I could pass the long hot afternoons. Zakariyya had come from the mountains and settled in Khowkha with plans for the motor trade. The town, he told me, was in grave difficulties following the dispute between Yemen and Eritrea over the Hunaysh Islands. Local fishermen were used to hunting in the rich waters around the islands but recently armed men had stolen a boat and others had been fired on. 'Things are not good,' he said. 'A few weeks ago, a German tourist was arrested for tape-recording the sound of the sea. They said he was an Eritrean spy.'

Officially, a skirmish had been fought over ownership of Greater Hunaysh and the matter had gone to international arbitration. But 'official' is a word that rarely means much in these waters and unofficially the story was murkier, far murkier. Hunaysh had been a way-station for smugglers for many years. Henri de Monfreid came regularly in the 'twenties with his cargoes of guns and hashish. More recently, the island became an arms market for the Eritrean rebels, now in government, and a drugs depot for Saudi Arabia.

'There is a cave on the island,' Zakariyya told me. 'A big cave that is large enough for a helicoptor to enter. There was an Italian pilot who flew drugs in from Djibouti and guns for the rebels. Then fast boats would take them on, either across to the Eritrean coast or to Yemen and Saudi.

'The problem is that the Eritreans don't want this smuggling now. They can buy their guns legally and this uncontrolled island is a danger to them. So they want to control it.'

It was a story that a fisherman confirmed next day when I walked north along the narrow strip of sand. He was trying to pull his boat up and called me to help grapple with the slippery wood, freshly greased with shark oil. When we had done it, we sat on a grass mat beside a large pile of white coral that he had removed from his nets.

'I live here,' he said proudly. 'My wife and daughter went to live in Italy and they write to me sometimes. "Come and stay in our house." Pah! If I go there I will see some things I do not like. God is generous: when I catch fish I buy rice and eat, if there is no fish I can eat the breeze. What do I want with Italy?'

Some skinny cats hung around. There were some plastic bags tied in the bush and piles of nets but little else. Quite probably he had nothing else.

'Why do you walk here?' he asked. 'What is it you want?'

I thought about that. 'I am walking to see what I can find on the sand – maybe the skeleton of a whale or a dolphin.'

He nodded. 'The dolphin is here. Sometimes the fishermen catch him in their nets and he cries. I tell you, he is a son of Adam that one. He cries real tears and if you taste them they are of salt like ours. So we release him.'

He complained about the poor fishing. He was too old to go to Hunaysh but now no one could go, everyone was fishing along this coast.

'You must not ask about Hunaysh,' he said. 'They will think you are a spy. The people will tell you that the Eritreans want the islands so the Israelis can build a place for tourists – that is nonsense. It is smuggling. Hunaysh is where they keep guns and whisky. It is always like this. Even many years ago there was a Frenchman came. He had his own boat and landed at Qataba, the next village up the coast.'

That interested me. 'A Frenchman smuggling guns?'

'Yes, and bringing people over from the Dankali lands. It was a difficult time and the Imam was fighting the tribes here in the Tihama.'

I suddenly realised he was talking of a time long gone and that the Frenchman would have to be de Monfreid.

'Why did he come here?'

'To Qataba, they say he brought some people across. These men would fight the Imam then run to Ethiopia, then return and fight again. But I was very small. I remember seeing a thin man, dressed like one of us.'

Later I walked on to Qataba, and in the sandy banks between the town and the sea I found the skull of a dolphin. The men building dhows on the beach pointed out the blowholes at the base of the beak. 'He has the mind of a man,' said one. 'We will not eat him.' They were quite unsurprised by my claim to have spoken of finding a dolphin only half an hour before. Such miracles were nothing new to them.

'One time I needed money,' said a young man of African appearance. 'I wanted twenty dollars to buy some things, but how could I get such a large amount of money? In the evening I walked to Khowkha and along the way I found a cow's skull. It is like nothing. There are many of them. But this time I picked it up and carried it with me. At the town I met a tourist and he asked to buy the skull. I told him it was worthless and offered to give it but he pressed some money into my hand. When I looked I found it was twenty dollars! Truly, only God knows all.'

Under the tutelage of their father, the younger boatbuilders were busy putting a new keel on a dhow, using a strip of red silk to ensure a tight fit. He took over when needed, always aware of what each of them was doing and ready to demonstrate. The main tool was a small adze which he handled with all the dexterity of an artist's brush.

'We have many orders for boats,' he told me when I asked if business was good. 'But the problem is this tool.' He held up the adze. 'It is a very special shape, only used by us boatbuilders. We used to buy them in Aden during the British time, but now there are no more. Can they be bought in your country?'

I had to admit that I did not know. He shook his head. 'Inshallah we will find some one day.'

The night after Tim was supposed to arrive but did not a violent storm burst over Khowkha and cut the town off. In the morning the Red Sea was red, the rain had washed tons of silt out from the mountains, staining the sea in brilliant blood-red stripes. At noon the wonderful old qat market, in a caravanserai through a stucco archway, was coming to terms with a grim fact: no qat. The calamitous rain had prevented the muqawwats returning to the mountains the previous night and it was unlikely that any cars would come. Disconsolate groups of men stood around the puddles, muttering to each other about the inflated prices the traders were now demanding for yesterday's leftovers. And I stood there with them, hoping to buy qat for Zakariyya and his family, and I knew I could not face an afternoon without the leaf.

When I first went to San'a, I used to play tennis occasionally at the British Club and sometimes against a young man of the 'My Body is a Temple' religion. He was vehemently, almost violently, opposed to qat. He had the belief that his body was perfectible: if only he could eat the right things, do the right exercise and beat me at tennis – something he did with sickening regularity – then all would be well. This young Adonis was quite determined to be addicted to nothing, and that is exactly what happened, he became addicted to not being addicted. It seems there is nothing quite so compulsively irresistible as self-righteousness. But once that was achieved, it only took one slip to shatter his self-belief. A cigarette accepted from Mister Nick-o-Tine in a moment of weakness and he gave up his religion to become a heavy smoker. He even tried qat. Unfortunately, he still won at tennis.

Incidents like this take on a mythic proportion in anti-drugs lore. That one cigarette, that first snort of coke or heroin rush – a fatal first step on the road to ruin. Instant addiction. But even a hard drug like heroin needs time and patience and dedication. 'It takes at least three months' shooting twice a day to get any habit at all,' wrote William Burroughs in *Junky*, a book based on his own experiences as a heroin-user. 'I think it is no exaggeration to say it takes a year and several hundred injections to make an addict.' You have to want to be an addict. If only there were a quick way to get hooked: the instant addiction idea probably did more to promote drugs than all the coke barons put together.

As for qat, I had tried it once without effect, then in Tim's seventh-floor view room I became hooked without even touching it. Situations are far more addictive than substances.

And so, as I stood in the mud in Khowkha souk, I reflected on my considerable irritation at the prospect of a qat-free day and I realised that my first successful qat experience had been qat-free, in which case I could in no way be addicted to anything but five hours of indolent conversation which has yet to be listed on any international convention or schedule of dangerous substances and so must be harmless. In which case, why not? I scouted around the dealers and paid an exorbitant price for some of the previous day's leftovers.

# 19

It was not altogether a surprise when Tim was a day late and arrived with two old friends, Abdulwahhab and Faiz. After a memorable lunch in a crowded restaurant where Tim caused panic by setting fire to the table-cloth of the San'a Airport Fire Brigade (they were on their annual outing), we reached Mansuriyya at sunset where Abdulwahhab and Faiz dropped us off and we took a taxi to Sukhnah at the base of Jebel Bura.

The driver interrogated us as we raced at twenty miles an hour along a dead-straight corrugated track.

'You're Christians, are you? Is it true you make wine from pigs?'

Sukhnah appeared as a few neon lights in a wall of darkness. The driver tried to take us into town but found the road blocked with piles of earth and masonry.

'Just up there,' he growled. 'Hotel Ghaleb.'

Nothing could hide the desperate decrepitude of the town. Over the once white walls, neat archways and slatted shutters had crept a ragtag army of breeze-block, iron and string. Though never much of a place, Sukhnah had briefly blossomed when Imam Ahmed decided that the hot springs were good for his aches and pains. He would come and spend long periods here when San'a grew cold, a sort of hill station at the bottom of the hill – in Ahmed's upside-down world, at least, it made sense. For some periods he ruled the country from his bath and even called his one and only press conference here.

Without a great patron, Sukhnah scrapes a living from the sick who come in dwindling numbers, most preferring to go to bigger bustling spas like Hammam Damt and Hammam Ali.

At the hotel, the boy took Tim's passport for registration first and we were shown to an upstairs room lined with Tihami iron beds. These strange modern versions of a traditional item of furniture are high beds strung with plastic cord and with a low rail on one side that serves no purpose but to trap your head under during the night. The older wooden variety, in contrast, are delightfully carved and strung with rope or plaited palm fronds, the design being exactly identical to that found in Harar.

We settled down to finish our qat. Tim was just beginning to tell me that Bura was famous for its ginger and he planned to fill his bag with it when there was a knock at the door. The boy re-entered and asked for my passport. I handed it over and he left, but within a minute the door opened again. This time two armed men walked in, followed by another dressed in white zenna with a pistol stuck in his belt.

'Whose is this?' he asked, holding out my passport.

'Mine.'

He glared and opened it. Lying between the pages, neatly pressed after all the weeks, were three twenty-dollar bills.

'What is this?'

Now I sat up and so did Tim. I think the same thought had hit us simultaneously: he thinks it's a bribe.

I stood up, smiling. 'I'm sorry, my brother! I left the money in there and forgot about it.'

He did not return the smile. I took the money but he kept the passport and began to flick through it.

'You are a tourist? You say you are a tourist? But you come to Yemen by boat from Djibouti. Is that what tourists do? No.'

I could see that he had the book open on the page of my Eritrean visa. It had been two years before and London had stamped 'State Government of Eritrea', but the immigration officer at the tiny port of Assab had put 'Provisional Government' as though it had existed so long in exile it was somehow truer, more real, in London. Either way, they had managed to get the word Eritrea stamped all over three pages for the sake of a one-week visit.

The officer was not about to commit himself to naming the country out loud but instead tested me on dates. 'When did you arrive in Mokha? What day did you leave Djibouti? Why does it not say on your Yemeni visa "tourist"?'

There was a discussion over this. The visa had been smudged a little and the wording was unclear, plus the handwriting was poor and almost indecipherable. When the other men crowded forward to read and Tim, with his fluent Arabic, managed to convince them, the officer changed tack.

'That is unimportant – where is your tasrih? Show me your pass?'

This really was ridiculous. Before 1990 and Yemeni unity, it had been necessary to get a pass to leave San'a – a pure formality but one forgotten at your peril. Now these officious words took us both back ten years. I could see the suspicion in his face, the absolute conviction that we were dangerous, and I thought of all the travellers' tales of Yemeni xenophobia, tales I had chosen to ignore.

'Why are you here, in Sukhnah?'

'We want to bathe at the springs,' said Tim. 'Perhaps climb up Jebel Bura and find some fresh ginger root – do you know if it's still grown there?'

It all sounded horribly unconvincing and the officer ignored the question. 'You do not have permission to climb Bura. You do not have permission to be in Sukhnah. This is very bad for you. I must telephone Hodeidah and speak to the commandant there.'

Now we were worried. As soon as that call was made, the possibility of an escalating situation was all too obvious. Tim began to explain how we had once been teachers in San'a and he still lived there and the school director would vouch for us.

'Listen,' said the officer. 'Give me the number of the school. I will talk to Hodeidah and to the director of this school.'

And then Tim pursed his lips and frowned and turned to me and said in English, 'I don't suppose you remember the number, do you?'

My smile never wavered. 'The chances that he'll actually phone them are nil – it's just to save face. We hand over a number, any number, and he comes back and says, "Okay, off you go." Can't you see? He knows he's made a mix-up over this tasrih business, he just wants a face-saving get-out.'

Tim did not seem convinced but he scribbled down a number and handed it over. The officer pushed it behind his jambiyya. 'I will go to the telephone now,' he said and marched out, followed by the firing squad.

We sat in silence for a moment, then Tim said, 'I really can't believe this – it's as though the bad old days have come back.'

'Do you think we're under house arrest or anything?'

'Let's find out.'

We got rid of the qat and strolled out of the hotel. The boy followed us, murmuring assurances that all would be well. In the tea-shop our case was already being discussed; everyone was very relaxed and friendly and not at all in the mood for lynching an Eritrean spy. We began to relax too, but it didn't last.

I saw the hotel boy's eyes flicker towards the street and turned to see the officer and his men marching up. He came under the awning and stood over us, gripping our passports.

'That number you gave me – it is not a school. You come now to head-quarters.'

The officer led the way with the soldiers behind us. We passed a few shops, simple tin shacks selling cheap towels for the baths. Shopkeepers and customers stared at us. I could hear the rumour mill starting up: people were whispering to each other. We walked past the baths, a tumble-down stone building, and came to the old Turkish government headquarters. This was the largest building in Sukhnah, a massive rambling ruin of arch-ways, galleries and broken shutters. In one upper room, above the archway where we entered, there was a light, but the rest was in darkness. The court-yard was filled with rubble and in places the colonnades had collapsed. This, I realised, was where Ahmed had stayed during his sojourns in the town: we were in the court of the mad tyrant.

A soldier gripped my arm: 'Up here – the steps.'

There was a flight of stone steps, the balustrade lying down below in pieces and the steps crumbly and uneven. We went up towards the light and came to a doorway leading to a large room with windows overlooking the courtyard. The floor was covered in red lino and in the centre was a single grey metal desk on which stood a large Bakelite telephone. There were two chairs. At the far end was an archway, curtained to hide some inner sanctum.

As we entered, two men grabbed their rifles and sprang to their feet. They had been lounging under the windows with their qat. The officer marched us up to the desk and indicated the chairs.

'Sit down,' he ordered.

Slowly the room filled with people: tribal soldiers draped with bandoliers, a dwarf, a fat bearded man with his hands tied together with electrical flex, a boy carrying a tray who had followed us from the souk, and various soldiers who between them might have possessed one serviceable uniform but were well-equipped with Kalshnikovs. They stood around the desk, a wall of faces, some pushed through at waist-height, all discussing our case and filling in new arrivals on the latest developments. 'It was a false number – now they have to telephone San'a themselves.' I realised that the commandant was coming and he would appear through the curtained archway. I also realised that my liberty depended on Tim remembering a telephone number.

This did not give me any cause for hope. Tim was frowning and trying to light a cigarette. 'Now what was it? Two-seven . . . no . . . two-five . . . no, hang on. Let's do this properly.' He reached in his pocket. The wall of men stiffened. Tim took out a scrap of paper about one inch square and a pencil stub. 'Now, if I write down all the numbers I think it could be.' He had managed about eight combinations, all completely different, when the curtain was swept back.

It's the Incident at Deraa, I told myself, Peter O'Toole as Lawrence of Arabia in the hands of the Turks, a sadistic bully swaggers in wearing bloodstained khaki and riding boots against which he flicks a hippo-hide whip. 'So, English Spy Pig,' he snarls, 'we meet again. Only this time there will be no conveniently unlocked door at the rear for your escape.'

Instead of this, the curtain fell back and in shuffled Wee Willie Winkie.

'Salaam aleikum,' he said dreamily, nodding gently at the men who moved back to give him room. He was wearing a long night shirt that reached to his bare feet and rubbed his grizzled scalp with his hands as if just roused from a pleasant slumber. 'Where are the passports?'

The officer handed them over and once again Tim's passed inspection but mine did not. His dreamy manner was gone now, the pages were flicked back and forth as dates were cross-checked.

'You were in Djibouti for one week and in that period you visited Eritrea, didn't you?'

'No!'

'You have visited Eritrea before, you have a visa.'

'That was long ago. I have never been back there.'

'Why did you come from Djibouti by boat? If you are a tourist, then you should come in a group by plane.'

'I like boats and I hate aeroplanes.'

'That is most unusual. What time did you leave Djibouti?'

'Around lunchtime.'

'And when did you reach Mokha?'

'Next morning at breakfast.'

He glanced at the officer who nodded. The passports were put on the desk. 'Please, you telephone the school and I will talk to the director.'

Tim pointed out that it was ten o'clock at night on a Thursday, the eve of the Yemeni weekend; it was highly unlikely that anybody would be there. 'Try.'

He dialled the first number. 'Two – that's right – what's next? Oh, I can't read my own writing – is that a three? Okay, let's try three . . . '

Eventually it rang and somebody answered. 'Hello, is that the school?' It took a while for a decision to be reached, but it was not the school. Tim tried the second number with the same result, and the third. The wall remained transfixed but there were dark mutterings at the back. On the fourth number we made contact. The school's night guard, Saleh, answered. I sat back smiling, but our troubles were not quite over.

He remembered Tim, of course, hadn't he spoken to him only last week? Where are you? Tim explained that he wanted Saleh to speak to the commandant about us. Did he remember Kevin from a few years ago? Brown hair, wife and two children, drove a habba, lived in an old Jewish house in al-Qaa. The coaching of our guarantor was quite blatant, but no one objected. As Tim handed the receiver to the commandant I could still hear Saleh bleating, 'But I don't remember him – it's before my time.'

The commandant frowned and spoke to Saleh at length then replaced the receiver.

'There were times,' he said thoughtfully, 'when such formalities were unnecessary. In the time of the Prophet, blessings be upon him, and the first caliphate, a man was free to roam the earth as he desired.' He picked up the passports and toyed with them. 'But those days are gone. As you know, some are up but they will come down. Did not you British say that the sun would never set on your empire? And the Americans who are

[273]

supporting these Eritreans – will not their power reach a peak and like the sun sink once again? Of course, it is so, only God is all-seeing and all-powerful and we hope for a day when these,' he waved the passports and handed them back to us, 'are unnecessary.'

The wall, which had been enthralled, now collapsed with relief. The foreigners were free men. The man with the flex unravelled it from his wrists and I realised he was another guard who just happened to like tying himself up.

'God willing,' said Tim, 'in that time the Yemeni currency will come to exceed that of America in strength. The rial will be more powerful than the dollar.'

This went down admirably, though some uncharitable soul at the door muttered that even if the foreigner was not a spy, he was almost certainly a lunatic.


At seven next morning, I woke and looked through the uncurtained window to Jebel Bura. It was a magnificent prospect. A broad plain of fields and low trees led to the foot of the mountain which then rose for 6,000 feet, like a golden bolt of shot silk. Between the jagged peaks of the summit ridge, tiny specks of houses could be made out, and on the southern side a lower ridge, known as the Land of Food, led across to the even higher massif of Jebel Raymah.

Our plan was to visit Sukhnah's baths in the morning, before catching a lift with any passing muqawwat as he returned up the mountain that afternoon. The following day we would walk along the top of Bura and down the northern flank into the remote valley of Rijaf, a marvellous forest which I had visited a decade before. On that occasion I had walked in from the coastal plain and seen only a part of the valley, now I wanted to approach from the summit and see the entire forest, one of the few such places in all Arabia.

A good hot bath is seen by Yemenis as the perfect prelude to a large lunch and qat. The bath exhausts you: starts you off on that languorous dreamy feeling that the qat continues. The leaf acts on the taste buds to sensitise them: water can taste sweet and tobacco smoother than honey. But before those pleasures are possible, you must go to the fire.

Sukhnah has fire. The baths have no nice domes, no clean linen, no beds or cushions, but they have fire. There are three pools of black water and the last is built directly over the eye of the spring. We entered to find ourselves on a tiled floor where an old man was being manipulated by a muscular assistant. Every now and then the man would groan miserably. Other bathers stumbled around in voluminous underpants or sat on a wooden bench breathing heavily with their eyes closed. We changed into our futas and spent an hour building up to the last pool. When my shoulders finally went under, my head seemed to double in size and begin to throb. I got out almost immediately and slumped on the floor next to two old men.

'As Christians,' one was saying, 'they are bound to go to Hell where they will pick fruit like the heads of devils from the zaggum trees before tasting the eternal scourge of fire.'

To which his companion replied: 'But does not the Koran say: "Whosoever believes in God and the Last Day and does what is right shall have nothing to fear or regret"?'

They turned to me. 'Why do you not become a Muslim?'

It is a question that is asked constantly in Yemen. There is no unfriendliness about it, more the sort of concern you might show to a blindfolded man crossing a busy road. Only at that precise moment I felt as though I had tasted the eternal torment of scalding water, my skin was screaming, my chest constricted, and between my legs was something that I didn't recognise but thought might be a zaggum fruit. This is the inferno, I told myself. Next the purgatorio.

Actually, lunch was quite good. There was a large room open to the street on two sides. Just inside were a number of shallow charcoal-burning trays on which pots of meat and marag were bubbling. Another area held a clay oven where bread was being baked on request: blobs of dough, with a few sinuous flicks of the wrist, becoming flying discs that were neatly dropped on a convex basket, then deftly stuck on the inner wall of the red-hot oven. In a minute they were ready to be hooked out with a bent piece of wire.

Most customers eschewed the solitary table and ate off the floor. Most also brought their own radishes and bananas. We ate well: sweet fatut made with wild honey, then a scalding salta, spitting chillis, and a glorious marag.

Finally came sweet tea and a stagger back to the hotel room, leaving word at various points about cars to Bura.

Our qat was Ba'imi, from the top western slope of Bura. 'You'll lose your mind on this,' warned the muqawwat, wrapping it in brown paper and string. 'Believe me, it's not like any other stuff you've tasted.'

But qat-sellers always say such things and we only remembered his words when twenty minutes after starting, I felt the sort of adrenaline surge that only an unexpected visit from Cedric could have matched. 'Bloody Hell!'

Tim looked across, cornflower blue eyes glittering. 'What?' Then it hit him too and he began to smile. 'Oh, good qat.'

My tongue began to tingle. I had never eaten anything like it. Ideas and words poured from both of us in reckless precision, not a syllable out of place but nothing planned, leaping from topic to topic with crazy logic. And all of it seemed new and innovative.

Later on a local stopped in to say hello. He told us Ba'imi was famed for such effects but few people knew of it because the production was so small. Some was rushed to Hodeidah on the coast but the more celebrated, and more plentiful, Shami qat tended to hide the Ba'imi.

He told us how he had chewed in Saudi Arabia. 'I was a chauffeur for a prince and one day we were driving along and he asked me where I was from. I told him, Yemen. So he opened his case and said, "If you are Yemeni, you had better have this." And he gave me some qat.'

'But it is illegal – did he take it himself?'

He shrugged. 'Why would he have it, if not to chew it?'

We asked about the journey to Bura. 'You need to head for Maghraba but there will be no more cars today. Tomorrow is market day and you will find one.'

In the hour after sunset, Solomon's Hour to the Yemenis, we were in a silent reverie. Across the border, I was thinking, the legal status is different, but does that mean the physical and mental effects are different, too? Qat in Britain makes young people want to dance all night, in Saudi Arabia it makes them criminals and drug addicts, in Yemen it draws them together and cements relationships.

'In qat,' said Tim suddenly and with mock portent, 'the silences don't matter.'

The paper wrappers were empty, the qat all finished. With the quiet sadness that always comes at the end, we strolled down to the town and drank milky, spiced tea.

Next day's market was a chance for Tim to enquire about his ginger but we could find no one who had heard of it. There were tree pods from Iran, civet oils, sesame seeds, camel muzzles, pink sweets and yellow sweets, there was even a concoction of ambergris and honey which smelled like faeces. 'A sovereign remedy for thinness,' said the seller from under a wide-brimmed straw hat. But Tim was sceptical. 'I tried it once before and the seller warned me that if I took too much I'd blow up like a balloon – an enormous butter-ball rolling around the souk.'

The seller waved his arms about in annoyance. 'No! No! It doesn't take effect as fast as that!'

'But I never gained an ounce.'

'Then it wasn't true ambergris – like this one.'

As for ginger, the seller knew what the word meant but had never heard of Bura producing it.

'Who told you about it?' I asked Tim.

'Oh, it's true – no doubt about it. I mean this man may not know his own mountain, that's not my fault. I'd have to check where I saw it: was it in the crops register of Sultan al-Muzaffar?'

'When was he around?'

'He died in AD 1295.'

He became angry with me for laughing and we wandered around separately after that, much to the confusion of the locals who kept coming over and saying, 'Your friend is over there.'

We joined up again to have lunch and buy qat – not Ba'imi, neither of us was yet ready to face such an overwhelming experience again. By early afternoon we were sitting on rope beds in a shop next to the Bura road. The shopkeeper, Ali, had taken us in hand and was organising various small boys to keep him informed on car movements in the market.

'One will come, if God wills,' he said.

The shop's stock was meagre but obviously carefully chosen to fit local needs. There were soap powder, Brylcreem, bullets (British or Egyptian), biscuits, cooking oil, straw hats, matches, cigarettes, small plastic bags of cold water (most could not afford the bottled mineral water), Coca-Cola, Chinese batteries, flouncy frocks for small girls and Czech machine guns. That was everything – except the sacks of flour kept in a lock-up over the street. People came and poked their heads round the door to see us.

'Russians?'

A man drove a sheep away, holding its back legs as if it was a wheelbarrow.

'Koreans?'

This man was a qat-seller who never made enough to buy good qat for himself. 'Like going to a banquet every day and only eating houmous,' he said. 'Are you Azerbaijanis?'

A hollow-cheeked old man with mournful eyes rolled up. 'Tell me, you speak English and you speak Arabic. So, what is the difference between a fart in English and a fart in Arabic?'

We began to laugh but he kept a straight face.

'I'll tell you. In English you say – ' he pursed his lips and emitted a thin, little squeak. 'But in Arabic, ha!' He pouted up and blew a tremendous raspberry. 'There! When the Yemeni went to London with his wife and they were walking in Ox-ford Street, she let out a violent fart that knocked her poor husband off his feet. "What are you doing?" he shouted. He was very angry. "It is all right, my darling," said the wife, "they don't understand Arabic."'

Ali almost choked on his qat but recovered to tell the Story of the Historic Fart, a much-repeated tale of the man, Abdul Aziz, who let rip in a qat chew and, covered in shame, went to India for ten years. After such a long period, hoping to be forgotten, he returned and crept back to his village. In the street he spied an old woman talking to a young boy. 'When was I born, Grandmother?' asked the lad. 'I don't know exactly,' replied the old woman, 'but it was in the year that Abdul Aziz farted.'

This was the first hour of the qat and one for such joking; everyone is so relieved to be finally sitting and tucking into their leaf that an outpouring of good humour is assured. I've seen sprightly old men leap to their feet and hold mock wrestling matches with equally aged rivals. Sticks of qat go flying at unsuspecting friends. Once, in a house in San'a, a man came in with a cardboard box and placed it in the centre of the room.

Silence fell. He pulled back the lid and out jumped a pair of hyaena cubs which ran round the room biting everyone.

Our own comedian that afternoon was on his way to the Land of Food and, to our regret, was soon called to climb up on the back of a habba laden with boxes of sardine tins. In rural Yemen, in places too small to warrant even a shared taxi, the merchants' four-wheel-drive pick-ups are the sole means of transport – and no matter how laden it's rare for them to refuse anyone.

An hour before sunset we were called out to a Landcruiser bound for Maghraba. We thanked Ali and said goodbye, then climbed into the cab. There were two men already inside and I was tight against the door, one hand dangling out the open window the other gripping the dashboard. There was an instant comradeship amongst us, qat and cigarettes passed around, conversation bouncing along, much as we did on the stony trail. Behind us on the sacks of flour and various parcels were half a dozen more travellers; we could hear someone singing merrily and the chatter of voices.

Yahya the driver was a muqawwat who went every day from Maghraba to Hodeidah with a load of Ba'imi qat. Once the leaves were picked, bundled and loaded it would be around eight in the morning. He would reach Hodeidah by midday, be back in Sukhnah by four and home by ten. Seven days a week. The rewards were good, he had a new Landcruiser, but the risks enormous. The road, he warned us, was in a very poor state towards the top, the result of a dispute between two sheikhs who both said the other should pay for repairs.

Muhammad 'the Small' was a UNICEF worker, heading up with several thousand polio vaccinations to give to the children on the mountain. His colleague, Hussein, was the jolly singer we could hear.

Bura had been entirely hidden all day by mists and even now, as we approached, there was no sign of its rock walls and spires in the last hazy light of day. But once we began to climb, the veil was pulled away, the moon rose and Bura was there above us.

Leaning out the window, head smacking painfully on the frame, I could see a tremendous wall of rock flanked by spurs and spires that soared up to a wolf's grin skyline. There seemed to be absolutely no way even a footpath could climb this vertical face, but slowly we laboured upwards, turning corners to find steep gulches or ascending ledges. The wheels spat shards of granite. We lurched, slammed into holes, roared out. The young men on the back were ordered down and ran ahead. In places they manhandled boulders out of the path or filled holes, then shouted guidance as we clawed up.

On a flat section, Yahya stopped to rest the engine and we climbed down to be greeted by Hussein's exaggerated salute. 'Thank God we are here!' he shouted. 'And we will say it again if we reach Maghraba – the road is bad from this point.' He was a Sergeant Bilko, a clever clown, the jester at the qat chew: he told the boys a potted potty history of the moon, then a shaggy dog story about a muqawwat with a speech impediment.

We restarted and Hussein's warning proved to be no joke. At every hairpin bend we made a two-bite attack: first a mad rush up on full lock, stop with a crunch at the rock wall, engine fails, lights go out, a sickening reverse towards the edge as he grabs at the key, stop, wheelspin and go. And the edge always seemed to be on my side. I leaned out and looked down: forty, fifty, a hundred feet, to a terrace not one yard wide or a mess of boulders.

Tim was asking Yahya about ginger. 'Yes, it grows here.' Tim gave a triumphant smile and delved into the finer points of the root's cultivation. Yahya showed the flower shape with his hands, his hands leaving the wheel – the wheel that was being wrenched by the road – and we lurched towards infinity only for Yahya to haul us back. We ran at a hair-pin, rose sharply, stalled and rolled back. Lights returned with the power.

Tim asked after Abdulrahman al-Bura'i, a thirteenth-century poet noted for his religious zeal and the mountain's most famous son. Muhammad the Small recalled a tale of how Bura'i was starving and only a Jew took pity. Later, when a great storm came, only Bura'i's house and the Jew's were not destroyed.

'How does it go?' said Tim. '"No exile is the exile to the latter end of the earth" – that's Bura'i, isn't it?'

My impression was that the tyres had crossed the edge for a moment.

Yahya could not talk without his hands. He lifted them off the wheel. '"The exile is the exile to the tomb and the coffin,"'

We whacked a rock, the wheel spun, we veered. I closed my eyes.

'"He hath claims on the dwellers in the places of their birth."'

We were clutching at a scree slope of crumbling boulders that had been hastily constructed by the youths.

'"Whoso wandereth the world, for he lacketh him a home."'

Tim was bright with interest. 'Where did Bura'i live on the mountain?'

Yahya had to point and look far across the blackness. There was a sort of staircase ahead made of blocks, something like the side of the Great Pyramid of Cheops. Tim blinked. 'I say, this is rather steep, isn't it?' Then was knocked back into Arabic by a thump from below. 'Have you had much rain recently?'

I couldn't take any more. 'Look will you shut up and let him drive!'

He thought for a moment. Yahya was saying that the rains had torn much of the track away only a week before. As if to confirm it, the rear wheels did an elegant glissando across a bare rock face. Tim nodded at me. 'Perhaps you're right.'

It was now apparent that we were moving up the side of a vast stack of terraces that led to the top. Silhouetted against the night sky were stone houses on a saddle of land between peaks. After a section so bad that everyone except Yahya walked, we roared into town.

There was a tight tangle of houses stretched along a narrow ridge. Parking space was limited to a square the size of a helicopter pad. I glanced over the far side and saw only clouds below; above us on the crag were lights.

'That is Ruqaab,' said Hussein. 'You will pass through it on your way to the wadi.'

He and Muhammad the Small invited us to sleep in their office, a tiny room filled with chest freezers for the vaccines. We all lay down to sleep on these freezers or on the floor but Hussein wanted to tell jokes which he did, despite a voice from another house bellowing: 'Ya, Doktur! It is shameful to laugh at night!' It seemed strange that the complaint was not about the nature of Hussein's jokes – all completely filthy – but the sound of us laughing.

At dawn I was the first outside, shivering on the edge of the terrace, waiting for the sun's rays to climb down from Ruqaab and warm the village. Below was a sea of cloud and, though I followed the track down with my eye, I could not find where it disappeared. It was as if we had clambered into the sky and drawn the ladder up after us.

[281]

Life begins at daybreak in such villages and soon donkeys were clattering past on their way to fetch water. The men wore rough woollen zennas and leather belts, while the women had long-sleeved black tunics, touched at the hem and wrist with gold threads and secured at the waist with a large cummerbund of twisted white cloth. The embroidery continued around the ankles of their trousers. On their heads they wore piles of red and green scarves, the topmost folded flat over the others – a style similar to that of some Burmese hill tribes. In many areas of Yemen traditional costumes survive only amongst the older women, but here the young girls were dressed like their grandmothers, and with their honey-coloured skin and perfect oval faces they were like tiny Modigliani madonnas.

After a breakfast cooked by Hussein – 'I'm an artist with beans' – we were passed into the care of a donkey drover who was heading up to Ruqaab, his beasts letting loose a morning chorus of frenetic farting that disguised any human indiscretions – be they in English or Arabic.

The path was a clear, smooth flight of steps spiralling up through fields of coffee. There were few qat trees – this was grown slightly below Maghraba. An old lady popped her head above a wall to greet us, grinning beneath a pile of red sparkly scarves. Her face would have been at home in any Silk Road souk east of Kashgar.

The summit of Bura is a central spine off which extend numerous limbs, all prickly with spires of rock. So deep and indented are the valleys that dense cloud can be trapped there through the day, apparently impervious to the sun's attempts to lift it. With this torn curtain of cloud below us, we walked in bright sunshine, and far away in the west lay the Red Sea.

'Sometimes we can see the ships on it,' said an old man who had caught up with us. He pointed out the coffee trees. 'Do you have this in your country?'

When we said not, he offered a poem.

> O coffee of Yemen! O pearls!
> O treasure upon the trees!
> He who grows you will never be poor.

He left us behind, bare feet padding quickly on the stones and far nimbler than our clumsy boots.

An hour later we passed under a stone lintel and entered Ruqaab where we found the male population waiting for the qat-runners to follow us up from Maghraba.

The stone was yellow and gave the village a feeling of warmth which the shadows of its lanes did not have. Only about 7,000 feet above sea level, the difference in temperature between sun and shade was astonishing. We decided to wait for qat too and found ourselves shuttling back and forth across the street as we first overheated, then froze.

I walked up to the old Hakuma, the government building put up by the Ottomans during their second occupation of the country. People leaned out of windows where marigolds grew in old milk powder tins, old men swaddled in white shawls on doorsteps, youths bright-eyed and cheeky, making a walking motion with their fingers at me and roaring with laughter: 'Where's the Johnny Walker?!'

The faces were so varied and different, it seemed incredible that this was a remote mountain in remotest Arabia: there were stout Caucasians, curly-haired Indians, green-eyed Turks, an Assamese, even a Khmer – all from good Bura'i stock.

Yemeni history is full of legendary excursions and conquests to far-off realms, and perhaps none is as fascinating and unlikely as that of Shammar Yuhar'ish, a Himyar king of the third century AD. His conquests are said to have extended to Chinese central Asia where he founded a city of 60,000 Arabs and also destroyed what is now Samarkand – hence the reputed meaning of the name 'Shammer destroyed it'. But we ridicule such claims at our peril: Himyaritic coins have turned up in Chinese burial chambers.

The arrival of the qat-runners brought a cheer from the company. They were coming along below us and behind was a mysterious backdrop of cloud-shrouded peaks and vertical ladders of terraces leading to mountain-top villages. I lingered long enough to take a photograph, then followed the others who had immediately run down to the market.

Qat-selling was a cheerful scrummage that lasted only fifteen minutes, then the runners were bundling up what was left and heading off along the ridge. We followed them, picking our way through villages where lop-eared, sad-eyed cows sat on the front doorsteps and voices shouted instructions to us from upper windows. 'Wadi Rijaf? – you must go to Mughaarib.' But Tim had got more information on ginger – we had to find

[283]

the house of 'The Sons of the Leopard'. 'They grow it and will sell you some.'

The ridge became narrower and more uneven: great smooth tors of stone stood in our path and we scrambled over slabs of red rock in which strange circular hollows appeared, as if huge and powerful fingers had once pressed there. Below on both sides, steep flights of terraces fell dramatically into cloud. In one place I counted the steps to seventy-one but lost track in the gathering mist. By rough calculation I estimated that such a flight was dropping about 900 feet while extending only 300 – an extraordinary feat of engineering. But vertical height is nothing to such people. A schoolboy caught up with us on his way home: every day he walked four miles and climbed down 1,400 feet to reach school. He invited us to stop for qishr at his home, a white-walled cottage poised on a saddle of land between two crags – a saddle just wide enough to contain the one-room building. Every inch of available space was utilised, even a flat boulder perched above a sheer drop had become a home to the hollow tree-trunks used as bee hives.

We thanked him for the offer but declined. He encouraged us to accept, full of adult aplomb at ten years of age, and quite able to cope with invit-ing two foreigners for coffee. But we were keen to press on and a late qat-runner showed us where the track dived down to avoid the impassable crag ahead.

Once we had descended a few hundred feet we joined a path along the coffee terraces and entered a green labyrinth. Here the path was just a series of stepping stones projecting from a terrace wall. Mature coffee trees reached up from the field below and over our heads, the unripe beans within our reach. A few late flowers delicately scented the air. In places where the path crept around a rock face a terrace could be a foot square, little more than a plant pot built of small stones on any available ledge large enough to hold no more than a single coffee bush. Where the rock allowed, cisterns had been built, each a few feet in diameter but many times deeper. Concave stone roofs covered them and a hole in the centre allowed water to enter; I guessed they were sited at places where rainwater naturally gushed down during storms. During the wet season when the water is fresh, the people drink from these cisterns, but later only well water is used.

By one such cistern or sabil, two men sat waiting for their qat-man who had been keeping us company. He unshouldered his sack and sat down. This was a world that felt strangely enclosed and separate from that below, and in it distant sounds became curiously close. The effect was like one of those old western films when the scene is the wild expanses of Montana but the voices seem to be indoors.

We went on. The path turned sharply up, a 500-foot flight of twisting steps that left us gasping for breath. At the top was a hamlet and two more men awaiting their runner.

'Don't you have mountains in your country?' asked one, rather alarmed by my desperate attempts to extract oxygen from the thin cold air.

'Nowhere like this.'

He was, we discovered, one of 'The Sons of the Leopard', but had bad news for Tim. No ginger. 'You must come during Ramadhan – then it is ready. However, in Mughaarib you may find some.'

We passed through the village, a tight little knot of houses and steep stony lanes covered in straw, then a further hour's walk brought us to Mughaarib.

In all places in Yemen, a visitor gets some sort of reception: children run out, men shout greetings, a snarling dog attacks – but none was quite like Mughaarib.

The houses were huge stone monoliths, much larger than in other villages, and all gathered around a broad paved street – broad in Bura terms at least, it was wide enough for a donkey dual carriageway. Our arrival was noted long before we entered and as soon as we did, a screaming troop of children surrounded us: girls laughing and clapping their hands, crop-haired boys with aged faces whooping and leaping. We were propelled to the centre of town, tiny fingers pinching at our legs. There wasn't an adult in sight but eventually a youth appeared and invited us into his house for a glass of qishr. We instantly accepted.

He led us up a flight of steps and through a series of low wooden doors into a back room. Here the small windows looked out over flowering trees to an empty sky and the walls were spotlessly white. There was one item of furniture, a wooden rope-strung bed of immense dimensions worthy of a Gulliver among the Lilliputians. Under the windows was a long rug and at one end sat an elderly white-bearded gentleman, puffing quietly on a hookah with a copy of the Koran at his side.

[285]

'Ahlan wa sahlan,' he greeted us, rising to shake hands and indicating that we should sit next to him. 'Do you know Martin from Switzerland?'

We confessed that we did not which disappointed him. Everyone in the village knew Martin from Switzerland, particularly the children who had forced the front door and now poured into the room screeching with triumph. Beatlemania had come to Bura.

Some older youths removed the youngest and the girls, suddenly over-come with shyness, removed themselves, except for one pretty toddler who fought to stay. She had the same black tunic and white cummerbund of her elder sisters, plus a red dot between her eyes and large golden ear-rings. The children who remained – I counted thirty-two – formed a semi-circle around us, sitting cross-legged.

Qishr was served to us and our behaviour noted with excited whispers.

'Look! That one smokes but this one does not!'

'See how fast he drinks – he is thirsty!'

'Why do they wear those boots?' (We had left them at the door, of course.)

'Oh, their feet are softer than a baby's.'

'Are they Yemeni? They are carrying qat.'

'You donkey – these are Syrians.'

At a word from the old gentleman they were all chased out, but instantly crept back. I drank four glasses of qishr and felt myself falling asleep. We had been walking for five hours, mostly either up or down. But the boys were keen to tell us about Martin, a man who had done a great job in teach-ing his name and also the rudiments of environmentalism. 'Martin says that Wadi Rijaf has 1,800 types of plant,' one youth said. 'There are leop-ards, hyaenas, land crocodiles and baboons – everything!'

'It is the only place in all Arabia like this,' cried another, and soon they were all shouting out about their wadi and how wonderful it was. It was touching to hear it: I had once tried to do the same as Martin in the village school in southern Sudan and I knew how hard it was to break down tradi-tional hostility towards dangerous beasts and create enthusiasm for the familiar.

'It is a garden of heaven down there,' said the youth. 'You will not believe your eyes. There are pools of water for swimming and butterflies like birds.'

[286]

'Is Ali Snake still there?' asked Tim who had, like me, seen the lower part of the wadi some years before. Ali Snake was a famous character and the sole resident, together with his ever-increasing family. His roof had been slept on by most of the handful of visitors who had seen the place.

The youth nodded. 'He is there.' A woman's voice called from outside the room and he said to us, 'Your lunch is ready.'

Our polite protestations were brushed aside and a large tray of chicken and rice brought in. There was no need to clear the children, they had gone, good manners dictating that only those eating remain. A small fuss over spoons – 'Foreigners eat with spoons! Quick, run to the kitchen!' – was dealt with and we ate a delicious meal.

The temptation was then to accept the offer of a qat chew and a sleep before continuing the next day, but the thought of the wadi was irresistible. Idyllic as the room was with the gentle bubbling of the pipe, the light on the kindly faces and the sound of the mob outside, we were both anxious to see that wonderful place. I wanted to sit by a pool and chew qat while the butterflies sailed by. It was a unique place and still some hours' walk away; we decided to press on.

I could hear the children howling as we put our boots on. When we emerged on the stairs, a great cheer went up and the few that had shoes threw them in the air. We were swept to the edge of the village on a tide of good will, then abandoned.

Mughaarib, we discovered, was on the edge of a side valley that ran into Rijaf and down that ravine we had to go: a 4,500-foot drop, covered in about a mile and a half. Every step was two more feet down and after a few hundred such steps, our knees began to quiver like jelly. When we reached a large outcrop of rock that promised a view down to Rijaf, we decided to call a halt and have some qat. A steady stream of women came past us, heading up to the village with heavy loads of firewood.

'That must happen every day,' I said. 'I thought Rijaf was protected in some way.' It was our first intimation that all was not well.

A youth driving a donkey stopped to chat and I asked why some of the smaller girls wore a red dot between their eyes.

'It is so we know they are girls when they wear boys' clothes,' he said mysteriously.

'But why would they do that?'

[287]

'If they fall sick many times, perhaps.'

It is a common superstition around the world that bad luck can attach to a person and some sort of identity change becomes necessary. Usually this involves a new name, even in Ruqaab we had spoken to man whose family name meant 'bad', a name often taken after a run of misfortunes. The ancient Egyptians, like Indian brahmins, had two names: one for the public and another, the real one, kept forever secret. In traditional societies right across the Indonesian archipelago, the simple question, 'What is your name?' was once a dangerously presumptuous enquiry that no one would answer directly. When I first arrived in San'a and took up residence in an upstairs flat of an Old City house, I happened to meet the landlord's daughter on the stairs. She was veiled but chatted for a while, asking me how the flat was and where I was working. Emboldened by this, I introduced myself and asked her name. There was a strangled cry from under the veil and she disappeared down the stairs in a fluster of skirts.

Changing of identity by clothes is an alternative means of tricking the attentions of the evil eye and it can happen both ways: in Yemen a newborn son whose previous brothers all died might be dressed as a girl and even have his ears pierced.

Tim switched to English to play the sceptic. 'They probably got it from Hindi films.'

But the youth heard and understood.

'Aiwa! Fil-m Hindi! The idea came from those films.'

'And, of course, these mountains are full of Indians,' said Tim teasingly.

'Aiwa! Even my neighbour is from Beit al-Hind: his grandfather's grandfather came from India.'

I sniggered.

'And my friend here,' said Tim trying to think of an insult comprehensible to a donkey drover from Bura, 'he is from a place . . . a place where they eat porcupines.'

The youth nodded. 'Aiwa! Even here people eat the porcupine, too, though I myself do not.'

At that, Tim gave up.

The youth went on, leaving us to contemplate the landscape, especially the narrow strip of green forest that was visible between the cliffs at the mouth of the side valley. Wadi Rijaf was down there, only an hour's walk,

[288]

and I was imagining a cooling swim in a rock pool. We were still sitting in broad sunlight but glancing back I saw that Mughaarib and the mountain had completely disappeared in cloud. A few heavy drops of rain splashed down. It was getting late in the afternoon and time to ease our aching knees back into action for the last few hundred feet of descent.

Tim took things at a sensible pace but I was too impatient to get there, rushing down the path at breakneck speed. The valley closed in towards the bottom. The stream was waterless but around patches of cool white sand stood large trees, bound together with tangles of creepers. There were no birds or butterflies to be seen but I put this down to the approaching storm. I had my eyes on the ground, hoping for a leopard print, but it was not that which stopped me. It was a noise. A distant rattle of metal against stone.

I stood for some time, trying to work out where it was coming from. In this vertical world of rock faces and sudden twists in canyons, sounds were difficult to pinpoint. I decided it must be coming from the ridge above. But when I reached the main wadi, I saw, to my horror, a quite different cause.

The side wadi emerged fifty feet above the bed of Rijaf. From the rocky sill a slope covered in bushes and trees led down to a ribbon of white smooth boulders and sandbars – the old riverbed, but there was no water in it. Beyond this the land rose in a dreadful scree of blasted rock, earth and smashed vegetation to a level scar that slashed across the far hillside. Above this was a second slope of ravaged forest where the route had been blasted into the hillside. A few hundred yards down the valley was a large wire-fenced road camp where a man with a pneumatic hammer was attempting to split a large boulder. In a valley only three hundred yards broad at most, the intrusion had been cataclysmic. The stream where butterflies as big as birds had flown was dry and choked with debris. Further up the wadi the road had yet to penetrate but it was clearly not far from happening. In this world of verticals, nothing could be more alien, more utterly hostile, than the deadly stab of that flat line.

I stood in shock. Tim joined me. Neither of us could understand how this could be done. I even wondered if we had come to the wrong valley, but as we scrambled down into the stream, the view revealed the familiar shape of the huge hump-backed rock that dominates the lower part of Rijaf. There was no doubt.

We scrambled up the far scree slope and onto the road. A few road-workers stared at us. The cacophony of the mechanical hammer in that confined space was terrible after the peace of the mountain – and I had thought we were leaving civilisation behind. Now I wanted to turn around and climb straight back up. We did not. We walked on quickly. On the right were ledges of deep moss through which grew dwarf trees. Far away we could hear baboons laughing, but there were still no birds or butterflies.

After a couple of miles we reached a small stone house around which the road had gouged a path. This was the house of Ali Snake. One of his sons came out to greet us.

'My wife has just given birth to a boy,' he said, full of excitement. 'I'm sorry, I'd invite you in for tea but there is nowhere to sit at the moment.'

We began to talk of the new road and his good humour evaporated. 'Look what they have done! They said they would build a wall to hold the earth up but they have not. When the rains come, the soil will wash down. They took a thousand of my coffee trees. They have diverted the stream. The road workers brought malaria. They have ruined this place.'

'But why? Why build a road here?'

'It is European money,' he said. 'The sheikh in one of the villages on top of the mountain wanted a road and this was the only way to reach it.'

'What of the wild animals?'

'The leopards have gone. As soon as the machines came they all went – no one knows where. So the baboons have become a problem. They eat all our fruit and we want to shoot them but the government say that we cannot as Wadi Rijaf is protected! What does it matter – without the water, everything will die anyway.'

'But the forest – what is left – they won't let that die, will they?'

He turned his hands over in a gesture of despair and snorted. 'If they wanted the trees to live, why not bring gas bottles for the people of the mountain to cook with. They are poor and they cut the trees down – what else can they do?'

We stood in the gathering gloom of dusk looking at the places where his papaya and banana trees were falling into the road cutting.

'What have you called your son?' Tim asked, trying to cheer him up.

He smiled. 'Radwan – it is a Yemeni name, you won't know it.'

'It's a good name,' said Tim. 'And I do know it. Radwan is one of the angels who guard paradise.'

We sat at the new agricultural research station at the end of Wadi Rijaf and I felt truly miserable. The whole idea of coming back seemed tainted now.

'Maalak?' asked one of the roadmen who had arrived in a truck. 'What's wrong?'

'This qat was planted on a graveyard,' I said, unable to smile.

If there was one memory of Yemen's nature I had treasured, it was that of our trip into Rijaf a decade before. Judith and I had camped at the mouth of the valley, cooking fish on an open fire and drinking water from the pool. Next morning we had watched baboons and picked up porcupine quills as we walked up into the forest. There had been hornbills and kingfishers that I had only seen before in Africa. But we had never gone far into the forest and I had long thought of returning to do just that.

'In some ways,' said Tim, trying to cheer me up, 'it'll be a good thing to write about – make people see how difficult conservation is.'

'We did this,' I replied. 'European money did this. I don't care about writing, I just want to get out of Wadi Rijaf and never come back.'

Like the noise of the hammer booming in the valley, my emotions were amplified by the qat. I could only think of escaping and it was not long before I had my chance: the roadworkers came and got back in their truck. 'We're going to Bajil,' they said. 'You could get a taxi to Hodeidah from there.'

We climbed up on the back. The entire vehicle was smeared with diesel waste from a black tank. I got on the spare tyre, trying but failing to keep the thick greasy stains off my clothes. When we hit the first bump, the air valve stabbed me in the backside, tearing the scab from where the last air valve had been. I stopped thinking of anything then, just chewed my qat and waited until four hours later when I slumped, belly-down, on a bed in a Hodeidah hotel room.

# 20

Hodeidah has long had a tricky relationship with outsiders: in short, none ever wanted to come and when they did they wanted to leave immediately. The British Army handbook for Yemen, 1917, states simply that it is 'dirty, unsanitary and unhealthy', the perfect post for disreputable Turkish officers dismissed quickly as 'trim but cowardly', 'corpulent' and 'slovenly in attire'. Tourists often find themselves taken there, largely because it is at the end of a tarmac road. A German I met in Khowkha was puzzled. 'Why did they take me to that rotten town? It was horrible.'

He had a point. On our first morning, crippled with calf cramp, Tim and I hobbled into the Old Town and slumped down at a tea-stall. The streets here are gently undulating ribbons of dust and detritus. One-eyed dogs skulk in every shadow. The tea-stall was built of packing cases and covered with a lacy negligee of small black flies that rose and fell gently on some undetectable breeze. We sucked at some tepid brown liquid, heavily sweet-ened with condensed milk, while a gang of small boys stood and watched, occasionally croaking, 'Hey, you!'

It is perhaps unfortunate that this squalid, filthy part of town should contain Hodeidah's finest buildings because few visitors ever get to see them. But a stroll around reveals beautiful old harem windows, fragments of scalloped arched stucco and doorways intricately carved by Indian craftsmen into arabesques. Above one we found the date 1297 AH, about 1880, and the words, 'God is a sufficient and most excellent protector.' At the sides of the door little wings emerged and curved up into posts for tying donkeys. I could imagine the coffee merchants in the silky striped zennas of old, paying courtesy calls on each other with bundles of qat, a small boy trailing behind with the master's hookah pipe over his shoulder. In places the doors had been overtaken by the rising streets. One house had four doors cut, each less beautiful than the last, like a measure of the town's slide in fortunes: first a carved lintel two feet off the ground and finally an ugly metal plate up two steps. 'Someone should do something,' said an old man who saw my interest. 'These old houses will be nothing soon.' But no one does much, it's too hot to bother. From nine till four the sultry air clings like a close cover of warm humid felt. At the headquarters of the secret police on the seafront, men sat in the broken windows, staring dully at passers-by. They were waiting, like us, for two o'clock when Hodeidah gets its injection, the little kick that makes the sluggish blood circulate, keeps life going until the night breeze seeps in.

By one o'clock the clapped-out taxis and mini-buses that drift aimlessly around the streets suddenly begin to turn north as if governed by a mysterious magnetism. You start to notice the streets are less busy, a few rattling saloons hammer past, the drivers with a determined gleam in their eye. Hailing transport of any kind becomes a problem, prices rise. When we did get something, there was no need to say our destination. The driver grinned. 'You want Shami?'

'Yes, we want.'

We went out past the lines of lorries waiting for goods to be cleared from customs, each with its fuel tanks brightly painted with scenes of tropical islands, then through a gap in a white wall towards a group of low tin-roofed buildings where a huge crowd was milling around.

There seems to be little, if any, academic work done on the various types of qat and their difference in effect. To the expert they are as distinct as wines: at one extreme is Sauti, the gut-rotting moonshine, and the other is Shami, the champagne qat of Yemen, one of only two varieties that almost everyone agrees is superior. The other is from Wadi Dahr near San'a.

Shami is always associated with Hodeidah but that is purely because the town is its main market in Yemen. In fact it is grown in a mountain region called Mahabishah some hours north by speeding Landcruiser. These highlands are particularly suitable for making money from qat – put simply, they are near Saudi Arabia. There are top quality leaves grown here that are rarely sold in Yemen, the entire production slips across the border – types like Shammakh, said to be so wonderful its broken stems exude the fragrance of incense.

Anyone involved in Shami makes money hand over fist, excepting the customer. Rich Hodeidi merchants might spend over 20,000 rials a day on bunches for himself and family – double a teacher's monthly salary. Such men cannot afford the stigma of the proverb, 'He never threw a bunch of qat at anyone', so they buy in bulk and distribute generously. Others impoverish themselves trying to maintain a Shami habit on a Sauti income.

We pushed through the heaving mass of people, men on iron benches with canvas sheets full of qat, others shaking rubtas under our noses. 'Here! Here! Malih! Good qat!'

At the more upmarket shops, the sellers sit on the counter with the qat well hidden. One customer was laboriously writing an I.O.U. for 6,500 rials on the back of a cigarette packet. The qat was in front of him: brilliant fresh leaves and shoots about six inches long – all eatable. He handed over the scrap of cardboard and began to collect the qat together but the muqawwat slowly, with infinite contempt, tore the note to bits and threw them over his head.

'But you gave me credit before,' protested the man.

The muqawwat was unmoved. 'Don't you know about the man who taught a donkey to talk?' he shouted. 'He still needed the stick to move it.'

The jibe roused the man to good-natured fury. 'And when he hit it, the donkey turned around and said, "You beat me once more and I'll bite your arse."' And with that he shouldered his way through the laughing mob in search of a cheaper deal.

We took over negotiations on behalf of the qat in question but the price had mysteriously risen to 12,000. We asked for half the bundle and handed over 3,000.

The psychology of bargaining is subtle and capricious. Start too high and your fate is sealed as far as that muqawwat is concerned: condemned forever to buy over-priced leaves. Too little risks his wrath – which is what happened. He threw the money back.

We went around to the side where his brother was selling. The same qat came across. We handed over the same sum of money. While he counted, we pulled the qat closer to us, out of his reach. The brother shook his head sadly, waving the money at us. 'Come on! I cannot sell at this price.'

Now we were in business. I reached out to take the money back. 'No problem, we have no more.'

And he drew it away. Our hand strengthened. Tim dragged two hundred rials from his pocket as though it were the last left to him on earth – the bit he had kept back to buy a decent funeral. The audience of other buyers, keen to see low prices, now swung behind us and he wilted, grabbing the extra two hundred and waving us away with a grin.

After a good lunch we sat in the hotel room. A boy had brought armrests and cold water. Tim rewarded him with four or five shoots, cleverly guaranteeing speedy service in future.

Our session was now like all the others around Yemen at three o'clock every afternoon. The doors and windows closed, mattresses under us, left elbow on hard bolster, right knee drawn up, the movement of hand to mouth as steady as the swing of a priest's censer. 'We have no entertainment,' the people often say, 'and so we take qat to pass time.' That is untrue. Build all the leisure facilities you like, qat would not disappear. Qat takes boredom, empty hours, and makes them magical. Each session must be like the last and every session the same. A set of identical movements that become a ritual, a misbegotten liturgy that transforms time.

By nature, the drug cannot work the miracle itself. All drug-users know that repetition reduces the effect and so doses increase. But safe drugs like qat do not allow an increase. There is a man in San'a who can fill both cheeks with leaf simultaneously but he is an exception – undoubtedly mudmin, addicted, as they say in San'a. Qat limits its own consumption by the way it is taken and it is the ritual itself, the session and all its certainties, which gives the kayf to the long-term user. To pop a pill in would be meaningless and unsatisfying.

In northern Thailand I once stayed in a village on the Burmese border where a Frenchwoman had a small guesthouse. She had been there for some years and had visited a small settlement in the next valley regularly. Both villages had produced opium for many generations but only the elderly people smoked it. Then a couple of French tourists arrived in the second village. They were heroin addicts, keen to indulge in cheap kicks. Supplies of the powdered, purified form were arranged over the river in Burma. The Frenchmen showed people how to get a bigger hit by injecting. Soon the entire village was dangerously addicted, including the new-born babies. Health and social problems began to destroy the old way of life: damaged houses went unrepaired, parents sold children into prostitution in Bangkok, and the land was neglected. Finding their idyll somewhat less than idyllic, the two Frenchmen promptly abandoned it.

It is impossible to know whether such a tragic course of events could occur with cathinone extracted from qat. One looks at the history of coca leaves and cocaine, opium poppies and heroin: the potential might be there. Cathinone is a powerful psychoactive substance. And yet in Yemen qat cannot be separated from its social context: the drug is necessary but only in the same way that frankincense has been needed at rituals for millennia. It is a prop, a token, something that symbolises more than it contains: the people have their faith in God and paradise and that he has sent them this leaf in which His name is written. Yemen, at least, would be secure from scientific 'improvements' to the flower of paradise. In AD 1543, Abdullah ibn Sharaf al-Din, son of the Imam who first banned qat then accepted it back, wrote:

> Do you not see the pen of the Merciful One
> has written His name upon its pages?
> Eat it for what you wish to attain
> from this world and the next.

The west could learn a great deal from the Yemen and its elegant ability to control a drug without recourse to laws, enforcement or scientific fiddling.

And so we ate our Shami qat. Conversation flowed, as if it had been dammed up for a year, not just since the day before. The room filled with smoke. After dark we took a melancholy stroll through Hodeidah park to a tea-shop. On all the benches sat silent groups of other melancholy people, absorbing the world once more after being locked away all afternoon. It was as though those few hours of contentment and ease could only be borrowed from the rest of the day, leaving it as barren and sterile as the sands around an oasis. I remembered Baudelaire's words on hashish: 'it gives power of imagination and takes away the ability to profit by it.'

Three days of Shami qat and Hodeidah were all that we could manage. We talked a little about San'a and what I planned to do. When I mentioned the idea of arranging a perfect crowning session, Tim thought for a moment and said: 'How would you like to chew in the Imam's Palace in Wadi Dahr?'

This astonishing building is the iconic image of Yemen. A plug of sand-stone rock rising vertically fifty feet to a palace, a traditional San'a tower house with daubs of white zig-zag patterns across the walls and latticework shutters across the windows. Once the summer residence to Imam Yahya, the building has languished since the Revolution for want of a new role in the modern world, yet the setting, deep in the spectacular gorge, is superb.

'You remember Hassan?' Tim went on, 'Well, I believe a friend or rela-tive of his has got the key.' We telephoned Hassan that night and he promised to enquire. Next day we set off: Tim had to return to San'a to work and I knew it was time to see the city.

The drive from Hodeidah speeds directly across the Tihama, then through the narrow Gate of the She-Camel and into the valley that winds up into the mountains, becoming ever narrower and more spectacular. For once the other passengers were a silent group and I did not feel like talking either, happy to recognise places and recall memories: the waterfall where Tim had stood on a snake; the market where a British animal-lover had once bought an injured donkey only to borrow a gun and shoot it, much to the local people's surprise; and higher up, after a long climb, my favourite garage, sadly closed. In 1988 I had stopped for petrol and asked in the office: 'What drinks do you have?' Four faces swivelled towards me. One of the men stood up and took a bunch of keys off a hook. 'Come!'

We went up a steep iron staircase to a room on top of the office which he unlocked. Inside was a 2,000 gallon water tank with a pair of doors cut in one side. He unlocked these and opened up to reveal four bulging sacks. 'Do you want red or white? Help yourself.'

The first sack was the white: it contained King Charles Canadian gin and Russian vodka; the second was the red: Japanese Scotch whisky and Blackbeard's Dark Rum. I hovered over the third sack. It didn't look as though it contained bottles. The man nodded. 'Take something from each sack,' he said, as if it was Santa's lucky dip. I reached inside and pulled out a hank of marijuana. With a grin he held the fourth sack for me to rummage inside. My hand felt down to the bottom and got hold of some-thing metallic and round. It was a hand grenade. Also there I could feel a pistol and a short machine gun, an Uzi.

'Buy four bottles and I'll throw in a hand grenade as a free gift,' he said generously. It was the only time in my life I turned down a promotional offer from a petrol station.

Sadly this remarkable retail enterprise was shut down. The pumps, never much used by the clientele, had been removed and the buildings were derelict.

We continued up and up into the darker, more brooding highlands of Haimah and Bani Matar where massive sulphurous clouds loomed over naked horizons of rock and the sun scratched scarlet lines across the terraced earth. At a dinosaur's back of smooth solidified lava, the road crept over a natural sill and into the plateau. It was cold now and the windows shut tight. We came into the long dark basin of Bani Matar where the villages were barely discernible from the wrinkled strata on the mountain rim and the light puckered at the horizon in lines of violet and grey between the black rock and sky.

There was one last army checkpoint for weapons, then the climb to the edge of the San'a bowl.

'Praise be to God on our peaceful arrival,' murmured the driver, then San'a appeared below us, the city lights filling the land between mountains. Ahead, buoyed on a shimmering haze of neon, Nuqum mountain seemed to hover like a shadow about to fall and in the centre of the orange stain was a black hole – the Old City suffering a power failure.

We coasted down and along Zubayri Street, past new high-rise buildings that I did not recognise or remember: ugly blocks of concrete, housing airline offices and new banks, vast twelve-storey monsters with every window topped off with the semicircular tracery of coloured glass, hundreds of them lined up floor by floor, identical red, blue and yellow panes rising like a plague of jelly fish in a polluted sea. There was plenty of time to survey the architectural decline of San'a, the traffic was worse than London: streets choked with fumes and giant gleaming Landcruisers among the usual battered taxis, all their drivers leaning out of their windows bellowing insults and sitting on their horns because the lights were red and they were stationary.

'Where is Bab Shu'ub?' asked one other passenger, a mild-mannered man who had never visited the capital before. He spoke eloquently of his disorientation and fear at arriving in such a place.

'I'll take you there,' said the driver, taking pity. This suited us and we went along, getting out near the edge of darkness where the Old City began, then walking in.

The old mud wall survives in scraps here, a failed chocolate mousse that is slowly being repaired to its former glory. The Gate of Shu'ub is gone, however, and all that marks the boundary now is the step onto the cobbles from the tarmac then you are inside San'a proper.

Two tall rows of houses, some leaning inwards some out, lead directly to al-Zumer mosque. On the ground floor are the blue metal doors of the shops, mostly closed at this time; above are the windows of the houses splashed around with white zig-zagging patterns, a ghostly cobweb of Miss Havisham wedding lace, dustily draped to eight floors high. There were no lights, except for candles and oil lamps, much as it was before electricity arrived in the 'seventies.

The street was busy with people hurrying home; men heading back from their post-qat tea, faces pinched and thoughtful; sweepers manoeu-vring piles of market rubbish; packs of dogs waiting under parked cars for when the humans have gone and the streets become theirs. Tim's house, once my own, was halfway along, that familiar battered wooden door, studded and scarred with a rope hanging like a red tongue from a hole by the lock, the rope that pulls the heavy wooden latch across inside. We ham-mered and the old lady who had lived on the first floor for as long as anyone can remember pulled on the rope by her room and the door swung open silently before us.

What came to me clearly as I stood in the dark at the bottom of the stairs was the familiar smell of this house: the tingling aroma of tobacco and coffee from the old lady's room. 'Come and take your breakfast,' she would shout as I went off to my lessons. 'A puff of smoke and a sip of coffee.' Then I would be light-headed and reeling on my bicycle.

The stairwell was cool, its temperature never varies, be it a baking summer's day or freezing winter night. And there was the strange sound effects produced by its five spirals: some oddity of construction that takes the cluck of a chicken in the neighbour's yard and places it sixty feet up in the air. After moving in I had often been woken in the morning to believe some animal was loose on the landing.

These houses are built to a pattern: ground floor for animals, first for storage, second a diwan for weddings and gatherings, third bedrooms, fourth perhaps more bedrooms or a living room and kitchen, fifth a qat room with an enclosed roof terrace, and finally a small view room for smaller qat sessions. All these rooms are hung upon a central spine, the stone stairwell lit by tiny chequerboard windows.

Tim had apparently trimmed his needs since I had last visited: the fridge was gone, the cooker traded down to a burner, only two serviceable mugs carefully washed ready, a jar of Syrian goat cheese balls in oil, a box of Omani frankincense and some tinned porridge oats beside the tin of Golden Syrup with its picture of a dead lion and the legend, 'Out of the strong shall come forth sweetness'. We sat next door in Tim's living room with its dusty cushions and stripy carpets. Nothing appeared to have moved since I had last seen it in 1994. His orange reading lamp still precariously balanced on a pile of books by the door, next to it an alabaster incense burner, a stone arrow head and a spent cartridge case. On the ledges other memories of trips and people were arranged: a plastic model toilet that shoots you in the eye with water when the seat is lifted, a line drawing, a dagger, and a stone penis from Carthage. Tim picked up a book lying there and read from Imru-l-Qais, one of the great poets whose work was hung on the Kaaba at Mecca.

'Stay, both of you! Let us weep over the memory of a love and a lodging, At the fall of the sandhills between Al-Dukhul and Hawmal.'

There could be no better place to find the perfect qat session than in San'a, for the city is the home of the most refined qat culture anywhere. It starts with the markets: San'a has more of them. Each side of the city has three or four major ones, all specialising to greater or lesser degrees in the qat brought from the lands behind it. In any one of them can be found qats from at least four or five different areas, a large souk, such as at Hasaba, may boast more than ten and within those will be great variation. You can go to Souk Ans on the south side of Bab al Yemen and buy Ansi, bulky leaves that can fill even the most capacious of cheeks. You can take the little alley into Al-Qaa market, the old Jewish quarter. Photographs of this market from fifty years ago show it has hardly changed at all: the same stride-wide alleyway carpeted with old qat leaves and dust, the same wooden shuttered cubby-hole shops where you can buy a bag of Wahasi, cheap and cheerful stuff, or arm-long sticks of Dhula'i, the last six inches soft and pliant. Do not be tempted by those little bunches packed in banana skin cases, that is Sauti from up around Shahara, and a nasty little number as far as I'm concerned the qat equivalent of meths. Twice I've sampled it and one time led to sleepless paranoia, the other to sleep but on waking I found the room filled with giant white worms that wriggled away when I screamed.

Not far from here is Souk Kuwait, next to the hospital, where there are top-notch stems from the Wadi or the staple diet of San'a sessions: Hamdani from north-west of the capital. Buying qat here, surrounded by a crowd, with the muqawwat keen to avoid a case of mass bargaining, I was once spoken to in Turkish, the numbers used these days almost as a secret language by the sellers.

Then there is Hail, Ferwa, Assir . . . and dozens of smaller places. More than any other city on earth, San'a is clearly gripped by qat fever. In this city, I thought, I would find something very special: a session to revive old memories and to end the journey. And the very day after arriving, I seemed to have the answer.

There is a small staircase that continues upwards from beside Tim's kitchen. The first step is about two feet high and two inches across, a step perhaps to a rock climber but not anyone else. This flight curls round to the roof terrace and then narrows, your shoulders press against the uneven plaster, there is no light except from a crack under a small wooden shutter out onto another patch of roof. Then continue up to a lobby landing and turn to the double doors into the mandhar.

It means, literally, a view room, a belvedere. It feels like a crow's nest or a boyhood dream of a treehouse. There are two windows, both double squares of cracked glass in wobbly frames that let the yellow miasma of dust come shooting under them during storms. The window at the end looks west across the Old City to Jebel Aiban, the other faces north towards Hamdan and its strange volcanic cones of ash. Higher up, above the stone shelf, are two tall thin aqds, the window most typical of

Yemen and especially San'a. They are constructed from a plaster framework, tracing shapes of leaves and flowers, sometimes even the word Allah or Muhammad, and into the spaces are put coloured glass. In the late afternoon the dappled colours climb across the faces and up the white walls.

On that first day, I was in the mandhar at three, and pacing, tying and retying my futa, listening for Tim's step, sitting, standing, unable to settle until I knew that door was closed for the next four hours. It was not politeness that kept me from starting without him – I had my qat and my water – it was my own subjugation to the rhythm of the session. To start and be disturbed was unthinkable.

Then I heard voices from below and I hurriedly sat and opened my qat up, as if totally relaxed and ready for the afternoon. In San'a the best qat is usually sold in long sticks, baladi they call it, which simply means 'from the country'. If it is top quality there may be just one stick and a few lesser stems tied at the bottom, the 'packing' that is called lughm, the land mine, because it gives you a nasty surprise. The long stem will be one of the main shoots of the tree, possibly the central topmost stem – in which case it is the best. This baladi qat needs sorting at the start of a session, breaking down into manageable lengths of a foot or so: side shoots taken off, old dusty leaves ripped out and discarded. I began to sort through and arrange it, but I could hear a familiar voice approaching, then a familiar face at the door and someone bundling into the room, hand outstretched.

I had last seen Hassan at a qat chew in North London two years before when we had sat in his study, awkward for lack of proper furniture in a land of armchairs and sofas. He had been studying in England but he had missed his homeland and we had taken our qat in mourning that we were not where we wanted to be. Unlike Khaled who had so enjoyed London, Hassan had never wanted to stay in England. Now we were both where we wanted to be.

Once the door closed, I relaxed. Across the rooftops I could see men in another mandhar settling down like us, as men and women were doing all over the city, separately for the most part. We made ourselves comfortable and Hassan told jokes, as is only right and proper at the start of a qat session.

'A man took his son to a psychiatrist,' he said. 'The father says to the psychiatrist, "My son believes he is a worm and whenever he sees a chicken he runs away. Can't you do something?" The pyschiatrist tries his best, he spends weeks with the boy slowly convincing him he is definitely not a worm. Eventually the father comes and takes him away. The boy says he is cured. Father is very happy. Outside the hospital they run into some chickens and the boy flees in panic. The father catches him and shouts at him, "I thought you were cured! I thought you said you were definitely not a worm!" And the boy says. "Yes! Yes! I am cured. I am definitely not a worm – but the problem is, do the chickens know?"'

The mention of madness reminded me of Yufrus mosque near Jebel Saber and the young man I had met there. I took out my notebook and asked Hassan to read what the Imam had written but, like all the others I had asked, he was unable to read the mysterious lines.

Seeing my disappointment, and keen to help, he began to talk about Alwan, the founder of the community at Yufrus. 'He was a scribe to the Rasulid kings and my own family goes back to that time – to the Rasulid king, al-Mujahid.'

He smiled and added modestly. 'I know little about it except that he was the fourth or fifth in the Rasulid line, I'm not sure. But Yemen has had many kings – it is really nothing so very special and it is a long time ago.'

But I was interested. Something Tim had said on Jebel Bura about the Rasulids being avid gardeners had chimed when Hassan mentioned his Rasulid ancestry.

'Look in that pile,' Tim suggested, pointing to a dusty heap of volumes. 'Al-Khazraji . . . I think he's in there somewhere.'

I rummaged through and found a copy of *The Pearl Strings*, chronicles of the Rasulid court, written by another court scribe, al-Khazraji.

Al-Mujahid was indeed the fifth Rasulid king, ruling from 1321 until his death in 1363. His reign was marked by astonishing natural phenomena and ominous portents: a woman gave birth to a goat with both male and female sexual organs, a man was laid in his grave and then the grave was found empty, al-Mujahid himself was only saved from death by a jinn that his own father had magically fathered. And if the great, glorious heyday of their dynasty was already over, the Rasulids showed no awareness of it, neither Mujahid nor his son and successor, al-Afdhal.

Gifts came from overseas: 'curious plants and birds' from the Lord of Calicut; four elephants and rarities from Ceylon; 'eatables, drinkables, wearables, scents and rarities in profusion, also horses, mules, hunting dogs, and birds of the chase in great numbers' from a Karimite merchant; and more elephants and wild beasts from the Lord of Dehlek.

Sciences like astronomy and navigation flourished, but the consuming passion of the dynasty was plants. Al-Khazraji mentions many new species: 'white jessamine, yellow jessamine, roses and other things besides' all planted in the Sultan's gardens. The mangosteen tree came from Sri Lanka, three kinds of pepper tree from Cambay and Sind, the screwpine and opium poppy from India, too. The second Rasulid king, al-Muzaffar, even retired to his gardens near Ta'izz in order to pursue his experiments in the cultivation of exotic species, handing the reins of power to his son.

Al-Mujahid was a keen horticulturalist too, creating 'delicious gardens', 'unusual pavilions', and 'hydrogogues'. His reputation was as the most learned of the Rasulids, 'a prince wise, sagacious, munificent, intelligent, awe-inspiring, learned, acute, sharp and witty', says al-Khazraji and the panegyric is over and above what he reserves for the other monarchs, as though this time he really meant it.

Here, I decided, was a man who would have attracted those strange new plants whose leaves and fruits had such curious power over men's minds. Almost all the legends and histories give dates for the introduction of the qat and coffee trees as during the Rasulid era. Perhaps both had first been planted in the Sultan's garden, the Brocade House, at Ta'izz and some enterprising visitor had pinched a cutting or two.

'I am as the lion when he flashes his eyes,' wrote Mujahid himself. 'I am as the lion when both deaths and objects of desire overflow in my right hand. I spend treasure and hoard it not; the place where every suitor seeks is in our direction.'

Outside the window, golden bars of light were poised between the ridge of Jebel Assir and the gardens of the Old City below. Tim chuckled at my fanciful notion: the qat was running in my brain just as it had when Khaled had claimed London to be a paradise and I decided to leave on this journey, just as it had when I redesigned my car to be a travelling oriental pavilion. Now I had Mujahid receiving the gift of qat trees at his court, planting the specimens in his Brocade House, even selecting and propagating until he had the perfect tree.

Nothing they said could deter me from this: I would have my qat session in the palace of the last king of Yemen in a grand room with ornate stucco arabesques above the windows, aqds of exquisite artfulness, some old pipes once smoked by the Imam, opulent acres of cushions. We would bring a lutanist and he would sing. The qat would be the best from the Wadi, the five-foot long sticks that come from Souk Zira'a. And Hassan would be there, representing his illustrious ancestor by whose grace we had those leaves in our hands.

Hassan, who had been enjoying my flight of fancy while it remained historical, now began to look uncomfortable as I wandered freely into the present.

'I'm sure it will be all right,' he said. 'But actually, my relative, the man with the key to the Rock Palace, unfortunately he is in prison. But don't worry,' he hastened to add, 'I'm sure he will be released soon. We can do it on Monday. Really.'

He explained the problem. His relative was sheikh of an area of San'a and the previous evening a car had been found burning in his street. It was not his car and he knew nothing about it, but as sheikh he was responsible and so arrested. The way Hassan told it, this was purely a formality, something no more remarkable than interviewing a witness. He would be out next day and we would arrange the session.

As the sun slipped away and evening came, we fell silent: the hour of Solomon upon us and our thoughts deeper. This was the room I had come to a dozen years before and sat, slightly contemptuous of the qat, but slowly becoming absorbed in the session, the light swelling and fading in a measured rhythm as the hands rose and fell, someone smiling and the flash of emerald green in the corner of his mouth, a broken traffic light forever signalling go.

In the 1930s, when travellers Ameen Rihani and Constantine had criticised qat in verse, it was Imam Yahya himself who felt moved to reply:

> Like a melting emerald on beautiful teeth,
> What could be better to moisten the mouth?
> Is it treacherous, as it was said to be?

It cures loved ones, relaxing the weary soul.
It is a source of energy.
Thought is sharpened to a fearful and burning brilliance.

When Monday came, I was ready. We bought expensive qat in the big pink plastic sheets that only Wadi qat ever gets wrapped up in. We had lunch at the best salta restaurant where the maestro chef Ali orchestrates lunch from his podium, a soup spoon in each hand, keeping time above the leaping flames. At two o'clock we were waiting for Hassan to pick us up.

He came at three, and his face told me all was not well. 'I am sorry, Kevin,' he said. 'My relative was released and ready to meet us, but this morning they have arrested him again. Let's go to a house I know in Bir Azab.'

So we sat in a delightful room of opulent cushions gazing out on a pool where a fountain played and Hassan explained that this was perfection for the San'ani qat-chewer, not the tower houses such as the Rock Palace. I wondered if he was trying to let me down gently, offer an alternative.

'Even now, if you look at the new villas people are building, it is this style they are following.'

I knew this to be true. Although qat is often taken in a room at the top of the house, this is really nothing more than a brave attempt to make the best of a cramped environment. When the Ottomans arrived in 1538, they extended the city walls westwards to include the lands of Bir Azab, between the Old City and the Jewish quarter of al-Qaa. With this expansion came the opportunity to build new types of house, lower and more intimate with a central courtyard and pool overlooked by a room with folding doors, something like the house we were in.

In Ottoman times the leaf was still very much associated with religious scholars, 'food for the pious' it was often termed, but the stage was set for a concrete link between what the savants were seeking and what the common man wanted. The new houses offered places where qat could be taken in idyllic circumstances. In 1757 Jamal al-Din al-Shahari wrote effusively on the delights of such dwellings: the ornate plasterwork and door carvings, the views across gardens full of pools, vine trellises and fountains that spout to twice a man's height. 'These mafrajes present a wonderful sight,' he wrote. 'Especially when the sun falls on them and they are dappled with the colours of crystal, glass, trees and so on.' Al-Shahari was writing from memory, however. Having fallen foul of Imam Mahdi Abbas, he spent ten years in a San'a prison, dreaming of those fabulous pavilions of pleasure that were just a few tantalising yards away.

We sat watching the fountain: a breeze lifted the leaves of trellised vines and set rainbows drifting through the spray in the courtyard, a cat lay asleep beside the carved wooden doors, the house and garden poised in delicate balance with the qat leaves as a go-between.

'It is very pleasant,' I agreed with Hassan. 'But I still want to try the Rock Palace . . . if you don't mind?'

He sighed. 'We will try. Who knows what will happen? God is generous.'


Hassan called at Tim's house two days later. 'He is still in prison, now with his brother. There is some negotiating to do, then he will be out.'

'Negotiating? I thought he had nothing to do with it.'

'He is a sheikh for that area and he should know what is happening. Maybe he does know something and they have arrested his brother to put pressure on him.'

This was justice based on collective responsibility – tribal law, the same system that meant a man could not travel freely to his village without checking what feuds lay between him and his destination. Another man's crime could become his own punishment, should he be in the wrong place at the wrong time.

'Shall we visit him?' I asked.

Hassan looked a little alarmed. 'No! I don't think that would help him. We will wait. Do you really want to take qat there? It is empty now – no furniture.'

I nodded, thinking of Rimbaud's line, 'You follow the red road to come to the empty inn', and also of T.E.Lawrence, wandering through an abandoned desert palace in the hope of catching the scent of the spices once buried in the walls.

'I know it might not be the greatest mafraj, and I haven't found a musician to play for us, but I'd still like to try.'

'Don't worry,' said Hassan. 'Stop trying to influence what will happen. If it happens, it happens. If not, no problem.'

It was all becoming irrelevant anyway because my visa was about to expire. Time had run out.

At three o'clock on Sunday, I sat in the window of Tim's diwan. The street outside was still full of people: youths with wheelbarrow-shops selling cheap and secondhand clothes, the man who sells boiled potatoes, women in the raspberry-red floral shawls and tie-dye veils that are unique to San'a, all hurrying along in groups to their afternoon qat parties. Hassan's estate car came nosing through and parked. We trooped down and joined him.

'Ready?'

Tim and I nodded. We had eaten a salta lunch, bought good qat. We had some tapes to play to make up for the absent lutanist. We were ready.

The streets of San'a at three are at their most dangerous as men rush to their qat sessions. Hassan drove carefully, out past the university and the medical school into the lands of Hamdan where black cones of volcanic rubble are piled up as if the creation had just finished but all the tidying up had yet to be done. There were vineyards and qat fields tucked away in these hills, all rather yellowing in this rainless season, waiting for the floods of March and April. The sky was a faultless blue, a hint of depth to the colour as the sun arched into afternoon.

The road drops gently for about two miles after leaving the San'a limits, then begins to rise. The horizon closes in, the road bends at ninety degrees, but we went straight on, bouncing up onto the stony ground. I glanced at Hassan but he was concentrating on driving, a little smile on his lips.

The ground was red, worn into little ruts where cars had passed. The horizon was suddenly very close, a red line where the land ended and then the sky came folding under and we stopped dead, a foot from the precipice.

'There,' said Hassan. 'Look.'

Five hundred feet below, sheltered by sheer rock walls of smooth sandstone was the fertile oasis that is Wadi Dahr. Above were gritty wastes of crag and hill, the strata breaking through occasionally like broken bones through the dry skin of a desiccated carcass. But below every inch of land was accounted for, each field parcelled by mud walls, and in those fields, shimmering slightly, were the pale green trees of qat.

The far cliff, a half mile away perhaps, was riven by deep fissures and strange undercuts. The cliff led across to the valley end, turning west in one last desperate attempt to continue. And there on the point of the lower corner in the wadi was a bastion of rock and the palace neatly fitted on top of it as though it had grown there.

'See it!' said Hassan. 'I promised you would chew at the Rock Palace.'

'Is your relative there?'

'Ah! No. I am sorry to say he is still in prison. We will chew at the palace but not in the palace.'

'Where?'

He grinned but did not answer, simply got out of the driving seat and went round to the back of the estate. He opened the rear door, climbed inside and pulled it shut. 'Here. We will chew here. It is better, I think. The view is better than the view of the Imam. He is down there, he can see nothing!'

Tim and I climbed over to join him. I started to laugh.

'Why are you laughing?' Tim demanded.

'I wanted to take qat in paradise – the most beautiful place in Yemen – and we're in Hassan's car boot.'

'Ye-es,' said Tim, enjoying the situation as much as Hassan. 'But don't you know they say, "If your heart is at peace, even a donkey's arsehole can be a mafraj."'

'I never heard anyone say that.'

'You weren't listening.'

I looked at their laughing faces and out over the golden filigree of light on the shoulders of the hills of Hamdan, and I felt truly content to be there in the car boot.

'The trick is to know when you're happy,' I said, using the wheel arch as an armrest.

'There was a man who chewed every day in Hajjah,' said Hassan. 'This is a true story. And he was a big dreamer, really. He dreamed of being a rich man and so at every session he wrote out pieces of paper saying, "Please send me one million rials" and threw them out the window. One day a soldier picked up the paper and took it to the Imam – Ahmed at that time. You know Ahmed could be a generous man when he felt like it. When he read the message, he laughed and ordered 50,000 rials to be sent around to that man immediately.'

He began to grin as he remembered what had happened. 'Really, the man was very pleased but after some months he had spent all the money – on qat, of course – and so he sat down and wrote his note again, only this time he wrote, "Please send me one million rials – but not via the Imam."'

'People are never happy for long.'

'They become restless. Then, like you, they travel. In Islam a man must travel – he must perform the hajj pilgrimage to Mecca. That is a requirement.'

I looked out over the valley and the caves on the western wall where the Himyaritic tombs are said to lie. Whatever had embarked man on his restless search for something better, a paradise on this earth, it had also prevented him from ever enjoying anything but the briefest moments in that blessed state. The sufi al-Hallaj claimed that a true believer could reach God in his own mind, without needing to perform the journey to Mecca. But his heresy brought the death penalty in tenth-century Baghdad. The authorities were quite clear: the journey had to be done and no amount of meditation, with or without chemical assistance on hand, could ever take the place of that fact.

# A Qat Glossary and Consumer's Guide

ARABIC

Most of these words will be understood throughout Yemen, a few are
Sanaani dialect.

*General:*

**aqd**  coloured semi-circular window placed above a normal window
**bint al-wusaa'id**  fly cushion
**diwan**  a larger room than a mandhar, often used for large qat sessions
**futa**  sarong
**gamariyya**  term often used for an aqd, but more correctly an alabaster
    window
**jambiyya**  dagger, lit: side weapon
**kayf**  inadequately translated as the 'high', kayf has overtones of intro-
    spection and melancholy
**khazzan**  lit: 'to store' qat in your cheek, e.g. 'Are you coming to store at
    our house today?' 'Atkhazzan indana al-yawm?'
**mada'a**  hookah or hubble-bubble pipe
**madka/madaaki**  bolster
**mafraj**  a restful room for taking qat, preferably 'adeni', i.e. facing south
**mandhar**  a small high room with a view
**maula'i**  expert (in qat)

**mudmin** qat addict
**mukayyif** having the kayf or high
**mukhaddar** drugged
**muqawwat** qat-seller
**qasaba** the pipe hose
**qat** botanic name: *Catha edulis Forsskal*
**shaaqus** small high ventilation window for qat room
**shanini** a cold draught, hated by qat-chewers
**takhzin** qat session, also majlis al-qat
**wusaada/wusaa'id** back cushion


*Buying it:*

**ahmar** red qat (reddish tint to stem)
**ais** ace, top quality
**'aqid** 'tight'. Qat that forms a good wad in the cheek.
**arbat!** tie it up! (I'll have it)
**a'sab!** wrap it up! (It's a wrap)
**baghra** grown fast with lots of water. Pale green and weak. The 'alcohol-free lager' of the qat world. Looks nice but is completely gutless.
**baayit** yesterday's qat. Tired-looking, black edges, leaves fall off if shaken gently. Don't buy it – except if there's nothing else, of course.
**baiyad** white qat (lighter leaves than the red)
**baladi** long sticks of qat
**durjama** doorjammer? A rare word of dialect from San'a, possibly Turkish in origin, describing a really-fine wad that fills the cheek.
**haariq** 'burnt'. Heard in Aden where the qat has travelled but not in San'a
**khashr** loose sticks of qat
**lauz** lit: almonds. Top quality, with a certain nutty texture.
**lughm** lit: land mine. The packing that makes a qat bundle more bulky.
**malih** good, fine
**m'bowdar** qat that has been covered in pesticide – many Yemenis now habitually wash qat before chewing and spin dryers are a popular way of drying the wet leaves. Simply wrap in a towel and give them 500 rpm. Qat that has been washed before market is highly suspicious.

**milham** big leaves. Just a matter of choice – muqawwats often ask which you prefer.

**mudhahal** 'rusted'. Red spotting on backs of leaves, to be avoided if it covers the chewable leaves.

**mukabbad** qat that catches in your throat. Often cheaper red qat does this. Shares the same root as kibda – 'liver'.

**mushamma'** the plastic wrapper

**mushimm** qat that has been tied tight and left in the sun. Slight scent of apples. Not always a total qatastrophe.

**mutrib** 'dusted'. Leaves covered in pale brown dirt have been treated the traditional way, by throwing dust over the tree to keep insects off. Often a good sign, but may need washing – something that purists claim changes the taste.

**nazzi** small leaves

**qatal** loose leaves and stem tips, usually sold in bags. 'The qat which dogs have pissed on,' as they say when haggling.

**qafla/qifaal** top, soft part of qat stem

**ra's (pl: ruus)** loose heads of qat stems, usually bagged

**rubta (pl: rubat)** a bundle of qat stems

**shakl** a pair of bundles (term used in the south)

**zabib** lit: raisins. Expensive qat with a hint of raisins in the texture.

**zid addi** Give me more! (very useful when buying qat)

**zowj** a pair of bundles


*The session:*


**Ain qad al-Turk?** Where are the Turks? Said to a silent chewer and almost like 'A penny for your thoughts.'

**Akramak Allah!** God reward you! Said after someone gives qat to you.

**Karaama sahiila** Generosity is easy (the answer to above)

**askub li** pour for me

**bardak** water cup. A Sanaani dialect word of Turkish origin.

**Hayya Allah man jaa** God give life to the one who comes! Said by the host to an arriving guest.

**Allah yuhayyik!** (the answer to above)

**nukta** joke
**as-saa'a as-Suleimaaniyya** Solomon's Hour – after sunset
**Sahh!** (give me) water!
**zebj** joking. First hour of a session


*After the session:*

**Raazim** the qat monster. A sprig under the pillow is said to ward him off.


SAN'A QAT MARKETS (not a complete list):

**Al-Qaa** Sauti, Wahasi, Hamdani, Matari – cheap stuff with some bargains. Convenient for Ali's salta restaurant, *the* place to have lunch before
qat.
**Asir** on the Hodeidah road and popular with travellers. Usually has some
good stuff from Beni Matar.
**Baab al-Sabah** Convenient, though horrible at the Tahrir Square end, but
walk down to the Saila, dry watercourse, and there may be good stuff
sold out of the Hilux pick-up trucks.
**Ferwa** Mainly qat from Hamdan. Experienced and desperate buyers only.
**Hasaba** Large qat market. Lots of Hamdani. Plenty of choice but franti-
cally busy. This is where a flock of crows dropped stones on an invading herd of African elephants back in the sixth century. An auspicious
qat site and with some excellent Hadhrami restaurants.
**Hayel** Lots of reliable qatal to choose from.
**Kuwait** As Zira'a but the second-grade stuff, also excellent quality. As
elsewhere the shops sell better quality than the street-sellers but are
more expensive.
**Suq al-Milh** Central in Old City. Lots of poor Haimi, some Hamdani
Ahjari and Dhula'i. A convenient place to buy but not a wide choice.
**Suq Ans** Good choice but Ansi qat is bulky stuff if your cheek is unac-
customed to it. A very good Hadhrami restaurant near by.
**Zira'a** Top-notch qat from Dhula and Wadi Dahr. Most expensive market
but worth every rial.

*Other types of qat:*

There are hundreds, generally named after the growing region, but the names most commonly heard are:

**Rada'i** Found widely in the south in non-qat-growing areas. Pretty rough but often all there is.

**Shami** The premier qat of Yemen is not found in San'a but Hodeidah and smaller nearby towns like Bajil and Mansuriya. Noted for the way it 'kicks in' after twenty minutes. 'Bagma' is one common type of Shami.

**Yafa'i** The most potent qat in Aden is Yafa'i, but only during the months April to September.

AMHARIC

(Many are Oromo loan words and most are used interchangeably in Amharic, Oromo, Harari and Gurague)

**akara** bundle of qat
**aterara** bouquet of qat offered to another person
**bercha** qat session
**bulti** yesterday's qat
**chapsi** to drink alcohol after qat
**chat** (qat) botanic name: *Catha edulis Forsskal*
**faqa** cheap, poor quality qat
**geraba** short pieces of qat and loose leaves – poor quality
**ijabana** lit: 'qat opens your eyes' – a morning chew
**jezba** an addict – a mild insult.
**jima** qat (Oromo)
**katira** night-time session
**lulukacha** a mouthful of qat
**merkana** the later stages of the kayf when the high is tinged with melancholy
**owa** fresh qat, opposite of bulti
**rabsa** a gift of qat sent outside (usually to servants)

# Bibliography

This brief list offers a few possibilities for further reading which are not made explicit in the text.

*On Qat:*

Ahmed Abdulrahman al-Mu'allami, 'Al-qat fi l-adab al-yamani wa l-fiqh al-islam'. Beirut, 1988.

Ingrams, D. and L., *Records of Yemen*. Neuchatel, 1983. A vast collection of colonial paperwork and travellers' reports on all subjects, including that of qat.

Institute of Drug Dependency Factsheet 9 (1994): a good source for further reading in academic journals and press cuttings.

Kennedy, J., *The Flower of Paradise*. Reidel, 1987. Undoubtedly the best academic book on qat and very readable too. Kennedy's level-headed investigation is an inspiration.

Rudgely, R., *'The Alchemy of Culture'*. British Museum Press, 1993. Wide-ranging and thought-provoking study about drug use around the world and through history.

Serjeant, R., and Lewcock, R., *San'a', An Arabian Islamic City*. World of Islam Festival Trust, 1983. A goldmine of information on the city and Yemen generally, including a section on qat.

Weir, S., *Qat in Yemen*. British Museum Press, 1985. An interesting study based around the people of Jebel Razih in northern Yemen.

*Early Travellers:*

Boxhall, P., 'Diary of a Mocha Coffee Agent', in *Arabian Studies I*, Serjeant, R. and Bidwell, R. (eds). Cambridge-London 1974.

Brodie, F., *The Devil Drives*. Eland, 1987. A classic biography of Burton.

Burton, R.F., *First Footsteps in East Africa*. Reprinted by Dover Publications, New York, 1987.

Hansen, T., *Arabia Felix*. Collins, 1964. A readable account of the 1761–67 Danish expedition to Yemen and the work of Forsskal.

Henri de Montfreid, *Hashish*. Has been republished at various times (in USA as *Adventures of a Red Sea Smuggler*) but is currently out of print. *Secrets of the Red Sea* is harder to find but just as interesting. An American journalist, Ida Treat, also ghost-wrote *Pearls, Arms and Hashish* (1930) – the book about de Montfreid that inspired its subject to have a go himself.

Nicholl, C., *Somebody Else*. Cape, 1997. Closely researched and detailed account of Rimbaud's African years.

Rimbaud, A., *A Season in Hell*, translated by Oliver Bernard. Penguin, 1962.

Rimbaud, A., *The Collected Works of Arthur Rimbaud*, translated by Paul Schmidt. Picador, 1988.


*Other References:*

Buxton, D., *The Abyssinians*. London, 1970.

Daum, W. (ed)., *Yemen 3000 years of Art and Civilisation in Arabia Felix*. Penguin, 1988.

*The Koran*, translated by N. J. Dawood. Penguin, 1956.

Pankhurst, R., *Economic History of Ethiopia*. 1968. Contains a detailed account of the building of the Addis-Djibouti railway.

Thompson, V., and Adloff, R., *Djibouti and the Horn of Africa*. Stanford University Press, Stanford, 1968. Also contains a section on qat in Djibouti.

# Index